Cambridge Studies in Contentious Politics

General Editor

Doug McAdam *Stanford University and Center for Advanced Study in the Behavioral Sciences*

Editors

Mark Beissinger *Princeton University*
Donatella della Porta *Scuola Normale Superiore*
Jack A. Goldstone *George Mason University*
Michael Hanagan *Vassar College*
Holly J. McCammon *Vanderbilt University*
David S. Meyer *University of California, Irvine*
Sarah Soule *Stanford University*
Suzanne Staggenborg *University of Pittsburgh*
Sidney Tarrow *Cornell University*
Charles Tilly (d. 2008) *Columbia University*
Elisabeth J. Wood *Yale University*
Deborah Yashar *Princeton University*

(Continued after Index)

Violent Resistance

Militia Formation and Civil War in Mozambique

CORINNA JENTZSCH
Leiden University

CAMBRIDGE
UNIVERSITY PRESS

CAMBRIDGE
UNIVERSITY PRESS

University Printing House, Cambridge CB2 8BS, United Kingdom

One Liberty Plaza, 20th Floor, New York, NY 10006, USA

477 Williamstown Road, Port Melbourne, VIC 3207, Australia

314–321, 3rd Floor, Plot 3, Splendor Forum, Jasola District Centre, New Delhi – 110025, India

103 Penang Road, #05-06/07, Visioncrest Commercial, Singapore 238467

Cambridge University Press is part of the University of Cambridge.

It furthers the University's mission by disseminating knowledge in the pursuit of education, learning, and research at the highest international levels of excellence.

www.cambridge.org
Information on this title: www.cambridge.org/9781108837453
DOI: 10.1017/9781108936026

First published 2022

A catalogue record for this publication is available from the British Library.

Library of Congress Cataloging-in-Publication Data

ISBN 978-1-108-83745-3 Hardback

For jboy

Contents

Figures

Tables

Acknowledgments

This book has been long in the making. Since my initial fieldwork trip for this project in 2010, Mozambique has experienced (among other things) two rounds of general elections, two destructive cyclones, the return of war, and the emergence of a new war in the country's north – in addition to a pandemic. In researching and writing this book over the years, I have benefited from the support of many people. First of all, I am deeply indebted to all my respondents in Mozambique who so generously shared their precious time to answer my questions; their stories not only made this book possible, but also taught me lots about politics and life more generally. Some of my respondents are no longer alive today; may they rest in peace. Since my respondents shared sensitive material, I kept all their names anonymous, unless they were public figures; I hope they forgive me that I cannot give them the credit they deserve.

I had the initial idea for this book after a talk on Sierra Leone's Civil Defense Forces, and militias more generally, by Macartan Humphreys at Yale University. I began researching the topic, came across a fascinating article by Kenneth B. Wilson on Naparama in Mozambique, and decided to further study these militias. Before my first fieldwork trip to Mozambique, Ken Wilson provided me with crucial advice and information on how to research Naparama. I am extremely grateful for my dissertation advisor Elisabeth Wood's early encouragement to pursue this project. Her exceptional mentorship and guidance throughout my graduate studies and beyond and her help in the book publication process were crucial in completing this book. I sincerely appreciate the advice and insights I received from my dissertation committee members Stathis Kalyvas and Mike McGovern; Stathis helped me to stay focused on finalizing and publishing this book. I would also like to extend my sincere thanks to Ariel Ahram, Bjørn Bertelsen, Matthew Kocher, and Eric Morier-Génoud for their generous advice on the project and Michel Cahen for carefully reading and commenting on parts of the manuscript.

In Mozambique, I thank Domingos do Rosário for the affiliation with the Political Science Department at the University Eduardo Mondlane in Maputo. Special thanks go to Ivo Correia, Victor Igreja, João Paulo Borges Coelho, Ben Machava, Sérgio Chichava, Gil Lauriciano, and Manuel de Araújo for their generous help in providing me with crucial contacts and invaluable advice. I thank seminar participants at the African Studies Center (CEA) at University Eduardo Mondlane and at the Institute for Social and Economic Studies (IESE) for their ingenious suggestions and Carlos Fernandes and Sérgio Chichava for organizing the talks. I very much appreciate the support of the provincial secretaries and district administrators in Nampula and Zambézia provinces who granted me permission to work in their districts, provided me with access to government archives, and supported my project. Armindo Félix Cassamuge, Elísio Vicente, Amos João Pires, and João Pereira provided excellent research assistance in Zambézia and Nampula. My friend and colleague Emily Van Houweling's support not only improved my project but also made my time between trips to the districts more enjoyable. Christian Laheij provided important support in difficult times. I also thank Tiffany Depew and Shannon Johnson for their hospitality and Lily Bunker, Doreen Cutonilli, and Alicia Mehl for their friendship.

I am deeply grateful for having had such great colleagues and friends who have provided outstanding feedback and emotional support over the years. As a graduate student at Yale University, I was lucky to benefit from the advice and friendship of Gina Bateson, Leonid Behner, Lihi Ben Shitrit, Yelena Biberman, Daniel Blocq, Erica de Bruin, Christine Cheng, Adi Greif, Lucy Joske, Kathleen Klaus, Meghan Lynch, Cory McCruden, Jensen Sass, Angelika Schlanger, Livia Schubiger, Ryan Sheely, Kai Thaler, and many others. When I moved to Leiden University as an assistant professor, many new colleagues and friends supported me and this project, in particular Nicolas Blarel, Ursula Daxecker, Imke Harbers, Jana Krause, Romain Malejacq, Juan Masullo, Jonah Schulhofer-Wohl, Lee Seymour, Danie Stockmann, and Nikkie Wiegink. Rebekah Tromble has been an invaluable mentor and Abbey Steele a great friend. Lena Laube deserves special thanks for always being there for me.

The book would not have been possible without funding from a National Science Foundation Doctoral Dissertation Research Improvement Grant and a Yale MacMillan Center International Dissertation Research Grant. The research project was approved by the Human Subjects Committee of Yale University under the Institutional Research Board (IRB) protocol number 110308177. I thank Bristol University Press / Policy Press for permission to include material from a prior publication (Jentzsch 2018a). I owe special thanks to my editor, Amanda Pearson, and her editing team at Pearson Ink for working with me on the final manuscript during a stressful time, and my editor at Cambridge University Press, Sara Doskow, for her helpful guidance throughout the publishing process. Three anonymous reviewers provided insightful and constructive comments and suggestions for revising the manuscript. My research assistant, Sofia Jorges, did an excellent job in making the maps, and Robert Sale prepared the index.

I wrote parts of this book while moving across the Atlantic and having two kids, and finished it while living through a pandemic. I often think of Sean Jacobs' advice that "life happens," which he gave me when I was a graduate student and thinking about having a baby while finishing my dissertation. Sean's advice to accept that not everything can be planned has helped keep me sane, and I sincerely thank him for that.

I dedicate this book to John. I remain deeply grateful for your unconditional love and support and could not have come this far without you. I am grateful to my parents, Birgit and Gerhard, for always cheering me on. Thanks to my sister Annika for her curiosity in chatting about this project and to my sister Britta for her openness to adventure when visiting me in Mozambique. It was fun talking to Jasper about writing a book. And Almeda's joyfulness is an inspiration for us all.

Abbreviations

CIO	Central Intelligence Organization of Rhodesia
FPLM	Popular Forces for the Liberation of Mozambique (Forças Populares de Libertação de Moçambique)
Frelimo	Mozambique Liberation Front (Frente de Libertação de Moçambique, Frelimo/FRELIMO)
GD	Dynamizing Groups (Grupos Dinamizadores)
MNR	Movimento Nacional de Resistência (early name for Renamo)
ONUMOZ	United Nations Operation in Mozambique (Operação das Nações Unidas em Moçambique)
PCA	Advanced Command Post (Posto de Comando Avançado)
PRM	Mozambique Revolutionary Party (Partido Revolucionário de Moçambique), aka Africa Livre movement
Renamo	Mozambican National Resistance (Resistência Nacional Moçambicana)
RUF	Revolutionary United Front
ZANLA	Zimbabwe African National Liberation Army

I

Introduction

Militias in Civil Wars

In the late 1980s, Mozambique was suffering from a civil war that had destroyed the country's infrastructure, resulted in severe violence against civilians, and contributed to widespread famines. It was at that time that a militia emerged, an armed group of volunteers from the civilian population that confronted the Renamo rebels who fought against the Frelimo government.[1] "The people revolted. They were tired of the war, so they volunteered to confront those who were waging war and end [the fighting],"[2] a local government representative explained to me in one of my many conversations about the origins of the group. *Naparama*, as the militia was called,[3] was created by a traditional healer in northern Mozambique, Manuel António, who claimed that he had received a divine mission from Jesus Christ to liberate the Mozambican people from the suffering of the war and learned of a medicine

---

[1] Renamo stands for Mozambican National Resistance (Resistência Nacional Moçambicana). Renamo fought against the party in power, the Mozambique Liberation Front (Frente de Libertação de Moçambique, Frelimo). The Frelimo party was the successor of the main liberation movement before Mozambique's independence in 1975.

[2] Interview with local government representative (2011-09-15-Gm1), Nicoadala, Zambézia, September 15, 2011. The interview citations throughout this book indicate date, location, the respondent's role during the war, and gender of the respondents: N (Naparama); F (Frelimo combatant); R (Renamo combatant); M (militiaman); P (religious leader); L (local leader including traditional chiefs and other community leaders); H (traditional healer); G (government representative); m (male); f (female).

[3] Depending on the local language and pronunciation, the spelling varies: Naprama, Parama, Napharama, Barama (see also Wilson 1992, 561n148). Finnegan (1992, 254) states that Naparama means "irresistible force" in the Makua language. "Parama" denotes the drug that is used during the vaccination, and "Naparama" denotes the people that received the Parama vaccine and is also often used as a second surname of the leader Manuel António (informal conversation with the late Naparama leader in Zambézia Manuel Sabonete, September 16, 2011, Nicoadala). I follow the spelling of Mozambican linguistic groups by Newitt (1995).

to turn bullets into water (Nordstrom 1997, 58).[4] António used the medicine to vaccinate militia members during an initiation ceremony. Naparama became the most important of many violent and nonviolent civilian resistance movements that emerged to stop the violence during a war that lasted sixteen years in total. The movement quickly spread across the country's central and northern provinces, growing from a couple of hundred to several thousand members in at least twenty-six districts across two provinces within a year of its formation in 1988–89.[5] António went "on foot if necessary, to 'wherever the people call me to help'" to train new members.[6] The people embraced this new force, and youths even dropped out of school to join the militia.[7] By 1991, Naparama controlled two-thirds of the northern provinces and returned stability to war-torn communities (Wilson 1992, 561).

Militias like Naparama are part of a broader phenomenon that is common across civil wars around the globe (Üngör 2020). By civil wars, I refer to armed conflict within a country between at least two parties subject to a common authority (Kalyvas 2006, 17). Militias, as defined in this book, are armed organizations that exist outside of the state's security apparatus; they emerge as "countermovements" against insurgents either on the initiative of community residents or state representatives (see Jentzsch, Kalyvas, and Schubiger 2015). Similar to communities in Mozambique, residents in Peru, Nigeria, and Sierra Leone formed militias to protect themselves against civil war violence. The civilian defense committees (rondas campesinas) fought against the Shining Path in Peru, the Civilian Joint Task Force (CJTF) countered Boko Haram in Nigeria, and the Kamajors quelled the Revolutionary United Front (RUF) rebellion in Sierra Leone (Zech 2016; Bamidele 2017; Hoffman 2011). Sometimes, governments take the lead in mobilizing militias to counter armed rebellion. The National Defence Force, for instance, supports the rule of Syrian president Bashar al-Assad (Leenders and Giustozzi 2019). The Iraqi government, together with the United States, collaborated with militias to counter Al-Qaida in Iraq (Cordesman and Davies 2008; Ahram 2011). Sudanese president Omar al-Bashir, ousted in 2019 by the Sudanese Armed Forces, was notorious for delegating violence to the Janjaweed to fight the rebellion in Darfur (Flint and De Waal 2005). And the Afghan government has worked with warlords and militias to defeat the Taliban (Malejacq 2019).

---

[4] Rachel Waterhouse, "Antonio's Triumph of the Spirits," *Africa South (Harare)* (May), 1991, 14.
[5] Mozambique's administrative structure includes provinces, districts, administrative posts, and localities.
[6] Rachel Waterhouse, "Antonio's Triumph of the Spirits," *Africa South (Harare)* (May), 1991, 15.
[7] República de Moçambique, Província de Nampula, Distrito de Mecubúri, *Relatório referente ao mês de Fevereiro de 1992*, March 3, 1992 (AGN, Nampula). The archival documents I refer to in this book come from two archives, the archive of the Provincial Secretariat of the Provincial Government of Zambézia, Quelimane, referred to as "AGZ," and the archive of the Provincial Secretariat of the Provincial Government of Nampula, Nampula City, referred to as "AGN."

This strikingly regular feature of civil wars, the presence of domestic "third actors," and its significance for order and violence during civil war is neglected in conflict and security studies. Although militias were active in nearly two-thirds of civil wars between 1989 and 2010 (Stanton 2015) and 81 percent of the conflict-years between 1981 and 2007 (Carey, Mitchell, and Lowe 2013, 254), they remain under-researched and under-theorized. Civil wars such as the one in Mozambique are often understood as dichotomous forms of armed conflict between states and insurgents. While scholars have studied why insurgent groups factionalize and fragment (Bakke, Cunningham, and Seymour 2012; Cunningham, Bakke, and Seymour 2012; Christia 2012; Woldemariam 2018), systematic analysis of armed groups formed to support the incumbent is more limited (Jentzsch, Kalyvas, and Schubiger 2015; Malejacq 2017; Carey and Mitchell 2017; De Bruin 2020). We know why states form and delegate violence to pro-government militias (Carey, Colaresi, and Mitchell 2015, 2016; Biberman 2018, 2019). However, our understanding of how and why *civilian communities* organize to form militias is in its early stages (Zech 2016; Blocq 2014).

I conceive of community-initiated militia formation as a type of collective action and an expression of civilian agency. Civilians are often seen as "extensions" of various armed groups in civil wars, not as actors in and of themselves. They are usually seen as facilitating armed group activities by providing access to resources such as food, money, recruits, and intelligence, rather than initiating any activity themselves. Recent research, however, has recognized the significance of "civilian agency" in civil war (Masullo 2015; Kaplan 2017; Krause 2018). Rather than passive victims, civilians respond to civil war in creative and organized ways, seeking to improve their own protection (Jose and Medie 2015). While they may have nonviolent means at their disposal, civilians can also opt for violent ones, such as forming militias to ward off insurgent (and state) violence (Jentzsch and Masullo 2019). By drawing attention to militias as a form of collective action, I emphasize the coordinated and organized nature of civilian responses to war and violence.

Recognizing how multiple non-state armed groups and civilian agency affect political violence, this book seeks to answer the following questions: Why do civilian-based, community-initiated militias emerge at particular times during civil war? What explains the spread of such militias across war-torn communities like Mozambique? Why are people drawn to participate in militias, even at considerable risk to life and limb?

1.1 WHEN, WHERE, AND HOW MILITIAS FORM

The book explains when, where, and how community-initiated militias form in irregular civil wars. While, based on existing scholarship, we might expect governments to mobilize militias when they are losing, or when they have the upper hand to retain their advantage, I argue that it is precisely when a military stalemate has been reached that communities themselves form militias. Stalemates pose significant risks for civilians as they find themselves between two forces, of which neither is able to protect them. Thus, we should expect communities to organize collectively and form militias when caught between evenly matched foes. This argument is important because it challenges our understanding of civil war as synonymous with rebellion or insurgency. Much of conflict research focuses exclusively on rebel groups and overlooks third actors such as militias (Metelits 2010; Weinstein 2007). The lack of attention to domestic "third actors" in armed conflict theories is largely due to the simplifying assumption that civil wars take place between two sides – incumbents and insurgents (Pettersson, Högbladh, and Öberg 2019). Taking militias into account resists the tendency to portray state–rebel relations as purely dyadic interactions, with consequences for theorizing and modeling how rebellions emerge, evolve, and succeed or fail. For example, third actors can overcome a military stalemate and upend the military balance between rebels and the state and thus influence how the war evolves and ends.

In a civil war, militias rarely form independently of each other. To fully understand why community-initiated militia form, we need to consider how such forms of collective action diffuse across community-boundaries. Ethnic, ideological, and cultural bonds between communities and successful militia activity in neighboring communities promote the initial diffusion of militias. However, as I show in this book, militias only take root when community and local elites' preferences overlap – a process I call "sustained diffusion." A militia cannot establish itself in a community with elite conflicts, as it may be used to challenge local state authority. In emphasizing the diffusion of collective action forms and repertoires, this book is part of a research agenda that focuses on the endogenous dynamics of armed conflict (Arjona 2016; Balcells 2017; Kalyvas 2006; Krause 2018; Staniland 2014; Steele 2017; Wood 2003). For example, I show that wartime collective action cannot be reduced to prewar structural factors such as ethnic group fragmentation, inequality, poverty, or state capacity (Cederman, Gleditsch, and Buhaug 2013; Collier and Hoeffler 2004; Fearon and Laitin 2003). Communities adopt successful repertoires from other communities over the course of a war, and inter-elite relations affect whether a community routinizes certain forms of collective action.

Finally, once they are formed, community-initiated militias need to grow to establish themselves. The peculiar nature of civil war gives rise to a context of uncertainty in which the consequences of civilian actions are difficult to calculate. Under uncertainty, people tend to make use of familiar knowledge to make decisions and plan their actions. Applying this insight to militia mobilization, I argue that community-initiated militias successfully mobilize members if they appeal to familiar preexisting social conventions. Reminding people of their own available resources provides community residents with the opportunity for self-empowerment and thus encourages participation. Militias' rootedness in the social and political fabric of the communities in which they mobilize brings about a considerable advantage over rebel groups in terms of recruitment numbers and support, which may explain militias' powerful impact on counter-insurgency (Peic 2014). Thus, though the book emphasizes the endogenous nature of civil wars, it also demonstrates that armed conflict is not a state of exception completely disconnected from prewar social and political institutions (Balcells 2017; Ellis 1999).

Beyond these theoretical arguments, I make two main contributions related to the study of war on the African continent. For the study of Mozambique, and southern Africa more generally, the book shows the limits of a perspective that privileges elite politics and the external interference of neighboring states in domestic affairs to analyze armed conflict. The historiography of the war in Mozambique has adopted a macro-perspective, paying particular attention to Rhodesia[8] and South Africa's goal to destabilize Mozambique through the funding and training of the Renamo rebels (Vines 1991; Minter 1994; Cabrita 2000; Emerson 2014). However, ethnographies of the war in central and northern Mozambique and recent research in conflict studies more generally have demonstrated that local conflicts, rather than the "master cleavage" of war, shape how communities experience and respond to civil war (Geffray 1990; Nordstrom 1997; Kalyvas 2006; Balcells 2017; Cahen, Morier-Genoud, and Do Rosário 2018a). Access to new sources about the war in Mozambique has made this analysis possible and fruitful (Cahen, Morier-Genoud, and Do Rosário 2018a). By making use of such new sources and studying community responses to the war, the book thus contributes to a broader debate on violent orders and state formation in the Mozambican context (Macamo 2016; Bertelsen 2016).

The second contribution relates to how the Naparama militia organized and mobilized fighters. I build on works in African Studies on prophetic armed movements whose access to (traditional) religious practices shapes the way they organize, mobilize, and fight. Such movements are strongly embedded in the social fabric of particular communities (Kastfelt 2005; Nicolini 2006). The Zimbabwe African National Liberation Army's (ZANLA) close links with the peasantry, for example, provided guerrillas with access to powerful spirit mediums, and embedded guerrillas into the local popular imagination (Lan 1985). The Holy Spirit Mobile Forces led by Alice Lakwena is perhaps the most iconic example of such a prophetic armed movement whose successes on the battlefield were tied to the spiritual powers of its leader (Behrend 1999).[9]

---

[8] I use "Rhodesia" when referring to the country before independence in 1980, and "Zimbabwe" when referring to the country thereafter.

[9] Prophetic movements can include both antistate and pro-state armed groups and thus have revolutionary or reactionary agendas. They also do not necessarily protect civilians in the communities in which they emerge. Lakwena's movement was the precursor of the Lord's Resistance Army of Joseph Kony that has perpetrated considerable violence against civilians in Uganda and neighboring states (Behrend 1999; Allen and Vlassenroot 2010). Similarly, reliance

I join Danny Hoffman (2011) in understanding such movements as developing and adopting an "experimental [military] technology," and define them as an innovative response to wartime violence that is shaped by developments on the battlefield (Jentzsch 2017). In Mozambique, the spiritual dimension of the war and Renamo's use of spirit mediums provided the background to the formation of Naparama, who reinvented preexisting social conventions to help people cope with the war (Wilson 1992).

1.2 PREVAILING APPROACHES TO STUDYING MILITIAS

Conflict scholars' narrow focus on rebels and the state has obscured the fact that incumbents and insurgents are rarely unified actors. Civil wars in Central and East Africa and East Asia have seen a proliferation of insurgent groups within the same war, often splitting from the same previously existing insurgent organizations (Stearns 2011; Woldemariam 2018; Staniland 2014). Scholars who analyze how and why armed groups fall apart have demonstrated that insurgent factions and changing alliances have an important impact on violence and the dynamics of war (Pearlman 2009; Pearlman and Cunningham 2012; Cunningham, Bakke, and Seymour 2012; Staniland 2012; Christia 2012; Bakke, Cunningham, and Seymour 2012).

The fact that state armed forces may be fragmented and states may rely on multiple auxiliary forces to fend off opponents from within the regime or outside of it has recieved less attention (De Bruin 2020). The overall number of "pro-government militias" – militias with a clear link to the state – rose during the 1980s and 1990s and peaked at over 140, and then fell during the 2000s (Carey, Mitchell, and Lowe 2013, 254). Political and military developments in Indonesia, Iraq, Iran, Pakistan, and India over the last decades have demonstrated the extent to which incumbent forces involve militias in counterinsurgency operations (Ahram 2011; Biberman 2019). However, in much of civil war research, incumbent forces are still assumed to be unitary actors (Carey, Mitchell, and Lowe 2013, 250) and treated as completely separate from civilian actors (Mazzei 2009, 6).[10]

---

on religious idioms and practices in West Africa has led to severe forms of violence against civilians (Ellis 1999).

[10] A first effort to assess the magnitude of the fragmentation of incumbent forces is Carey, Mitchell, and Lowe's (2013) collection of quantifiable data on militias across the world. The authors focus on what they call "pro-government militias" in the period from 1981 to 2007. The dataset includes militias that are active in civil war and non-civil war settings. De Bruin (2020) assembled a dataset on state security forces that include all paramilitary forces under the direct command of the military. Carey, Mitchell, and Lowe's (2013) focus is different, as it includes forces that identify with the state or receive support from the state, but are not part of the official security apparatus of the state.

Militias may form during peace or wartime, and their activities may be defensive or offensive in nature. In times of elections, for example, political elites may form or sponsor nonmilitary death squads, party militias, or youth militias to intimidate opponents (Campbell and Brenner 2000; Carey, Mitchell, and Lowe 2013; Raleigh 2016; Raleigh and Kishi 2020). But militias can also form to protect civilians against crime or other sources of insecurity. When the state is not able or willing to protect a community, vigilante groups form as a self-help mechanism to (violently) oppose "criminals and others whom the actors perceive as undesirables, deviants and 'public enemies'" (Abrahams 1998, 9). In democratizing states such as South Africa, vigilante groups can be an expression of unease over the strengthening of human rights, as crime fighters consider releasing a suspect on bail as a source of insecurity and state "failure" (Smith 2019). Vigilantism is therefore "an exercise in power" (Bateson 2020, 1) and is closely linked to how elites or communities attempt to shape political order.

During war, militias are involved in counterinsurgency and the protection of communities. While the majority of militias operate in peacetime, they are very common in civil wars. Carey Mitchell, and Lowe (2013, 255) find that 43 percent of all pro-government militias are active when the country experiences a civil war, and in 81 percent of country-years during which the country experiences a civil war, there is militia activity. In contemporary civil wars, militias have been cost-effective force multiplicators and help the state deny accountability for violence, as they can outsource such violence to militias (Carey, Mitchell, and Lowe 2013). But also in the past, during the anticolonial wars, for example, occupying forces frequently created and collaborated with local forces who knew the terrain well and were able to collect crucial intelligence (Coelho 2002; Branch 2009; Bennett 2013). Militias have always been important tools for state repression. States have delegated mass violence against civilians to militias throughout history (Ahram 2014; Üngör 2020). In addition, communities themselves often form militias to protect themselves, such as during the long and violent civil wars in Colombia, Guatemala, and Peru. These groups were encouraged or co-opted by the state or formed in cooperation with social and political elites (Mazzei 2009; Romero 2003; Remijnse 2001; Starn 1995). Usually, community-initiated militias recruit residents for nightly patrols, collecting intelligence, and warning the population of imminent attacks. In many cases, such militias professionalize and militarize over time, at times collaborating with the government or even substituting the army.

In this emerging research agenda on domestic third actors, many issues remain unexplored. Most scholars have focused on how and why states form militias and delegate violence to them. Such research implies that political elites form village guards or death squads to support their strategic efforts in counterinsurgency and state building (Kalyvas and Arjona 2005). However, militias can also form (and evolve) independently of such state initiatives. We know little about why communities form militias, what form these groups take, how they evolve during war, and what that implies for the dynamics of civil war.[11]

It is important to fill this research lacuna as militias have important implications for the dynamics of civil war and its aftermath, with seemingly contradictory effects. They are an important resource to defeat insurgents but contribute to the fragmentation of armed groups, which hampers negotiated settlements to end civil wars (Peic 2014; Staniland 2015; Stedman 1997). They empower civilians to protect themselves and at the same time fundamentally restructure the social and political order by providing what has been denoted as non-state governance (Blocq 2014; Malejacq 2016). They form to limit political violence but become violent actors themselves, often increasing the length and lethality of civil wars (Clayton and Thomson 2014, 2016; Hoffman 2011; Starn 1995; Mitchell, Carey, and Butler 2014; Aliyev 2020a, 2020b). Finally, though militias are often formed during war, they shape the political process in the postwar era, in particular when they are excluded from demobilization and reintegration processes and co-opted by political elites (Acemoglu, Robinson, and Santos 2009; Mazzei 2009; Coelho and Vines 1992; Hoffman 2003; Daly 2016).

1.3 HOW TO STUDY MILITIAS

The focus on community initiatives to form militias requires detailed evidence from subnational units on how armed groups originate and evolve. To develop a theory of militia formation and explore its validity, this book builds on a subnational research design that allows for within-case comparisons of militia formation over time and controlled comparisons of geographical areas with and without militia activity within the context of one civil war. With both analytical strategies, I carefully trace the causal processes to check the subnational evidence of competing cases against alternative explanations and identify the causal mechanisms at work. In this way, the analysis both develops original arguments and explores their validity in a wider context.

The research design builds on other works that have brought together two recent methodological trends in the study of armed conflict, namely, the within-case analysis method of process tracing and the use of subnational evidence for controlled comparisons (Petersen 2001; Wood 2003; Arjona 2016, 2019; Lynch 2013; Daly 2016).[12] Bennett and Checkel (2014) define one of the standards of good process tracing as the combination of process tracing with

---

[11] For important exceptions see Arjona and Kalyvas (2012) and Humphreys and Weinstein (2008) on the comparison of recruitment for rebel and militia groups; Gutiérrez-Sanín (2008) on the organizational forms of militias compared to rebel groups; and Mazzei (2009), Blocq (2014), Zech (2016) and Schubiger (2021) on the formation of militias.

[12] I provide more information on what process tracing is and how I use it in this book in Chapter 2.

case comparisons to improve the test of alternative explanations and check for omitted variables.[13]

Subnational evidence for controlled comparisons (or quantitative analysis) has greatly advanced research on armed conflict by studying the micro-foundations of violence and order (Kalyvas 2008b; Arjona 2019). A subnational focus can improve data quality, test causal mechanisms, improve the fit between concepts and measurement, and control for variables that can be held constant within the boundaries of smaller units of analysis (Kalyvas 2008b; Snyder, Moncada, and Giraudy 2019). I use the unit of analysis of the community for subnational comparison, a population in a defined geographical space in which regular face-to-face interactions take place. These interactions create stable direct social interactions that are maintained by common institutions, such as markets, schools, the police, and the administration.[14] Empirically, in this book, communities are rural villages.

Combining subnational comparisons and process tracing is particularly valuable because they help uncover causal mechanisms: subnational evidence provides the fine-grained data necessary to conduct successful process tracing (Checkel 2008, 122). Subnational comparisons also strengthen the validity of the findings from process tracing, as alternative explanations are not only checked against evidence within one case, but also across cases (Lyall 2015). In addition, combining fine-grained comparative evidence with a process-oriented lens allows for "comparison with an ethnographic sensibility" (Simmons and Smith 2017). Oral histories help to critically interrogate conventional explanations arising from comparative evidence and analyze how interlocutors themselves experience the formation of militias across communities.

1.4 HOW TO STUDY MILITIAS IN MOZAMBIQUE

The book focuses on the formation of a certain type of militias – community-initiated militias – and their diffusion across community boundaries. I make use of subnational variation in the formation and diffusion of community-initiated militias in northern and central Mozambique, known under the name of *Naparama*, during the country's civil war (1976–92). The insurgent group Renamo emerged shortly after Mozambique's independence in 1975 among disgruntled Mozambicans with the help of the Rhodesian intelligence service in

---

[13] This combination is not new, since many controlled comparisons make use of process tracing to develop a causal narrative of a particular case (Slater and Ziblatt 2013). However, while traditional controlled comparisons have focused on cases across national boundaries, subnational studies conduct these comparisons within national boundaries. Slater and Ziblatt (2013) criticize George and Bennett (2005) for not recognizing the complementarity of controlled comparisons and process tracing or within-case analysis. However, Bennett and Checkel (2014) recognize the complementary value of both.

[14] This definition builds on Petersen (2001, 16), who develops his concept of community based on Taylor (1982).

Rhodesia. Rhodesia and Apartheid South Africa, hoping to end Mozambique's support for liberation movements challenging their governments, backed Renamo, and disenchantment with Frelimo's authoritarian policies and one-party system further nourished the movement. By the early 1980s, Renamo extended the war into northern Mozambique. Facing increased levels of violence and abduction, and inspired by the war's spiritual dimensions, Naparama formed and spread rapidly across two-thirds of the northern territory.

By focusing on subnational variation within one civil war, the book improves upon cross-national studies, which implicitly assume that militias' presence extends to the entire country. I combine process tracing to analyze how the Naparama militia formed over time with a structured-focused comparison of how the militia diffused across districts. I identify mechanisms of mobilization by comparing the militia's mobilization success with the less effective mobilization of state-initiated militias. Using an in-depth approach, I facilitate theory building in a thematic field within civil war studies that has remained limited in scope (Jentzsch, Kalyvas, and Schubiger 2015).

I collected different sources of evidence during extensive fieldwork in Mozambique over thirteen months between 2010 and 2016. I collected quantitative and qualitative evidence from over 250 oral histories and semi-structured interviews with former militia members, rebel combatants, soldiers, government representatives, community leaders, and civilians, and more than 10,000 pages of government documents from the Zambézia and Nampula provincial governments' archives in northern Mozambique. I systematically analyze interviews for narrative patterns, and construct a dataset of violent events from government reports for the province of Zambézia to trace how and why the militia formed. This combination of evidence allows me to triangulate information and overcome challenges of studying a war that ended over twenty years ago.

The war in Mozambique serves as an appropriate context in which to build a theory of community-initiated militia formation as it resembles other civil wars where community residents organized militias for self-defense. In Peru, for example, community-initiated militias were crucial in defeating the insurgency in the 1980s and 1990s (Zech 2016). During the second civil war in Southern Sudan, tribal militias emerged to counter the Sudan People's Liberation Army (SPLA) and settle local conflicts (Blocq 2014). In Indonesia's Aceh province, ethnic minorities formed militias to protect themselves against rebel coercion (Barter 2013). In Sierra Leone, where rebels encountered a severely weak state, community residents resisted violence by both state and rebel forces through the formation of militias (Hoffman 2011). What these wars have in common is the state's inability or unwillingness to protect its population, high levels of violence against civilians, and a fragmented nature of war in which local conflicts partly replace the master-cleavage of the war. I therefore expect the findings from Mozambique to apply to a larger set of cases.

1.5 CHAPTER OVERVIEW

The book is organized as follows. In Chapter 2, I develop a theoretical framework to analyze how militias form. I suggest a definition and typology of militias for the purpose of this book, introduce the theory that guides the subsequent analysis, and provide an overview of the research design of the study.

In Chapter 3, I reflect on the unintended consequences of fieldwork in polarized societies, which may affect the autonomy of both the researcher and the researched. In a context of past violence and intractable conflict, research participants often have concerns about how the research impacts the autonomy of their daily life by potentially compromising their safety. On the other hand, research participants may try to make use of the researcher for their own political and economic objectives, compromising the autonomy of the project. In analyzing the simultaneous empowerment and disempowerment of research participants, the chapter discusses the methodological and ethical challenges of power and neutrality during fieldwork and joins others in showing that conflict research needs to be understood as a form of intervention in local affairs.

In Chapter 4, I argue that the warring parties' strategic aim of controlling the population provided the background for the formation of militias in Mozambique. The control of the population became an end in itself rather than a strategy to control territory. As a consequence, the population's forced resettlement became a major weapon of war. The war's focus on the people contributed to the rising level of community responses to the violence, which culminated in Naparama's formation.

Chapters 5, 6, and 7 are organized along the three parts of the theory – when, where, and how militias form. Chapter 5 shows that, while community responses to the violence were widespread, the Naparama militia formed at a strategic moment in time, when "community-empowering military stalemates" emerged. Tracing the process of how Naparama formed over time, I find that local stalemates shaped community residents' and local elites' preferences and gave rise to windows of opportunity for militia formation. Community residents were willing to engage in armed responses to insurgent violence as other options appeared inviable. Local administrative elites complained about insufficient support from the provincial government and supported alternative military solutions such as Naparama. This chapter draws on evidence from an over-time analysis of Naparama's formation in Zambézia province in Mozambique.

In Chapter 6, I assess why – though facing similar stalemates and other structural challenges – two adjacent districts in Zambézia province experienced the diffusion of militias so differently. I find that communities learned from neighboring communities about how militias formed and "diffusion agents" migrated to spread the message of militia success, which helped initiate militia diffusion. However, "sustained diffusion" – the persistence of militia activity in a district and integration of the militia into the local security apparatus – depended on the cohesion of elites. I explore the validity of my argument by analyzing Naparama's diffusion to a district in Nampula province.

Chapters 5 and 6 are based on the group level of analysis to explain formation and diffusion of militias, but they do not answer the question of why individuals participate in militias despite the risk. I demonstrate in Chapter 7 that militias successfully mobilize members when they appeal to common social conventions, create innovative institutions and provide an opportunity for self-empowerment. In particular, I show that the appeal to preexisting social conventions such as traditional healing facilitated the mobilization process as the new militia institution resonated with local communities and created a belief in agency, which enabled the large-scale mobilization of members. I develop these arguments with evidence from Nicoadala district in Zambézia province and explore their validity with evidence from the main district of militia activity in Nampula province, Murrupula.

The concluding chapter reviews my theory and evidence and derives implications for how civilian agency, violent resistance, and the rise of third actors affect the dynamics of civil war. I explore how the arguments shed light on similar developments in past and contemporary armed conflicts and reflect on Naparama's legacy for postwar politics in Mozambique. Overall, I show that, while this book explains when, where, and how militias originate, there is much work to be done to understand how militias evolve and develop their relations with governments, rebels, and civilians. Militias are important third actors in civil wars, but we do not yet completely understand the challenges that come along with their rise.

Third Actors and Civilian Agency

Moving beyond a Dichotomous Understanding of Civil Wars

Though the field of conflict and security studies has come a long way to acknowledge the fragmented nature of war and the multiplicity of armed groups, much of theory building and data collection is still based on a dichotomous understanding of civil wars breaking out between incumbents and insurgents. The focus on structural characteristics of civil wars drives this perspective as these factors are used to explain conflict onset and intensity, two core outcomes of interest in the study of civil war. Following a process-oriented perspective, this book aims to move beyond the dichotomous understanding of civil wars and analyze how civilians contribute to the fragmentation of war, forming and joining third actors that shape the war's dynamics.

Civilians in civil war are not passive bystanders. How armed groups relate to civilian populations has been the focus of much revolutionary theory and practice. Controlling the local population is an important gateway to resources and power for government and rebel forces alike. Political violence against civilians is used to achieve such control, which has contributed to a perspective on civilians as being stuck "between two armies" (Stoll 1993) or "between two fires" (Zech 2016). However, rather than inducing passivity, such an in-between status creates grounds for civilian agency. In both Guatemala and Peru, for example, civilians formed self-defense forces to protect communities from war-induced violence (Stoll 1993; Zech 2016).

This chapter develops a framework to analyze community-initiated militias in civil war and proposes a theory of when, where, and how these militias form. We have a good sense of how and why civilians support rebels or the state. However, we know much less about how civilians coordinate and organize to form their own armed groups. Such "third actors" in civil wars play an important role in redefining relations among state and non-state actors.

2.1 CONCEPTUALIZING MILITIAS IN CIVIL WAR

Though frequently used in scholarly and policy writing, the concept of militias has remained contested (Tapscott 2019; Schuberth 2015; Carey and Mitchell 2017). This is partly due to a normative connotation and an ahistorical under-standing of the term, particularly in writings on African state failure. The term "militia" has frequently been used to denote loosely organized, roving bands of violence-wielding thugs, often without a political project (Hills 1997; Francis 2005). While I acknowledge that "militia" is a fleeting category, I maintain that it is analytically useful to separate militias from rebel groups and other armed actors. This book focuses on militias that operate *during* civil wars (Malejacq 2017). I define "militia" as an armed organization that exists outside of the regular security apparatus of the state and emerges as a countermovement against insurgent organizations (see Jentzsch, Kalyvas, and Schubiger 2015). This definition excludes groups challenging or capturing the state militarily.[1]

My definition of "militia" improves upon existing ones that are either too narrow or too broad. In contrast to narrower definitions (Kalyvas and Arjona 2005; Mazzei 2009; Carey, Mitchell, and Lowe 2013), I do not require a link to the state to define an armed organization as a militia. Militias can form inde-pendently and ally with the state at a later point. They are also highly dynamic and may change alliances often (Staniland 2015; Otto 2018). Counter to broader definitions, in which "militia" also includes rebel groups and various other armed organizations in failed states (Zahar 2000; Hills 1997; Okumu and Ikelegbe 2010), my definition emphasizes that militias have features distin-guishing them from other armed organizations – in particular rebel groups.

An important difference from rebel groups is militias' reactionary agenda of guaranteeing security and protecting property. Militias do not promote a revolutionary agenda. Rather, they secure rules that already exist and present no systematic threat to the state.[2] The self-defense committees (*rondas campesinas*) in Peru, for example, did not "tie into a broader program for change," pointing to their "predominantly local thrust" and disinterest in electoral politics (Starn 1995, 565). Regardless of the paramilitaries' relative

---

[1] As the case of the United Self-Defense Forces of Colombia (Autodefensas Unidas de Colombia [AUC]) shows, militias sometimes put severe pressure on the government by influencing politics through the legislature, even if they do not challenge them militarily (Gutiérrez-Sanín 2008). Thus, militias are not necessarily allies of the government and occasionally evolve into challengers to the government. The definition includes such groups as the AUC if their challenge to the government remains political. Once militias turn into military challengers of the state (insurgent groups), they are no longer considered militias in the sense of this definition.

[2] Some rebel groups form their own militias to administer territory under their control and perform certain tasks such as providing security at the village level, rehabilitating the village, and con-structing houses or new public buildings. Examples of such militia forces are the *mujeeba* (also called *mujuba, mudjiba, mujiba, majiba, madjuba,* or *madjuhba*), the Renamo representatives and local police at the village level during the war in Mozambique (Jentzsch 2017; Hall 1990, 50–51). I discuss these militias briefly in Chapters 4 and 6.

strength and the Colombian state's weakness, the United Self-Defense Forces of Colombia (Autodefensas Unidas de Colombia [AUC]) sought to "reclaim," not "replace," the state (Mazzei 2009, 102). A second major characteristic is therefore militias' local character. Militias are often formed at the village level, are composed of local men and women, and operate in their own or neighboring villages (Kalyvas 2006, 107).[3] The Fertit militia during the second civil war in southern Sudan, for example, formed and operated in particular villages, as local leaders perceived rebel violence to be directed at their communities (Blocq 2014). The origin of the Kamajors in Sierra Leone also lies in the protection of particular villages and, later, of displacement camps (Hoffman 2011, 73–74). However, militias may evolve into more mobile forces as their resource base and alliances with other actors become stronger.

In sum, militias are important domestic third actors in civil wars, either directly supporting the state or substituting the state in certain regions. This does not mean that militias always protect the communities in which they operate; to the contrary, to protect the state, militias can perpetrate severe levels of violence against civilians.

2.2 A TYPOLOGY OF MILITIAS IN CIVIL WAR

Militias vary within and across civil wars, and also over time. Depending on the research goal, militias can be distinguished along various dimensions, such as their origin in relation to the state, primary objectives, and social base (Okumu and Ikelegbe 2010). To understand militia *formation*, it is useful to distinguish between militias on the basis of two factors: (1) whether the state or community members initiate the militia ("top-down" or "bottom-up" mobilization; Jentzsch, Kalyvas, and Schubiger 2015), and (2) whether the members of the militia engage in tasks that require their full- or part-time commitment (see Table 2.1).

---

[3] This understanding of "militia" is congruent with the historical uses of the term. Historically, the term "militia" refers to a reserve force comprising citizens with limited military training that is available for emergency service to the state. The reserve force supplements the regular army and is therefore distinct from the force comprising full-time soldiers (Mackey 2017). In addition, the historical uses of "militia" can also explicitly refer to defense groups raised locally and independently of the state army. Historical examples of such a frontier phenomenon include the vigilantes in the eastern and western United States (Brown 1975). Early examples of militias in other regions of the world include forces that supported the militia of clansmen that defended the border regions against invaders in Macedonia under Philip II (d. 336 BC), or the fyrd among the Anglo-Saxon peoples of early medieval Europe that comprised able-bodied free men giving military service. The fyrd served as a model for the North American militia in the colonial period that later also played a role in the Civil War. By the early twentieth century, militias were transformed into the National Guard. The able-bodied portion of the population between the ages of seventeen and forty-five received "universal military training" and then served as a reserve pool from which the military could obtain volunteers (Mahon 1983).

TABLE 2.1. *A typology of militias*

		Level of professionalization	
		High	Low
Initiator	State	State-initiated full-time militias	State-initiated part-time militias
	Community	Community-initiated full-time militias	Community-initiated part-time militias

The first factor resembles the public/private (Okumu and Ikelegbe 2010) or semiofficial/informal distinctions (Carey and Mitchell 2017) in other typologies. However, in contrast to these cited typologies, I differentiate between "initiation" and subsequent "control" of militias by communities and states. My typology only covers the distinctions of militias at the point of their formation, since explaining formation is the book's research goal. State- and community-initiated militias may change their patrons during the course of war (Otto 2018); oftentimes, this is the case when states co-opt community-initiated militias or distance themselves from state-initiated militias due to their human rights violations, or when community-initiated militias reach out for resources from the state. During Sierra Leone's civil war, for example, the government co-opted the community-initiated Kamajors, which transformed the militia into a full-time, militarized armed group (Hoffman 2011).

The second factor, the type of commitment that militias display, has empirical implications for their degree of professionalization and the tasks in which they engage. For example, full-time forces stay in barracks, are on duty day and night, have continuous access to weapons, and sometimes even have uniforms. They may leave the barracks for missions outside the town or village they are stationed in, which implies that they conduct both offensive and defensive operations. Part-time forces are more likely to reside in their own houses, be on duty during the night, and go about their regular activities during the day. Those forces may have limited access to weapons and no access to uniforms. Their activities usually include patrolling, intelligence gathering, policing tasks such as arrests, and defense in the case of an attack.

The two dimensions result in the following typology (see Table 2.1). State-initiated full-time militias are professionalized and state-directed, such as the Janjaweed in Sudan's Darfur region (Flint 2009). State-initiated part-time militias can be illustrated by the Guatemalan civil patrols who patrolled villages by night, but otherwise went about their daily routines (Remijnse 2002; Bateson 2017). Community-initiated militias rarely emerge as full-time forces but rather evolve into them. For example, the Kamajor militias during the civil war in Sierra Leone represented community-initiated part-time militias before they evolved into a full-fledged army and community-initiated full-time forces after they replaced the state army (Hoffman 2011). The typology simplifies militia formation processes and focuses on the state and the community as initiators of militia formation. These dimensions should therefore be understood as continua rather than dichotomies. For example, in addition to states and communities, political elites such as party leaders can form their own militias, which represent an intermediary type of militia.

Distinguishing between state- and community-initiated militias has empirical implications regarding militias' forms of organization and objectives. Concerning their form of organization, state-initiated militias typically have a clear link to the state through a commander appointed by the state military, training organized by the state military, and/or resources from the state. For community-initiated militias, commanders are typically chosen locally, training is organized by local social or political elites, and (initial) resources come from the local population.

A militia's objective depends on if either the state or the community initiates its existence. While the state's primary objective for creating a militia is to improve its control of the population and delegate violence to non-state actors (Carey, Mitchell, and Lowe 2013), community-initiated militias form to fulfill people's needs during war, such as improving security and protecting property from pillage by insurgents or criminal bands, as did the self-defense committees (*rondas campesinas*) in Peru (Starn 1999; Fumerton 2001). For incumbents, militias may provide a tool for local state building and population control and can turn into an important means of counterinsurgency by seeking to attract "turncoats" (Kalyvas 2006, 107; Kalyvas and Arjona 2005). Especially in (ethnic) insurgencies, the state might make efforts to win over collaborators ("ethnic defectors") (Kalyvas 2008a) and organize militias to fight the insurgency. Similarly, in wars between foreign occupiers and the local population, foreigners may mobilize local collaborators to fight against resistance movements (Branch 2007). For local communities, militias serve as a substitute to state forces that are unwilling or unable to protect a population in a certain region or a population of a specific characteristic. This self-help mechanism comes close to what the social historian Eric Hobsbawm (1969) calls "social banditry" – peasant mobilization to protect the status quo against those challenging it. "Social bandits" often do not join insurgencies since insurgents define their goals independently of peasants' needs.[4] Peasants, when they mobilize, often seek to protect what they have rather than demand social change (Scott 1976).

---

[4] The Sandinista insurgency in Nicaragua, which the Miskitu Indians thought did not represent their values and needs, illustrates the gap between insurgent objectives and a particular group of peasants (Hale 1996). However, when the Sandinistas came to power in 1979, they mobilized many other peasants in an effort to restructure the agricultural economy, which received much support (Ortega 1990).

The state may co-opt community-initiated militias at a later stage of the civil war, but this often depends on the strength of the state. While militias are associated with auxiliaries of incumbents in wars in which the state has a military advantage, in wars with equal capabilities among the conflict parties, militias take on a more autonomous role (Kalyvas 2006, 107n44).

The proposed militia typology helps to structure the phenomenon of militias and provide useful analytical differences. In this book, I explain how community-initiated militias form as part-time forces. To ensure leverage of the theory, I compare the formation and evolution of these forces to those of state-initiated part-time forces.

2.3 CIVILIAN AGENCY AND MILITIA FORMATION

When, where, and why do communities form militias? In wars that are characterized by high levels of violence against civilians, people can choose a variety of strategies to provide for their own security. Intelligence gathering, nightly patrols, systems to alert people of imminent violence, identifying protected spaces to flee to, or declaring a peace community are all forms of unarmed security provision organized by a community. In addition, security provision can take on the form of armed groups for defensive or offensive purposes. This book seeks to understand the conditions under which communities form such armed groups – militias. The first part of the theory considers the *timing* of militia formation. The second part analyzes the *location* of militia formation. The third part specifies the *process* of militia mobilization.

2.3.1 The Timing of Community-Initiated Militia Formation

When do militias form? The timing of community-initiated militia formation refers to the strategic context in which militias form. The strategic context shapes the expectations of community residents and elites about future violence and thus their preferences about what actions to take.

Community residents form militias when insurgent and incumbent armies enter a military stalemate at the local level, which I refer to as a "community-empowering stalemate." A military stalemate can be defined as "a situation where neither combatant is able to make noteworthy advances on the battlefield due to the strength of the opposing side, and neither side believes that the situation will improve in the near future" (Walter 1997, 347). This is a common definition of a military stalemate related to the balance of military capabilities (Licklider 1993, 309; Schulhofer-Wohl 2019, 7). A stalemate on the district or provincial level can coincide with a stalemate on the national level, although it does not have to. Usually, stalemates characterize the strategic situation in which governments and insurgents find themselves on the national level – a situation that prevents decisive victory of one side

(Fearon 2004, 276).[5] However, given the disjunction between war dynamics on the local and the national levels (Kalyvas 2003; Lubkemann 2005), local military stalemates may exist regionally when there is no stalemate nationally, and in turn a national stalemate may not reflect the strategic situation at regional or local levels.

There are two possible types of military stalemates. A military stalemate arises either when territorial control is relatively constant, which means that the level of violence against civilians by the incumbent is relatively low, or when territorial control changes frequently and incumbent violence is high (Kalyvas 2006, 207). In the first case, incumbents – the armed actor in control – use civil war violence selectively to punish those civilians who they suspect of supporting the enemy. In this way, armed groups seek to ensure that civilians collaborate and provide them with the necessary intelligence about those who support the enemy (Kalyvas 2006). Incumbents attempt to expand their base of popular support, as occurred in El Salvador with the decrease in state violence against civilians and the provision of basic services (Wood 2003, 132, 150). Thus, a "*local* political equilibrium" between the El Salvadoran government and the Farabundo Martí National Liberation Front (FMLN) emerged (Wood 2003, 150).[6] In such situations war economies flourish, as the warring parties seek to reap benefits from the ongoing war, as happened in Liberia when a military stalemate arose two years after President Samuel Doe's death in September 1990 (Ellis 1999, 25, 169; cf. Le Billon 2001).

The second type of military stalemate is particularly conducive to the bottom-up mobilization of militias as it allows for more civilian agency. In this second type, the military stalemate results in a war of attrition, during which both sides try to hurt the other as much as possible. After the war in Chechnya, for example, evolved into a stalemate in 2002, "Chechen fighters were 'no longer able to confront Russian troops head-on, but they remain determined to inflict as much pain as possible in the name of Chechen independence'" (Kalyvas 2006, 164n33, citing a report from *The New York Times*). In this context, states often adopt scorched-earth tactics as their main counterinsurgency measure to kill potential collaborators indiscriminately and destroy the insurgents' popular support base. This was the case, for instance, in

---

[5] Fearon's (2004) definition of a military stalemate is different from Walter's (1997) in that Fearon's model allows for fluctuating capabilities and therefore changing expectations about future success. In Walter's concept, a stalemate implies that no positive expectations exist about future decisive moves. I take a position between these two and assume that a military stalemate does not allow the contending parties to expect that they will prevail decisively over the other in the near future, but that capabilities may change and allow small advances that might prove advantageous in the negotiation process of a peace settlement.

[6] In El Salvador, this local equilibrium led some peasants to adopt a strategy of neutrality. These peasants saw themselves as standing between two armies and could only protect their lives and livelihoods by supporting both of them (Wood 2003, 153–54).

Mozambique during the anticolonial war, when the Portuguese colonial regime indiscriminately targeted potential collaborators of the liberation movement (Reis and Oliveira 2012). The high cost of military stalemates has led analysts to contend that conflict parties should prefer negotiated settlements to wars of attrition (Zartman 1989). However, problems in credibly committing to settlements in an environment of fluctuating state capabilities lead to prolonged civil war. The state's commitments are not credible, and the hope remains that one day one's own side prevails over the other (Fearon 2004).

Though civilians must bear much of the violence in such costly military stalemates of the second type, these stalemates can be community-empowering. Community residents form militias when indiscriminate violence is high, the incumbent's territorial control over a core area is relatively stable but constantly under threat, and peripheral areas change control often (see Kalyvas 2008a, 1059). In such a situation, incumbents find themselves virtually under siege; limited control over access roads leads to a lack of resources, which in turn leads to a failure of the incumbent to protect the population under its control.

Community-empowering military stalemates shape the preferences of communities and elites in the following ways. First, regarding community preferences, the population receives sufficient protection from neither the insurgent nor the incumbent forces. In such situations, neither cooperation with the dominant armed group nor defection to the enemy promises to improve civilians' security. By fleeing to an area between zones of control, civilians lose access to both their farming plots and relief goods, which also endangers their food security (Justino 2009). Civilians may think that they are better protected when they become combatants (Kalyvas and Kocher 2007). However, joining the insurgents is unlikely as people become alienated with the armed group that inflicts violence upon them. Similarly, people may avoid joining the incumbent security forces either because of the army's perpetration of violence against civilians or because joining does not promise protection as the fighting intensifies due to the lack of a military advantage. This difficult situation makes civilians vulnerable and war-weary, inducing a preference to form militias.

Second, from the administrative elite perspective, the population's frequent displacement disrupts the control over people, the delivery of relief supplies, and the provision of state services. Thus the local administration's primary goal is to protect and hold the population under its control. If the state security forces present in a community – these may include regular security forces or state-initiated militias – are too small or otherwise unable to fulfill this goal, and the administrative elites' demands for regional or national military commando support are not met, community residents and their leaders look for alternative solutions. This provides an opportunity for alternative forms of security provision. Administrative elites are forced to tolerate or even actively support the formation of armed forces outside the regular state security apparatus and with substantial influence of community leaders.

In sum, community residents form militias when community-empowering military stalemates emerge. The population sees no better option for survival than organizing its own protection in the form of militias. In the absence of military support from regional or national commandos, administrative elites are forced to tolerate or even actively support the formation of such irregular forces.

2.3.2 The Location of Community-Initiated Militia Formation

Where do militias form? The strategic context of militia formation indicates that the experience of violence and state responses to that violence shape people's expectations about future violence and, thus, their preferences about their own response to that violence. However, expectations are influenced not only by events that occur within one's own community but also by events in neighboring communities. Communities' decisions to form militias are often influenced by neighboring communities' experience with militias. In fact, like other forms of violent collective action – riots, rebellions, revolutions – militias diffuse across geographic boundaries, be they defined by national borders or local boundaries.

I distinguish between initial diffusion – the spread of a militia – and sustained diffusion – the integration of a militia into the local security apparatus. *Initial diffusion* of militias depends on the relationship between the communities among which diffusion occurs. Ethnic, ideological, cultural, and historical bonds between communities facilitate initial diffusion, in particular when these bonds are reinforced by the (temporary) migration of "diffusion agents" – community residents and local elites – between these communities. Moreover, when militias reduce violence in neighboring communities, community residents learn that forming militias serves them better than staying passive. *Sustained diffusion* depends on the institutional context of the receiving community. When elites are relatively unified, local officials integrate militias into existing institutions. Relative unity among elites prevents community-initiated militias from becoming the private army of individual leaders. The community and its leaders need to trust and support a civilian-based armed group during war to facilitate its widespread mobilization. When elites are united in their understanding of the new armed group's aims and strategies, community residents and local elites have more trust in the militia's ability to curb violence, and hence support the new institution, ensuring its success.

The notion that revolutions do not occur in and of themselves but need to be nourished by the spread of ideas and actions across geographic and group boundaries is a recurring theme in many different episodes of collective action. Diffusion of ideas creates solidarity and fosters identification with others in the same situation.[7] However, the concept of diffusion applies to much broader areas of scholarly research. Scholars interested in the evolution of policies, institutions, and organizations use diffusion to explain how ideas and models of action – opinions, attitudes, and practices – spread or disseminate across geographic or group boundaries. This research agenda assumes that "there are enduring, cross-boundary dependencies in the evolution of policies and institutions" (Gleditsch and Ward 2006, 912). Social movement scholars have adopted this perspective to inquire into the conditions and mechanisms of how both established and innovative collective action frames and repertoires across communities, movements, and nation-states spread (Givan, Roberts, and Soule 2010, 4; Strang and Soule 1998).[8]

Concerning the study of armed conflict, the regional and transnational dimensions of civil wars in Africa and Asia in the 1990s and 2000s triggered renewed interest in the geographic spread of civil war. Scholars have long recognized the interdependence of civil wars and nationalist movements (Lake and Rothchild 1998; Buhaug and Gleditsch 2008; Beissinger 2002). The movement of insurgent groups, refugee populations, and weapons across porous borders regionalizes civil wars (Salehyan and Gleditsch 2006; Salehyan 2007).[9] However, scholarly efforts to understand the process and precise mechanisms of how civil wars spread are relatively recent (Checkel 2013; Wood 2013, 233–34).

Dominated by studies of international politics, conflict scholars have analyzed the diffusion of violent collective action repertoires primarily as a transnational phenomenon rather than something that also occurs within states across community and group boundaries. By repertoires of collective action, I mean a set of forms of collective action available to a community or group (Tilly 1978; Gutiérrez-Sanín and Wood 2017; Ahram 2016). I focus on how and why a particular form of violent collective action (forming militias) spreads across communities during civil war. Militias can spread across community boundaries either through direct contacts traveling between communities or mediation through third actors (see Tarrow and McAdam 2005; Givan, Roberts, and

---

[7] On how the diffusion of ideas is necessary to form networks of solidarity for revolutions, see Gramsci (2000, 58): "This means that every revolution has been preceded by an intense labor of criticism, by the diffusion of culture and the spread of ideas among masses of men who are at first resistant and who have no ties of solidarity with others in the same condition."

[8] The concept of diffusion stresses interdependencies as a precondition for a phenomenon to spread across boundaries (Wood 2013, 233). Interdependencies between units can take on various forms. Diffusion can occur through personal contacts, which resembles contagion, or through impersonal contacts by way of stimulation of an external source (Boudon and Bourricaud 1989, 126–32). Tarrow and McAdam (2005) refer to these pathways as relational diffusion and non-relational diffusion, and suggest a third pathway, that of brokerage. In other works, brokerage is also referred to as mediated (or indirect) diffusion through a third actor that connects previously unconnected units (cf. Givan, Roberts, and Soule 2010).

[9] For an overview of research on the diffusion of civil wars, see Wood (2013).

Soule 2010). I call such actors who temporarily migrate and spread forms of collective action "diffusion agents." I explain why diffusion is sometimes sustained, meaning that the community integrates the new form of violent collective action into its collective action repertoire. Communities – influenced by surrounding communities or diffusion agents – may try to adopt various forms of collective action during war; what is more compelling is whether these forms persist and become institutionalized, thereby influencing the dynamics of war across time and space.

Diffusion depends on the relation between two units and on the characteristics of the receiving unit. Research on the diffusion of civil wars suggests that ethnic or ideological bonds between units or refugee movements, including rebel combatants, to a neighboring state make the spread of violence more likely (Saideman 2002; Salehyan and Gleditsch 2006; Salehyan 2007). Research on how policies and norms diffuse shows that diffusion depends on the coalition of actors in the receiving unit and their ability to translate new policies and norms into the local context (Acharya 2004; Gilardi 2010). This means that once a bond is established or reinforced between two units, sustained diffusion occurs when the coalition of actors allows new forms to integrate into the local institutional context.

Applied to militia formation, militias initially diffuse when two communities are linked via ethnic, ideological, cultural, or historical bonds. A crucial mechanism that accounts for diffusion is the temporary or permanent *migration* of diffusion agents who reinforce such preexisting bonds (see Franzese and Hays 2008). Diffusion agents spread stories about militias' success in decreasing violence against civilians, leading to initial diffusion to other communities. Through such success stories, community residents learn that active resistance rather than passivity helps to achieve security. Success can be understood as the perceived ability of a militia to create stability in a village so that community residents no longer have to flee to protect themselves from insurgent violence. In the diffusion literature, this mechanism is referred to as *learning* – the updating of previously held beliefs (Dobbin, Simmons, and Garrett 2007, 462).[10]

An empirical implication of this argument is that in order to learn from other communities, community residents have to define their situation as sufficiently similar to the one in which militias already exist to believe that a militia will also improve their situation (Tarrow and McAdam 2005). This may be influenced by the strategic situation in which the community finds itself. As outlined above, local military stalemates are necessary for militia formation; this implies that if the same conditions of local military stalemates exist in a neighboring community, then militias should spread.

---

[10] If communities form militias to signal their commitment to the state (Schubiger 2021), this might also be described as *emulation*, since communities do not necessarily change previously held beliefs (Elkins and Simmons 2005).

Community linkages and militia success in neighboring communities are necessary for initial diffusion, but they are not sufficient for the sustained diffusion of community-initiated militias. A last condition thus relates to the characteristics of the receiving community. The institutional context of preexisting security forces and authority structures is crucial for understanding when sustained diffusion occurs. Divisions among social, political, and military elites may prevent militia formation in the long term. Militias may change the balance of power within a community and – when tied to certain elites – risk that one group exerts more power than another. This risk may lead some elites to prevent or stop the militias from forming or isolate the emerging militia. In contrast, when social, political and military elites are relatively unified, militias do not risk upsetting the balance of power among elites and can be incorporated into the existing security apparatus.

An empirical implication of this argument is that militias that change the balance of power among elites serve the interests of elites only and resemble a private army. Unless the commanding elites have independent income, these militias typically have access to few resources and recruits, which limits their activities and potentially their life span. In contrast, a militia with broad-based support from a range of different elites has access to more resources, including the most crucial one – new members.

In sum, I expect that initial diffusion of militias occurs in communities that are tied to each other by ethnic, ideological, cultural, and historical bonds, and where one community experiences militias improving stability for its residents. Diffusion agents who travel from one community to another reinforce such bonds and tell the story of militia success. Communities learn from each other when residents are convinced that their situation is sufficiently similar to that of a neighboring community, such as in the case of a local military stalemate. Sustained diffusion occurs when social, political, and military elites are relatively unified in the receiving community, which prevents militias from becoming private, semiprofessional armies.

2.3.3 The Process of Community-Initiated Militia Mobilization

How do militias mobilize their members? The arguments above account for the formation and diffusion of militias by identifying the factors that change people's expectations about future violence and how they can respond to it. But once a community forms a militia, what makes the new organization grow? What are the mechanisms of social mobilization that operate in this instance? I suggest a causal path of militia mobilization that pays special attention to the social context. While the community level can explain militia formation and diffusion, it is at the individual and group levels that militia mobilization occurs (see Eck 2010, 10). Militias successfully mobilize when the militia leadership offers potential members a means to manage uncertainty about future events – about how best to protect oneself and one's family. Militias that appeal to social conventions that invoke collective meaning within the community help manage uncertainty and are therefore more successful in attracting members than other militias.

Many approaches to mobilization for violence rely on a rational cost–benefit approach, which implies that if the benefits of joining an armed group outweigh the cost, then joining is a likely outcome (Olson 1965; Tullock 1971; Popkin 1979; Lichbach 1995; Weinstein 2007; Humphreys and Weinstein 2008).[11] This assumes that probabilities of receiving such benefits and avoiding related costs can be estimated, and thus acted upon. However, the costs and benefits of participation in rebellion are often difficult to calculate due to the unpredictable nature of war. What dominates decision-making during war is *uncertainty* about future events. In economics, the distinction between risk and uncertainty goes back to Knight (1921) and Keynes (1921) and implies that while estimates about future events are possible in risky environments based on known probability distributions, uncertain environments are too unstable and unpredictable to lend themselves to rational calculations (Nelson and Katzenstein 2014).[12] In irregular civil war, uncertainty is present when indiscriminate violence against civilians by insurgents and/or incumbents is the dominant form of violence. This is the case in contested areas in which no social contract between armed groups and civilians exists, or in areas of complete control in which the rival armed actor has no access to information (Kalyvas 2006; Arjona 2016). In such contexts, without the available information to calculate probable consequences of their actions, the question arises as to *how* people make decisions about how best to protect themselves. Accordingly, the focus here lies on the *process* of decision-making, not only the *outcome* of that process.

The process of decision-making under uncertainty is shaped by existing familiar repertoires and scripts. Applying the conceptual distinction between risk and uncertainty to decision-making in international relations, Nelson and Katzenstein (2014) argue that in the presence of uncertainty, actors' decisions are rooted in social conventions – shared templates and understandings that coordinate action – rather than rational calculation. In situations of crises and social change, individuals' decision-making process can no longer rely on

---

[11] According to Kalyvas and Kocher (2007), however, the risk of joining the rebellion may actually be lower than the risk of remaining a noncombatant due to the nature of violence in insurgencies, which is predominantly indiscriminate, thus targeting innocent civilians. As combatants hide among civilians, the civilian population becomes a target for both sides. Instead of exposing combatants to more violence, insurgent groups may actually offer protection from such violence. This logic may apply to militias when we assume that insurgents inflict indiscriminate violence on the civilian population under government control, and thus the risk of nonparticipation in state-initiated or community-initiated militias equals or exceeds participation in such armed groups.

[12] Nelson and Katzenstein (2014, 365) argue that what is often presented as "uncertainty" in political economy should actually be called "risk."

established probability distributions. Rather, people rely on common know-ledge from their immediate social environment to stabilize uncertainty and guide decision-making.

Regarding armed group mobilization, Nelson and Katzenstein's theory suggests that social conventions help manage the uncertainty of war. This fits with two major lines of research in conflict studies. First, Gutiérrez and Wood's (2014) call for attention to immaterial and other-regarding incentives rather than self-regarding, material incentives for armed group mobilization in high-risk circumstances, including the noninstrumental, community-building use of ideology. Second, a growing number of researchers have emphasized that, in making their decisions under uncertain conditions, individuals are embedded in social contexts. Strong communities are important in facilitating recruitment through information, support networks, and normative commitments (Petersen 2001; Parkinson 2013). Shesterinina (2016, 417) shows how families and friends provide "access to information that is critical for making difficult choices about whether to fight for the group, escape the fighting, or defect to the other side." But communities do not only provide crucial information but also access to a repertoire of collective action. Kaplan (2017, 34) argues that uncertainty during war encourages civilians to strive for "autonomy" and organize themselves. He observes in the context of unarmed civilians' responses to civil war violence that "[a]n option to make daily life more certain and increase chances of survival is to turn to indigenous – meaning local – organiza-tions." Similarly, Arjona (2016) has shown that preexisting community organ-izations that regulate civilian life are an important condition for civilians' abilities to resist armed groups from intruding into their community.

My argument extends the second line of research, as I emphasize the social conventions – the "repertoire" or "script" – that communities can rely upon to respond to an uncertain situation. I bring together the question of individual motives with the nature of the group that seeks to attract participants to show that even though participants may be guided by various (non-)instrumental motives, it matters what *kind* of group they are asked to join.

Armed groups that rely on social conventions attract members through two main mechanisms: *commonality* and the *context for self-empowerment*. The first mechanism is commonality between the militia and potential participants: Building on social conventions, the militia is more familiar and less threatening to potential joiners. Such conventions are rituals and routines that transmit meaning to community residents and range from spiritual means to nonviolent forms of collective action. Relying on social conventions, militia institutions resonate with communities; which means that militias effectively frame their purpose of self-defense (Benford and Snow 2000). Resonance occurs when a militia's purpose is framed as credible and salient. Credible means that the framing reflects the militia's actual activities and that the militia leader has expertise to direct these activities. Salient means that the militia's purpose is central to the lives of the people and resonates with cultural narratives

(Benford and Snow 2000). For example, Ranger (1985) argues that in southern Africa, respect for traditional religion made liberation movements' ideology more relevant to peasant experiences and thus strengthened peasant support.[13] This implies that where militias bring with them "imported" ideologies and routines, successful mobilization is less likely. In addition to creating resonance, militias also need to provide innovation to motivate joiners. Community residents who neither feel protected by the state nor by the rebels "seek innovative courses of action" (Masullo 2015, 47) to overcome the limits of existing options. References to social conventions invite communities to adapt them to new social contexts, thereby creating a form of "invented tradition" (Hobsbawm and Ranger 1983) that legitimizes the new institution. The innovation may consist of new forms of legitimating leaders, new definitions of eligibility for membership, or new rules that govern participation.

The second mechanism, *a context for self-empowerment*, builds on the first. The reliance on repertoires rooted in the community facilitates people's autonomy in shaping their own future, creating a belief in agency and therefore a context for self-empowerment. This idea builds on Wood's (2003) concepts of "pleasure in agency" and "participation," which explain peasant support for rural insurgency in El Salvador. "Pleasure in agency" refers to participants' "ownership of successes of their collective actions" and expression of pride in the collective contribution to justice (Wood 2003, 234–35), while "participation" emphasizes the expectation of success of collective action, which raises hope and a sense of purpose (Wood 2003, 232). The concept of agency here refers to "protective strategies to retain autonomy, or self-rule" (Kaplan 2017, 34), as it has been used in works on civilian agency in nonviolent communities. The commonality and the innovative character of the new institution foster the sense of purpose and the expectation of success as it improves upon existing social conventions.

I stipulate that social conventions are a necessary condition for militia mobilization by providing commonality between the militia and potential participants and a context for participants' self-empowerment. A group that makes use of social conventions fares better in mobilizing members than a group that does not.

2.4 RESEARCH DESIGN

The research design for this book builds on within-case and cross-case process tracing, using subnational evidence from the civil war in Mozambique (1976–92).

---

[13] This process is reflected in social movement research on diffusion. The diffusion of collective action repertoires is only successful if these repertoires can be adapted to the local context and/or mixed with already established repertoires (Campbell 2002).

2.4.1 Case Selection and Data Collection

The goal of this book is to explain the formation of community-initiated militias across time, the diffusion of community-initiated militias across space, and the process by which such militias mobilize their members. To develop and explore the theory, I designed a subnational study of how community-initiated militias in Mozambique formed and diffused during the country's civil war from 1976 to 1992 between the incumbent Frelimo and the insurgent Renamo. In particular, I study the largest militia, Naparama, and its spread across the northern territory.

Mozambique offers an excellent opportunity for study. The history of the war provides subnational variation on the variables of interest – military stalemates, levels of violence and territorial control, ethnic heterogeneity, and institutional (dis-)unity (Vines 1991; Wilson 1992; Nordstrom 1997; Weinstein 2007). Moreover, it is puzzling why community-initiated militias formed in Frelimo-held areas in Nampula and Zambézia provinces, as popular support for Renamo in these two provinces was stronger than in the southern region and the level of indiscriminate violence against civilians lower (Roesch 1992, 464; Finnegan 1992, 72). In addition, militias in Mozambique's war have not been studied in as much depth as the insurgent forces, even though their formation and activity provide important insights into why Mozambique experienced such a wide variation of violence. In the two provinces under study, Zambézia and Nampula, both community-initiated and state-initiated militias operated during the war. Thus, it is possible to compare how different types of militias form and mobilize.

In order to collect the necessary data, I conducted thirteen months of fieldwork in the capital and five districts in two provinces of Mozambique between 2010 and 2016.[14] I carried out more than 250 semi-structured interviews and oral histories with community members, former militia members, soldiers, and insurgents, public functionaries, and community leaders. I collected more than 10,000 pages of district and provincial government wartime reports and other government documents. In addition, I spoke to journalists, politicians, and researchers in various cities about the history of the war and its legacy.[15] From the interviews and archival material, I obtained detailed information on community histories; levels of violence and territorial control by insurgents and the government; motivations for joining the militia; the relationship between the militia, government, and the population; and current activities of former militia members who demand compensation from the government for their wartime contribution.

---

[14] See map of Mozambique's provinces in Figure 4.1 and map of the Nampula and Zambézia provinces indicating the fieldwork sites in Figure 5.1.

[15] I discuss data collection methods in detail in the Appendix and the challenges of fieldwork in Chapter 3.

TABLE 2.2. *Overview of research design*

	Analytical strategy	Cases	Case selection
Formation	Within-case analysis	Naparama in Zambézia province	Militia presence varies over time
Diffusion	Controlled comparison	Lugela and Namarrói districts	High levels of war-affectedness;
	Case study	Mecubúri district	Militia presence varies across space
Mobilization	Controlled comparison	State- and community-initiated militias in Nicoadala district	High levels of war-affectedness; Militia presence varies according to type
	Case study	State- and community-initiated militias in Murrupula district	

2.4.2 Analytical Strategy and Methods for Data Analysis

To study the formation and diffusion of militias, I combine within-case analysis over time with cross-sectional comparisons. Within-case analysis is suitable to study the process of the formation of Naparama in northern Mozambique over time (the militia as unit of analysis). I use controlled comparisons for the cross-sectional analysis of why Naparama diffused to certain communities but not to others (the militia in a certain community as unit of analysis). I also compare the formation and evolution of Naparama with that of the state-initiated part-time militia (the militia as unit of analysis) (see Table 2.2).

I use process tracing to construct theoretical narratives that identify causal pathways, thereby confirming or disconfirming alternative explanations (Hall 2003).[16] Process tracing has elements of both theory generating and theory testing (Bennett 2008). It puts special emphasis on social processes by linking causal variables with different outcomes over time. It is therefore well suited for a theoretical framework that emphasizes causal mechanisms (Checkel 2008).

Process tracing has several advantages. First, process tracing is well suited to address the complex causes of militia formation and capture the endogenous relationships between different variables that account for how community-initiated militias form and diffuse. The method can help address complex causality, the problem of feedback loops, and endogenous relationships between variables (George and Bennett 2005). As a consequence, process

---

[16] Scholars in the social sciences have developed many different approaches to process tracing. The different approaches can be broadly divided into the generation of theoretical narratives and the generation of historical narratives (Caporaso 2009). While the former is guided by theory and seeks broader generalizations, the latter seeks to explain specific (historical) events. The approach I follow in this book is the former.

tracing can reduce the gap that emerged between the ontology and the methodology in comparative politics – between the acknowledgment that the social
world is characterized by a diversity of causal relationships and the methods
that are unable to meet these challenges (Hall 2003).

Second, cross-sectional large-n studies often suffer from poor data quality.
As a result, researchers may mis-categorize certain armed groups as militias, or
they may not distinguish between different types of militias due to a lack of
sufficient data on all cases. By focusing on few cases and studying them in
depth, process tracing improves data quality and can better uncover omitted
variables. Process tracing allows for causal inferences within the limits of a
single case or few cases (Bennett and Elman 2006). To improve causal inference
and explore external validity, I conduct out-of sample case studies for each part
of the theory (Lyall 2015).

Third, identifying causal mechanisms is a crucial part of theory building and
a necessary building block to advance the research agenda on militias and
compare militias to other forms of violent collective action. Process tracing
improves theory building by understanding how causal mechanisms work that
connect different variables to each other while holding many variables constant
(Checkel 2008; Gerring 2010; Kalyvas 2008b). Finally, process tracing is a
suitable strategy for an approach that is grounded in methodological and
theoretical pluralism (Checkel 2008). Contexts of complex causality are well
suited for approaches that remain flexible with regard to their theoretical
assumptions, as it is possible to explain different aspects of the phenomenon
under study using theories with different assumptions about human behavior.

Process tracing, as I apply it, has two steps. First, I use the method to check
which of the proposed values of the causal and outcome variables, as suggested by
the alternative hypotheses, is congruent with the observed values of these variables.
Second, I trace the mechanisms that link the causal variables with the outcome
variables. For each case (each militia or each militia in a certain district), I map the
potential factors that lead to community-initiated militias forming and diffusing
and analyze the extent to which they affected the outcome.

I analyze the interview and archival data, as well as my field notes, with
software for qualitative analysis (TAMS Analyzer, Weinstein 2012), which
helps code portions of the text files and then group text portions belonging to
predefined codes. The qualitative data from my first field site, Nicoadala district
in Zambézia province, informed the theory development. Data from the
remaining field sites is used to further explore the theory.

The following chapter discusses in detail the opportunities and challenges of
conducting fieldwork in such a polarized society as Mozambique, which is
important to take into account when analyzing information collected about a
war that ended more than twenty years ago. In the subsequent chapters,
I present an overview of the history of the war and the empirical analyses of
when, where, and how militias formed in Mozambique.

3

Intervention, Autonomy, and Power
in Polarized Societies

Challenges and Opportunities of Historical Fieldwork

The secretary of a small village in Murrupula district in northern Mozambique received me and my research assistant with a concerned expression on his face when we visited the village for a second time. Following our first visit, the police had arrested four people from the area and incarcerated them for six days. During our first stay, we had conducted extensive interviews with former members of the community-initiated Naparama militia, which was disbanded at the end of the war. At the time of my fieldwork, some militia units were trying to lobby for recognition of their war effort to receive demobilization benefits. The village secretary had made a connection between the imprisonments of the four residents and our first visit, since the four were arrested while helping to register former Naparama members (and other militiamen as well). The registration served the purpose of counting all former militia members in the area to pressure the government to formally demobilize (and pay) them. The Naparama leader of Nampula province who had introduced us to the Naparama militia in Murrupula district organized the registration. After the provincial Naparama leader had collected names and fees from about 250 militiamen and left, the police charged the local Naparama leadership who had helped with the registration with betrayal and arrested them. According to the police, it was unlawful to register militiamen and collect money from them. The arrested men were released after the provincial Naparama leader paid a significant fine to the municipality. Afterwards, people asked the local Naparama leaders to find out what happened to the money they used to pay their registration fees.

This story from my fieldwork in rural Mozambique in 2011–12 demonstrates the ways in which fieldwork in the aftermath of war can have unintended consequences and can create ethical and methodological dilemmas for the research process. The researcher's activities may provide a backdrop for social mobilization and opportunities for personal enrichment for interlocutors, who decide to take advantage of people's hopes of future benefits. Nampula's Naparama leader had not visited the local Naparama community in Murrupula since the general elections in 1994. Only when I asked him to introduce me to that community and we went there together did he reestablish contact with the former militia unit. In a way, I had encouraged the reestablishment of that contact, which the provincial Naparama leader abused for his personal benefit. That benefit had both monetary and political ramifications. During our conversations, he had tried to establish himself as the primary Naparama leader during the war, a fact that many other sources contest. It is likely that through this registration process, he was trying to mobilize Naparama to bolster his claim of being the one and only Naparama leader. As with other Naparama members (and also former members of the armed forces), he was disappointed that the government had neither recognized him as a war veteran nor provided him with demobilization payments. In fact, a considerable number of military members were not recognized as demobilized soldiers as part of the peace agreement signed in Rome in 1992 and were thus ineligible for demobilization benefits. These included members of the armed forces who were demobilized before the end of the war, members of Frelimo's auxiliary forces such as the Naparama, and the "popular militias."

These unintended consequences are linked to how legacies of war – social, economic, and political polarization and historical marginalization – influence how communities make sense of researchers' activities in their midst. As Sluka reminds us, research participants "are naturally going to try to figure out what you are doing here," and previous experiences with strangers in the community provide categories such as "spy, journalist, policeman, tax collector, and missionary" that may be mistakenly applied to the researcher (Sluka 1995, 283). Experiences from the war in Mozambique continue to impact daily lives, and contemporary concerns about the distribution of social, economic, and political benefits all contribute to the perception of the researcher as a powerful and ambiguous figure who can influence people's lives in positive as well as negative ways. Although some community residents may feel disempowered by the researcher's presence, others may attempt to manipulate the researcher's work for the purpose of their own economic and political empowerment.

This chapter reflects my attempt to navigate the polarized political landscape in Mozambique's society. Though I encountered many challenges along the way, I collected more than 10,000 pages of documents in government archives and conducted more than 250 interviews and oral histories with community members, former militia members, former rebel combatants, former soldiers, (former) government officials, politicians, and academics in five districts and the capital. I worked together with two Mozambican research assistants who spoke all the necessary local languages and had experience in data collection for international projects. They helped me with arranging interviews, translating from local languages into Portuguese, and explaining cultural particularities. As Mozambicans from the regions we worked in, but long-term residents of the city of Nampula and Quelimane, respectively, my assistants were sufficiently knowledgeable about the provinces we worked in (and their languages), but outsider enough to not be identified with a certain political position. In fact, as I outline below, in Nampula, my research assistant was perceived as a stranger just like me, which made our access to some respondents problematic.

Conflict researchers have recognized the ethical and practical challenges that research on violence entails (Nordstrom and Robben 1995; Wood 2006, 2007; Sriram et al. 2009; Fujii 2012; Mazurana, Jacobsen, and Gale 2013; Parkinson and Wood 2015; Cronin-Furman and Lake 2018). However, as Malejacq and Mukhopadhyay (2016) note, there is still little transparency and debate on how researchers form and manage relationships in the field and what kinds of ethical compromises and methodological adaptations they have to accept in order to collect the necessary data for their projects. Researchers in political science have learned from their colleagues in anthropology (and geography) for whom the position and impact of the researcher on the local community has become a central concern for how to "do" anthropology (Clifford and Marcus 1986; England 1994; Sirnate 2014). However, what is often obscured rather than openly addressed are the ways in which the researcher becomes a political actor capable of reinforcing existing power structures and, by disempowering or empowering local actors, influencing social realities in communities under study. This is significant, as the autonomy of not only the researched but also the researcher may be jeopardized, and there is a risk that local actors may manipulate researcher's presence and work. This is true not only for research in today's volatile conflict zones (Malejacq and Mukhopadhyay 2016), but also for research in (postwar) polarized societies in which political conflicts linger on and reinforce economic, social, and political inequalities (Gerharz 2009, 2).[1]

The limited understanding of the workings of power, and by extension the limits of researcher neutrality, is often due to the fact that field researchers are typically more concerned about the data that they extract from the field site and how to mitigate systematic bias than about what happens to the field site as such. This means that challenges of access to research participants or the "subtext" or "meta-data" (Fujii 2010) from conversations, such as lies, silences, and evasions, are considered "obstacles" rather than "a source of

---

[1] By "polarization," I mean, following Esteban and Schneider (2008, 133),

the extent to which the population is clustered around a small number of distant poles. This notion of polarization is particularly relevant to the analysis of conflict, because it stands for the idea that the tensions within a society of individuals or states result from two simultaneous decisions: identification with other subjects within the own group of reference and distancing oneself from one or several other competing groups.

In Mozambique, the sixteen years of war contributed to political polarization between sympathizers of the party in power, Frelimo, and the rebel group turned opposition party, Renamo, which, during the war, was referred to as "armed bandits" and largely seen as "terrorists" without a political project.

knowledge for ethnographers" (Wedeen 2010, 256). In fact, researchers may alter the field site and the data in ways that are difficult to account for and "reverse" during data analysis. As Goodhand argues, such intervention in conflict settings is not only a methodological challenge but also an ethical issue, as it "may affect the incentive systems and structures driving violent conflict or impact upon the coping strategies and safety of communities" (Goodhand 2000, 12).

It was puzzling to me that the social, economic, and political legacies of the war affected my interactions with rural communities in Mozambique, as the country is often hailed as a successful example of postwar peace building and reconciliation (Boutros-Ghali 1995). One could expect that (unofficial) reconciliation processes, national reconstruction, and the passing of time would have helped create confidence in people's futures (Honwana 2002; Igreja, Dias-Lambranca, and Richters 2008). However, the country remains polarized even decades after the end of the war (Weinstein 2002; Darch 2015). Fear of renewed violence still influences political and social life in rural Mozambican communities – for good reason, as the resurgence of violence in the center of the country in 2013–14 demonstrates (Darch 2015; Pearce 2020). Moreover, the spoils of recent discoveries of natural resources have not (yet) reached the ordinary citizen, leading to increases in already high levels of inequality (International Monetary Fund 2016).

In a society seeking to overcome its violent past and advance economic development, the ways in which communities tried to make sense of my as well as my research assistant's presence had two major consequences for the (perceived) autonomy of research participants and of my own work. The first was related to a narrative of suspicion and mistrust about me and my work that stemmed from people feeling severely disempowered with respect to their control over their own well-being. My presence was threatening to some community residents because I reminded them of other white foreigners who had mingled in their community's affairs throughout history. The second narrative was related to whether and how participants could manipulate my presence and my work in a ways that benefited them economically or politically. Some research participants saw my presence as an opportunity to escape from the uncertainties of their own lives regarding jobs, livelihoods, and political projects. In the remainder of this chapter, I analyze these two responses and what they meant for the perceived autonomy of research participants and my own work. I provide specific examples from my fieldwork to highlight the implications of residents' ambiguous responses toward neutrality and power during fieldwork in polarized societies.

3.1 DISEMPOWERMENT AND RESEARCH PARTICIPANT AUTONOMY

One evening in Mecubúri district in Nampula province, a local government representative told me and my research assistant that people had been talking and wondering what we were up to. In the days before, we had walked through some of the neighborhoods of the district town and conducted interviews with residents and local leaders. The government officer reported that some people were afraid we were spreading diseases, as a number of residents had recently suffered from diarrhea. Others thought that our presence meant another war was on the horizon. As the officer elaborated, it became clear that these fears had been triggered by several events that had occurred in the area, in the province, and abroad. A few days before our arrival in Mecubúri, in October 2011, Libyan head of state Muammar Gaddafi had been killed by rebels, and the youth leader of the African National Congress in South Africa, Julius Malema, had made divisive speeches (for which he later got expelled from the party).[2] Mozambicans follow the news of both countries closely, and in their eyes, the instability in Libya and South Africa was concerning.

In addition, in the officer's view, some events closer to home had exacerbated people's wariness about our presence. A theatrical performance attempting to explain that China would build and sell 5,000 houses to the community was understood to mean that 5,000 Chinese would "invade" and settle throughout the province. People were also concerned about news that, a month before, in September 2011, one British and four Americans with heavy weapons in their luggage were briefly held at Nampula airport.[3] The men claimed that they had come to rescue a boat from Somali pirates. Over the course of our conversation that evening in Mecubúri, we learned that we were not the only strangers who were treated with suspicion. NGO workers of a US-funded project seeking to improve access to safe water regularly distribute "certeza," a chlorine-based water-purifying liquid to prevent cholera outbreaks. However, whenever cholera breaks out, Mozambicans believe these workers brought the disease (Serra 2003).[4]

Our presence in the district seemed to fit into this ill-boding sequence of events whose origins and consequences remained uncertain.[5] As Gerharz (2009) confirms, people's suspicions about researchers' motives are often triggered by their memories of past violence. In highly polarized settings such as the

---

[2] David Smith, "ANC Youth Leader Julius Malema Thrown Out of Party," *The Guardian*, November 10, 2011.

[3] "Mozambique Holds US and British 'Pirate Hunters'," *BBC News*, September 19, 2011.

[4] "Mozambique: Cholera Disinformation Leads to Clashes," *Agência de Informação de Moçambique*, February 17, 2013; Paul Fauvet, "Mozambique: 17 People Arrested for Cholera Riots in Nampula," *Agência de Informação de Moçambique*, February 22, 2013. A related phenomenon is *chupa-sangue* ("drawing blood"), which residents claim has recurred over decades in regions of Zambézia and Nampula province whenever government or international agencies visited rural communities during vaccination campaigns. These agencies are accused of drawing blood like vampires and thereby causing deaths in the community (Chichava 2007, 392–99).

[5] While my research assistant was a Mozambican who spoke the local languages, he still was perceived as a "stranger" because he was from the city and did not have any relations with the local community.

civil war in Sri Lanka, residents of Colombo quickly accused Gerharz of being a Liberation Tigers of Tamil Eelam (LTTE) sympathizer when she discussed the humanitarian situation in LTTE strongholds (Gerharz 2009, 5–6). Since Gerharz' comments reminded people in the South of their suffering from seemingly unpredictable episodes of violence, it was difficult for her to highlight the suffering of the other side and at the same time claim neutrality. Similarly, in Mozambique, people did not want a return to war and wondered about the true meaning of my work since it focused on the history of the war.

Such suspicion created a situation that prevented me from establishing trust with and gaining access to some members of the community, crucial preconditions for any successful fieldwork. Drawing on research experience in Northern Ireland, Knox shows that gaining access in politically contested environments is often problematic because communities suspect that the real research objective is "unlikely to be viewed by local actors as neutral or altruistic" (Knox 2001, 211). In the highly contested political environment of Northern Ireland, "There was immediate suspicion about the ulterior motives of this research, which had the potential to block access at worst or severely curtail data gathering" (Knox 2001, 211). This is also true for the context of my research. The officer we met that evening in Mecubúri was nowhere to be found when we tried to meet with him for an interview the following day.

All these concerns were troubling, as, without realizing it, I had become part of a social and political context in which people feared that, as a consequence of interacting with me, they would further lose control over their health and well-being. The more I (or people like me) entered their lives, the less they felt in charge. At the same time as people overestimated my power, they underestimated their own. People's responses to my presence in their communities had a similar meaning as their resistance against the distribution of chlorine, which Serra (2003) interprets as an expression of severe disempowerment. As Serra's analysis reveals, resistance against outsiders in the form of suspicion and mistrust is an expression of people's distrust in state institutions, which they perceive as being absent and failing to deliver promised services.

The sources of such feelings of disempowerment and loss of autonomy in the central and northern provinces of Mozambique are varied. First, the history of the central and northern provinces is one of political marginalization by the government in Maputo in the south of the country (Chichava 2007; Do Rosário 2009). Frelimo, the liberation movement and party in power since independence in 1975, has been perceived as a southern movement; the independence movement's penetration of both provinces during the liberation struggle was slow and ineffectual or, in the case of Nampula province, completely absent (Legrand 1993, 88); and the peasant population opposed Frelimo's policies after independence. In Nampula, it sparked popular discontent when the Frelimo government constructed communal villages and abolished traditional authorities (Geffray 1990). In Zambézia, it was the disrespect for traditional values more generally that in turn provoked opposition (Ranger 1985, 189;

O'Laughlin 1992, 115). As a result, the region was and remains a Renamo stronghold.

Second, the particular character of the civil war, a typical guerrilla war, contributed to suspicion toward strangers in rural communities. Community residents responded to my presence in ways that reflect Sluka's (1995, 283) observation that people misapply preexisting categories (e.g., being a spy) to strangers who enter their communities, which was a common concern during the war in Mozambique and in many other wars (Vlassenroot 2006). Many people referred to the war as a "war between brothers." In contrast to the anticolonial struggle, members of either side could not be identified easily, as they all belonged to the same community. The enemy could therefore always be lurking somewhere in the community. Moreover, the Renamo rebels were actively supported by Rhodesia and Apartheid South Africa. White South African advisors were regularly flown into Renamo bases. Community residents linked that experience to my presence and wondered whether I had anything to do with the war, since I was so eager to speak to them about that time period. At the end of an interview with an older male community resident, I was asked whether the war would return once I left the village. When I worked in an area in Murrupula district, Nampula, where one of the main Renamo bases was located during the war, the chief of staff of the local administration told us that there had never been a delegation with a white person staying overnight. He urged the community police chief to inform residents so that they would not think something was wrong, as his village had been "an area of the enemy."

Moreover, although Mozambique has received much development aid and has also recently discovered more natural resources, people feel they have yet to benefit from economic development. Serra's (2003) analysis points to the arrogance and distance of NGO workers that creates discontent among community residents. In different regions of Mozambique, residents have been displaced by foreign companies, such as coal mining in Tete province or the Brazilian large-scale agribusiness project ProSAVANA, which adds to the impression that strangers meddle with people's affairs, to the detriment of their livelihoods (Abelvik-Lawson 2014; Lillywhite, Kemp, and Sturman 2015; Chichava and Durán 2016).[6]

Finally, much of the hesitance in talking to us was connected to current party politics and reflects the fact that the Frelimo party never lost its dominance in Mozambican politics despite having introduced multiparty politics in its new constitution in 1990 (Sumich and Honwana 2007). Some former government officials declined to be interviewed since they did not feel qualified, which suggests that they did not feel authorized to speak and were afraid of violating

---

[6] Amos Zacarias, "Mozambique's Small Farmers Fear Brazilian-Style Agriculture," *The Guardian*, January 1, 2014.

the official party line. In other cases, these officials made sure that I had respected the administrative hierarchy and attained permission from their (former) supervisors.

This past and contemporary experience of marginalization contributed to the perception of my research assistant and I as "intruders." I dealt with this situation in several ways to establish "research legitimacy" (Knox 2001). I always respected the social and administrative hierarchy when coming into a district I had never been to, and I introduced myself and my work to local leaders to receive "'approval' from key stakeholders" (Knox 2001, 212). In the districts I visited after Mecubúri, I asked for an elder who was respected in the community as a guide who could introduce me to people, or asked for referrals from research participants, a strategy commonly referred to as "snowball sampling" (Sluka 1995, 284; Knox 2001, 212; Cohen and Arieli 2011; Romano 2006). Mistrust between Frelimo and Renamo elites implied that I was to pursue relationships with several types of "gatekeepers" (Campbell et al. 2006): with Frelimo party and state structures and, separately, with Renamo party structures. I also respected people's wishes to not being interviewed alone; when I was interviewing men, their wives often sat next to them to listen in on the conversation. I also tried to visit communities several times to establish rapport (Browne and McBride 2015; Norman 2009).

Overall, I avoided talking about politically sensitive topics (Sluka 1995, 283) and avoided mentioning "politics." In the process of trying to make sense of my presence in their communities, residents wanted to make sure that I do not have anything to do with "politics," which has negative connotations in Mozambique, as in many parts of Africa, because people believe politicians lie and enrich themselves (Ekeh 1975). A businessman and veteran of the pre- and postindependence wars in Nicoadala in Zambézia province invited me over to his house for lunch to finally "forget about politics" and "just chat." He could not understand why I was willing to "suffer" and study political history rather than do business, as Mozambique was "the place to do business." Religious community residents were concerned about my political intentions. In Murrupula, the first question of a sheikh was which party I was affiliated with.[7] In Nicoadala, a pastor only agreed to meet with me once I assured him I would not talk politics under the roof of his church.[8] When I was confronted with these concerns, I emphasized my status as a student who is independent of party politics (Knox 2001, 212).

But as many field researchers have recognized before me, neutrality is difficult to achieve, and sometimes not even desirable (Nash 1976; Sluka 1990, 1995; Gerharz 2009; Malejacq and Mukhopadhyay 2016). The strategies I adopted mitigated many of these concerns, but posed some new methodological

---

[7] Interview with religious leader (2011-11-02-Pm4), Murrupula, Nampula, November 2, 2011.
[8] Interview with religious leader (2011-09-08-Pm2), Nicoadala, Zambézia, September 8, 2011.

and ethical dilemmas. For example, it was important to take into account the ways in which people introduced me to certain communities and to consider whether the presence of certain people during interviews influenced and changed the conversations. As Campbell et al. (2006, 115–16) argue, rather than trying to be "neutral" in general, it is important to emphasize your independence from gatekeepers. It also meant that some community residents might have felt compelled to talk to me because an authority figure told them to, and not because they themselves had volunteered. It was also important to consider "gatekeeper bias" (Cohen and Arieli 2011), and in particular the issue of sampling bias (Groger, Mayberry, and Straker 1999). These dilemmas required me to provide detailed explanations and to be transparent about my activities to ensure that people were comfortable talking to me, but I also had to consider the emerging methodological limits during analysis.

However, fieldwork challenges did not always arise out of people's concern about their own disempowerment and the limits to their autonomy, but also out of their hopes for political, social, or economic empowerment, as I discuss in the next section.

3.2 EMPOWERMENT AND RESEARCHER AUTONOMY

While the reports of mistrust and suspicion in northern Mozambique were troubling, the way in which they were communicated to my research assistant and me appeared to be for political currency. The local government representative who warned us about the concerns within the community in Mecubúri apparently used these stories to pursue his own agenda and fight a political battle against the district administrator. My research assistant found out that, for unclear reasons, the administrator was not well liked among local government employees. The officer we talked to was wary of the fact that the district administrator had given us permission to work without a guide accompanying us to interviews with community members. It seemed likely that he felt his position within the local administration was not taken seriously. As someone who was in constant contact with the local police and other local leaders, he used his monopoly on information to manipulate us for his political interests and divert attention from the fact that he himself mistrusted us. As mentioned earlier, throughout our time in that district, the officer avoided being interviewed, although he had agreed to do so earlier.

This politicization of mistrust and suspicion has a long history in Mozambique. During our conversation in Mecubúri, I learned that members of the "opposition" sprinkle "chlorine" (actually they use flour), which supposedly spreads cholera, on some people's doorsteps, implying that if the residents touch it, they will be contaminated. Thus, while the initial narrative about how cholera spreads expresses disempowerment and distrust of state institutions, this counter-narrative puts blame on the "opposition," a diffuse group of people who oppose the Frelimo government and may be sympathetic to Renamo. Overall, such suspicions reinforce political cleavages, which are understood in many parts of Mozambique as existential threats rather than aspects of democratic politics.

Politicization can occur on several levels. Another example of how current political developments affected my research was how Renamo leaders in the provincial capital of Quelimane reacted to my request for permission to interview former Renamo combatants in the province. Since at the time of my request, national Renamo leader Afonso Dhlakama had threatened to stage a (peaceful) overthrow of the government on December 25, 2011, provincial leaders of the party did not consider this a suitable time to allow such interviews.[9] When I tried again in February 2012, the provincial party leaders in coordination with Dhlakama himself granted me permission, as the political situation had since calmed.

But my work was not only politicized with respect to its potential negative consequences. Others played with my work's potential positive consequences, as I outlined in the beginning of the chapter. In a way, the Naparama leader who had organized the registration of Naparama after our departure from Murrupula was manipulating people's hopes of future benefits, which I had (unwillingly) raised in the first place. Former Naparama members were not only surprised but also humbled by the fact that someone wanted to talk specifically to them so long after the war had ended. I was able to conduct many interviews in Mecubúri and Murrupula with Naparama who walked many miles to meet with me. Naparama members hoped that my questions would precipitate their being registered to eventually receive demobilization benefits or at least funds for "projects."

This demand for recognition and "projects" had meaning for both the individual and Naparama as a group. "You can't talk to Naparama individually," a former commander of the militia told my research assistant and me one morning in Nicoadala. We had just introduced ourselves and our project during a meeting with the group's leadership. The commander informed us that the (former) Naparama high command could give us all the information we needed, and that the remaining former combatants would speak to us as a group. He claimed that individual Naparama were not mentally capable of talking properly about the Naparama, which would result in contradicting stories. They sought to restrict my access and allow me to interview only former members that they could "control" or combatants of high rank, while discrediting other members as not telling "the truth."

The Naparama commander clearly sought to control what version of the history of the community-initiated militia would be told. He did not want my research project to jeopardize Naparama's ongoing struggle to receive

<hr />

[9] Renamo party leaders in Nampula province, whom I contacted a few months later, did not see the political situation at the time as a problem and granted me permission to interview former Renamo combatants.

recognition from the government and compensation for the group's wartime efforts. This concern was not completely unfounded. As the commander later explained, he had been taken once to the Mozambican intelligence agency's office and charged for not providing a certain document that the agency had received from other sources. The commander was afraid that I would pass along information that the combatants told me to the intelligence agency, which would in turn interrogate the Naparama leadership for not having disclosed this information previously.

My research assistant and I emphasized that I was an independent student writing a thesis and that I was unaffiliated with parties or the government. But by emphasizing my student status the leaders concluded that the Naparama militia would not benefit from the study, and they therefore suddenly ceased to cooperate with us. In a last effort to solve what at that point seemed to be an insurmountable hurdle, I explained why I found my study important: most histories of the war had focused on Frelimo and Renamo while ignoring the important contribution of the Naparama. Since the militia leaders had been demanding recognition from the government for a long time, they appreciated that I highlighted the value of their contribution and thus agreed that all the leaders could be interviewed individually.

These examples of individuals and groups attempting to manipulate my research project represent instances of the aforementioned gatekeeper bias, but in more intentional and manipulative forms, which is common in fieldwork with marginalized or high-risk communities who have certain grievances that they want addressed. Access is traded for a certain version of representation that benefits research participants and the political groups to which they belong. Gerharz (2009), for example, mentions how the rebel group LTTE in Sri Lanka attempted to make use of the many researchers in order to polish its own image. In the eastern provinces of the Democratic Republic of Congo (DRC), Vlassenroot (2006, 197), working among armed groups, experienced how his "writings were used as proofs that [respondents'] claims or grievances were justifiable." Researchers thus can be used to improve a group's or an individual's reputation. Malejacq and Mukhopadhyay (2016, 1014) report how a handshake of one of the authors with an Afghan governor was broadcast on TV to counter "the governor's reputation as an uneducated countryman by exhibiting his connection to a foreign university professor."

While I was careful in all conversations to avoid making the impression that talking to me would result in political or monetary benefits, this hope was difficult to dispel. Part of the problem was that local leaders who helped to connect us with former combatants were insensitive to the ways in which they might create false expectations. In a rural area in Murrupula district, the secretary of the locality had called all demobilized soldiers for a meeting. When we started our interviews with some of the demobilized soldiers and explained what we were doing, they were disappointed because they had hoped to finally receive the benefits that they had been anticipating for such a long time. At times, it seemed as if local leaders had deliberately misrepresented the purpose of such meetings, because they realized that people would not show up if they knew the purpose of my research.

This misrepresentation created an ethical dilemma, as I depended on others to introduce me to community residents who had been involved in the war, but I did not have complete control over how people represented the purpose of my work. When researchers depend on core contacts and gatekeepers who can manipulate their activities and writings, this dependence inverts the power relationship between researcher and researched and constrains the autonomy of the researcher and her project (Vlassenroot 2006). Such power asymmetries in favor of research participants are especially pronounced in dangerous settings in which researchers depend on certain elites for their personal protection (Adams 1999; Kovats-Bernat 2002; Malejacq and Mukhopadhyay 2016, 1013). But they find similar expression in polarized societies in which researchers depend on certain individuals to gain access and trust.

3.3 CONCLUSION

These narratives from my fieldwork in central and northern Mozambique demonstrate how the autonomy of the researcher and the researched are closely interlinked. The people I asked to interview thought I had particular powers, both positive and negative. Some believed my mere presence and/or the subject of my work threatened their livelihoods and well-being. For others, my presence provided an opportunity for them to receive support for their visions of politics so that they could reach their political, social, and economic goals.

In such contexts, the researcher becomes a political actor within the field site and fieldwork becomes "a form of intervention" (Malejacq and Mukhopadhyay 2016), which curtails community residents' autonomy over their lives and well-being. As a consequence of the researcher's presence, the field site experiences a qualitative change, which is difficult to "factor out" of the resulting data during analysis. At the same time, community residents become "actors" in the research project, which may constrain the autonomy of the researcher (Vlassenroot 2006) and contribute to her "relative powerlessness," restricting her role to that of a "mascot researcher" (Adams 1999). For example, the Naparama commander of Nicoadala that I mentioned previously attempted to influence the research design by limiting access to certain individuals, thereby becoming an author of the study rather than its subject. A researcher therefore needs to consider how any negotiation of her position within the field site as well as potential biases due to gender and other characteristics of the researcher affect data analysis. Instances of empowerment and disempowerment (and their consequences) can only be recognized when discursive strategies such as rumors about the researcher, inventions, denials, evasions, and silences are treated as "meta-data" of fieldwork (Fujii 2010).

Rather than conceiving of ourselves as external observers, analysts, and critics of disempowerment, researchers need to consider the ways in which we may, inadvertently, contribute to empowering some and disempowering others. Even if (or especially when) researchers try to be neutral and retain distance from community life, they unwittingly become actors in local or national conflicts (Sluka 1990, 1995; Gerharz 2009). Some researchers have embraced the impossibility of remaining as neutral and impartial observers, in particular in violent settings. Malejacq and Mukhopadhyay (2016), for example, discuss the ways in which they have "intervened" in their respective field sites and engaged in "tribal politics" during their work in Afghanistan and Somalia, creating informal networks of informants who provided access and protection. Security concerns make research difficult in violent settings, but researchers in highly polarized postwar contexts can also intervene in local politics even though they are "only" observers.

Overall, the two narratives demonstrate that community residents react to strangers in deeply ambiguous ways. First, I argue they do not trust strangers who intrude in their communities with short-term projects that are contingent, conditional, and subject to review. Conversely, some projects provide jobs and seed money, which could improve people's lives. This again confirms Serra's (2003) notion that what people ask for is not a complete absence of the state and its services, but when external agencies intervene, they need to be more accountable and reliable.

By extension, what communities ask for is not that researchers stay away from them, but that they are aware of the political nature of their work. Researchers become part of a community and shape social realities in ways that may be neither anticipated nor intended, creating opportunities for both empowerment and disempowerment. Such reflection remains important, both for research transparency and research ethics (Parkinson and Wood 2015).

Chapter 4 introduces the reader to the historical context of the war in Mozambique and explores the historical roots of social, political, and economic polarization that shaped my fieldwork.

4

A War over People

An Analysis of Mozambique's Civil War

In 1975, Mozambique gained independence from Portugal after being embroiled in a ten-year liberation struggle. Soon thereafter, the newly independent country faced new instability. Mozambique's neighbor Rhodesia (present-day Zimbabwe) sought to ward off liberation movements that benefited from their sanctuary in Mozambique. Rhodesian intelligence forces trained discontented Mozambicans who had fled to Rhodesia in 1974 and formed an armed group, first under the name Mozambican National Resistance, or Movimento Nacional de Resistência (MNR), and later under the moniker by which it is known to this day, Renamo.[1] From 1981 onward, Apartheid South Africa also began supporting Renamo to destabilize its neighbors, since Mozambique had become an important sanctuary for the anti-apartheid movement, the African National Congress (ANC).[2]

After Zimbabwe's independence in 1980 and with South African support, Renamo expanded its activities across the entire country and gained in strength. In the early 1980s, Renamo moved into the central and northern regions and occupied vast areas, thereby threatening a partition of the country between north and south along the Zambezi River valley.[3] Popular discontent with Frelimo's restructuring of economic, social, and political relations, in particular in the northern provinces, fueled the ensuing war.

Frelimo and Renamo were only willing to engage in a peace process after the signing of a nonaggression pact, the N'komati Accord, between Mozambique

---

[1] In English writings about Mozambique at the time of the war, Renamo was often referred to as "MNR." For reasons of simplicity, I will use "Renamo" throughout this book.

[2] Mozambique borders Tanzania to the North; Malawi, Zambia, and Zimbabwe (formerly Rhodesia) to the East; and South Africa and Eswatini to the South. See the map of Mozambique in Figure 4.1.

[3] Fernando Manuel, "Para compreender o presente," *Tempo (Maputo)* (993), October 22, 1989, 6.

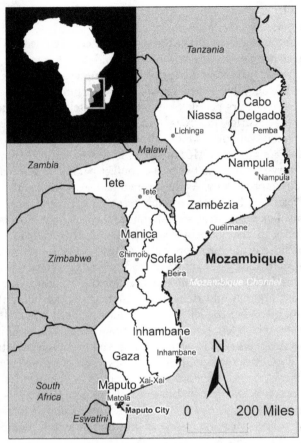

FIGURE 4.1. Map of provincial boundaries in Mozambique
Note: Cartography by Sofia Jorges

and South Africa in 1984, the end of Malawi's assistance to Renamo in 1986, and an apparent military stalemate in 1988–89. Peace negotiations culminated in the signing of the peace accord on October 4, 1992. Overall, it is estimated that the war cost over one million lives and displaced almost five million people of a total population of about thirteen million at the end of the war, both as a consequence of fighting and war-induced famine and disease (Hanlon 1996, 16). The war took a heavy toll on infrastructure, with 60 percent of primary schools and 40 percent of health clinics destroyed in 1992 (Hanlon 1996, 15).

This chapter analyzes the origins and the evolution of the war to provide context for the formation, diffusion, and mobilization of community-initiated militias. I analyze both internal divisions and regional contexts. I put particular emphasis on the relations between the armed actors and the population and the patterns of violence that – as I explain in more detail in subsequent chapters – influenced community initiatives to form militias.

Throughout the chapter, I make three interrelated, arguments. First, the war was a war over people. The control of the population became an end in itself rather than a means to expand control over territory. Kalyvas (2006) argues that selective violence by armed groups – the incumbent or insurgent – in irregular civil wars deters people from providing intelligence to the other side, which improves security in areas under control. Violence thus serves to strengthen civilian support, which allows for the expansion of territorial control. In the late 1980s in Mozambique, however, during a time characterized by a military stalemate between the conflict parties, Frelimo and Renamo developed a different strategy. As they were unable to significantly expand their control over territory, both sides forcibly resettled the population as a strategy of war to consolidate the areas already under their control. Rather than using selective violence to change people's incentives and deter disloyalty, Frelimo and Renamo chose brute force – population resettlement – to make disloyalty impossible (Zhukov 2015). I explore the evolution of this instrumental relation with civilians and delineate its consequences for the dynamics of war.

Second, both Frelimo and Renamo attempted to consolidate their control over people by involving residents in gathering intelligence and defending the local population, which led to the militarization of society.[4] Frelimo's counterinsurgency strategy was built on assigning military tasks to state-initiated militias who initially served political purposes. The government also trained civilians for local defense. Renamo enlisted traditional authorities and formed local police forces to ensure collaboration of the people in areas under their control. In developing this argument, I unpack how Frelimo's internal conflicts and domestic politics after independence put domestic and regime security at center stage of the party's political agenda.

Third, although Frelimo's military strategy was built on community defense, it failed to protect the population from insurgent violence. Renamo's military strategy was meant to control the local population rather than protect it from violence. Community residents thus suffered from high levels of indiscriminate and collective violence perpetrated by both sides. Due to the lack of material and ammunition in the central and northern regions, Frelimo and Renamo fought a "war of avoidance," attacking the population in zones under enemy control rather than engaging in direct battle (Legrand 1993, 98). As a consequence, community residents developed their own means of protection, such as peace zones and community-initiated militias to patrol residential areas. I analyze how characteristics of violence helped to form community-initiated militias and show how far these militias relied on preexisting social conventions for the spiritual dimension of the war.

---

[4] I develop this argument in more detail in an article on auxiliary armed forces and innovations in security governance in Mozambique's civil war; see Jentzsch (2017).

The first section analyzes the conflicts that evolved within Frelimo before and after independence. These internal struggles created popular discontent, which, in many areas, fueled the war at the local level. The second section assesses the impact of regional factors that gave rise to the formation and expansion of Renamo. The third section examines how Frelimo's counterinsurgent strategy improved or deteriorated the movement's relationship with the population. To control "internal and external enemies" of the state, Frelimo militarized society and Mozambique evolved into a police state. The fourth section reviews the extent to which Frelimo's inadequate response to the threat posed by Renamo led communities to develop their own responses to Renamo. One such response was the formation of the Naparama, the independent militia that later supported Frelimo in its counterinsurgent effort in Zambézia and Nampula provinces. The final section provides a brief overview of the peace process and the legacies of the war.

4.1 ANTICOLONIAL STRUGGLE AND INDEPENDENCE

When Mozambique gained independence from Portugal in 1975, the FRELIMO liberation movement[5] came to power, and it worked hard to retain that power. As a political movement, and subsequently as a political party, Frelimo recognized the importance of unity (De Bragança and Depelchin 1986). However, internal divisions about goals and strategies evolved, which enabled Rhodesia and Apartheid South Africa to build support for their regional agenda among discontented Mozambicans. From independence onward, the regime treated such "enemies of the revolution" harshly. Frelimo was able to consolidate its power over the long term by slowly creating a police state that made use of violence against those disloyal to its political project (Macamo 2016; Bertelsen 2016). A "politics of punishment" (Machava 2011) emerged that did not distinguish between internal and external security, giving rise to an increasing militarization of the party and society that also influenced Frelimo's counterinsurgency response to Renamo.

4.1.1 The Formation of FRELIMO and the Beginning of the Liberation Struggle

Mozambican historiography – including the way in which Frelimo has told its own story – has often been used for political purposes and is thus contested (Cahen 2008a). For Frelimo, Mozambique's official historiography has served the purpose of promoting and legitimating a unified movement and nation-state. A case in point is the beginning of the liberation struggle. FRELIMO was

---

[5] I follow others by capitalizing "FRELIMO" when referring to the liberation movement and using lowercase "Frelimo" when referring to the political party that was established at the movement's Third Congress in 1977. Mozambique History Net, "FRELIMO and the Frelimo Party, 1962–1991, Dossier MZ-0011," 2012. www.mozambiquehistory.net/frelimo_62-63.php.

formed on June 25, 1962 in Dar es Salaam, Tanzania, with Eduardo Mondlane – who had been educated in the United States and had worked for the United Nations – as the movement's first president.[6] The violent liberation struggle began in 1964, with, according to the official history, the infiltration of 300 FRELIMO fighters into Mozambique from Tanzania. On September 25, 1964, FRELIMO attacked the Portuguese administrative post at Chai in the northern region of Cabo Delgado (see map in Figure 4.1 and an overview of major historical events in Table 4.1). Alberto Chipande, Minister of Defense from 1975 to 1994, supposedly fired the first shot (Muiuane 2006, 31–43). Contrary to this official account, factions of movements that were not fully integrated into FRELIMO had already launched small-scale assaults in July and August 1964 in Zambézia (Cahen 1999, 45). These contradictions about the beginning of the liberation struggle hint at Frelimo's "victorious historiography," which demonstrates Frelimo's attempt at a triumphalist, coherent, and conflict-free chronicle of the liberation struggle and its aftermath (De Bragança and Depelchin 1986, 165).

Although the Portuguese government responded to the beginning of the armed struggle with heavily armed troops and a sophisticated network of secret police agents, FRELIMO gained popular support and made quick advances in Cabo Delgado, Niassa, and Tete provinces. The largest Portuguese counter-insurgency campaign – Operation "Gordian Knot" from May to August 1970 – failed due to FRELIMO's strong support among the peasants from the Makonde, an ethnic group in Cabo Delgado (Hanlon 1984, 35).[7] When FRELIMO advanced into the central provinces,[8] the Portuguese responded by

---

[6] There were three liberation movements before FRELIMO's foundation. These were the National Democratic Union of Mozambique (União Democrática Nacional de Moçambique, UDENAMO), the Mozambican African National Union (MANU), and the National African Union of Independent Mozambique (UNAMI). The foundation of FRELIMO replaced all three movements in 1962. However, UDENAMO and MANU were not completely dissolved and provided a forum for those that were expelled from FRELIMO or left FRELIMO at a later stage. Many of these factions were unified into the Revolutionary Committee of Mozambique (Comitê Revolucionário de Moçambique, COREMO) in 1965. See Cahen (1999) and Robinson (2006, 78–79). See also Mondlane (1969). For a critical analysis of the complicated early history of FRELIMO, see Marcum, Burke III, and Clough (2017).

[7] Bowen (2000, 6n10) points to how those early analyses of FRELIMO's history that claim its broad popular support are not based on detailed empirical material. Thus, it is difficult to judge how much voluntary popular support FRELIMO really enjoyed and how much coercion the movement made use of.

[8] Most of the early anticolonial activity focused on Cabo Delgado and Niassa, since Malawi impeded FRELIMO activity on its territory from 1964 onward, which made raids into Zambézia and Tete more difficult (Hedges 1989). FRELIMO managed to consolidate its power in the north and open another front in Tete province by March 1968 (Isaacman and Isaacman 1983, 86). In July 1972, FRELIMO moved into the central provinces of Manica and Sofala and in July 1974 (again) into Zambézia (Muiuane 2006, 167, 185). There was some FRELIMO activity in Zambézia in 1964–65, but it stopped after major logistical and political difficulties, and Alberto Mutumula, FRELIMO leader in Lugela in Alta Zambézia, was killed under mysterious circumstances in 1968 (Chichava 2007, 287–301).

TABLE 4.1. *Overview of major events in recent Mozambican history*

Date	Event
June 25, 1962	Formation of FRELIMO
September 25, 1964	Start of the violent liberation struggle
June 25, 1975	Independence of Mozambique
September 1979	Frelimo kills Renamo leader Matsangaíssa; Afonso Dhlakama becomes Renamo president
1980	Rhodesian independence; South Africa becomes Renamo's main sponsor
March 1982	Tanzania, Zambia, and Zimbabwe begin to provide military support to Frelimo
July 1981	Renamo reaches Inhambane
December 1981	Renamo reaches Manica
Late 1982	Renamo offensive in the Limpopo valley
December 1982	The war affects one-third of the country
August 1982	Renamo creates camps in Malawi
August 1982	Renamo crosses the Zambezi River into Zambézia and unites with the Mozambique Revolutionary Party (Partido Revolucionário de Moçambique, PRM)
Mid-1982	Frelimo offensive northward through Inhambane and southward through Manica and Sofala
Early 1983	Gaza and Maputo become areas of intense Renamo activity and they clash with the Frelimo army
April/May 1983	Renamo reaches Nampula
August 1983	Renamo reaches Niassa
March 16, 1984	N'komati Accords between Mozambique and South Africa
May 1984	Renamo reaches Cabo Delgado
August 1985	Frelimo attacks Renamo headquarters in Gorongosa and captures the "Gorongosa documents," which provide evidence for continued South African support
July/August 1986	Renamo offensive in Zambézia province
October 1986	End of Malawi support for Renamo
October 1986	President Samora Machel dies in an airplane crash over South Africa
Late 1986/early 1987	Frelimo counteroffensive in Zambézia province, supported by 3,000 Tanzanian troops
January 1987	Mozambique adopts IMF-sponsored structural adjustment program (Economic Rehabilitation Program/Programa de Restruturação Econômica, PRE)
December 1988	Tanzanian forces withdraw
March/April 1989	Frelimo regains control of all the district towns in Zambézia province
July 1989	Frelimo's Fifth Congress; Frelimo drops its commitment to Marxism-Leninism

(*continued*)

TABLE 4.1. *(cont.)*

Date	Event
July 1989	Frelimo launches a major offensive against Renamo's headquarters in Gorongosa
Early 1990	Frelimo army together with Zimbabwean troops step up pressure in Gorongosa and Sofala
Mid-1990	Frelimo operations resume in Tete, Sofala, Manica, and Zambézia provinces
July 1990	First round of peace negotiations
December 1990	New multiparty constitution takes effect
December 1, 1990	Partial ceasefire signed
June 1991	The Chissano government discovers a coup plot
June 1992	Twelfth and final round of peace negotiations
October 4, 1992	General Peace Agreement signed in Rome, Italy
December 1992– December 1994	United Nations Operation in Mozambique (Operação das Nações Unidas em Moçambique, ONUMOZ)
October 27–29, 1994	Presidential and parliamentary elections

massacring the population. One of the most notorious massacres occurred in December 1972, when elite troops killed 400 people from the village of Wiriamu in Tete province (Hanlon 1984, 36; Dhada 2016).[9]

The anticolonial struggle was not decided on the battlefield but ended following domestic developments in Portugal. Out of concern for Portuguese national debt and the danger of becoming embroiled in wars that could not be won, young army officers in Portugal formed the Armed Forces Movement, which overthrew the Portuguese dictatorship in April 1974 (Isaacman and Isaacman 1983, 106). The "Carnation Revolution," as it was later called, accelerated the decolonization process across the Portuguese Empire, including Mozambique (Lloyd-Jones and Pinto 2003). The coup made negotiations possible between the new Portuguese government and FRELIMO, culminating in the signing of the Lusaka Accord on September 7, 1974, granting Mozambique independence nine months later. After the transitional government period, FRELIMO's then president, Samora Moíses Machel, became the first president of independent Mozambique.

4.1.2 Internal Conflict within FRELIMO

During the independence struggle, FRELIMO faced internal conflicts about the goal and strategies of the movement, but debate remains regarding the precise

---

[9] Adrian Hastings, "Portuguese Massacre Reported by Priests," *The Times*, July 10, 1973. This massacre was committed by the elite troops of the Portuguese secret service in Mozambique, the Polícia Internacional e de Defesa do Estado (PIDE), called the *flechas* (arrows) (Hanlon 1984, 36), which received training from Rhodesia in an effort to improve the Portuguese counterinsurgency capabilities (see below). PIDE and the *sipaios* (colonial native police) are still remembered among the population as those who committed the most atrocities during the anticolonial struggle.

divisions. According to the movement itself and some analysts, the main rift was over the final objective – national independence or the socioeconomic restructuring of society. De Bragança and Depelchin (1986) – adopting the official Frelimo party language – call the first goal the "reactionary" line and the second the "revolutionary" line, which implies a class conflict within the movement between a black nationalist bourgeoisie and the revolutionary vanguard.[10] Echoing de Bragança and Depelchin's comments about Frelimo's conflict-less "victorious historiography," Hanlon (1984, 28) remarks that in reality, these two lines were difficult to separate. The more conservative line attracted many supporters and was not as homogenous as Frelimo attempted to portray it in its official history. Cahen (1999, 46n27) argues that rather than a conflict between the bourgeois and the revolutionary class, the divisions within FRELIMO represented a conflict with social and regional dimensions: the "rural modern merchant elite" among the Makonde ethnic group in the north was in conflict with the "urban bureaucratic petty-bourgeois elite of the Frelimo military" among the Shangaan, the *assimilados* (assimilated, Mozambicans with Portuguese privileges), and the *mulattoes* in the southern cities – these were not merchants, but worked in the bureaucracy or other services.[11]

This internal conflict influenced how the movement defined the enemy, the tactics of armed struggle, and the type of society to be constructed in the "liberated zones" during the armed struggle against the Portuguese (Isaacman and Isaacman 1983, 86; Frelimo 1978, 4–21; Cahen 2008a). Much of the evolution of FRELIMO's strategies, however, was a mixture of ideology and pragmatism. In terms of the military strategy, different factions advocated for urban uprisings, short-term insurrection in the countryside, or long-term mobilization of the rural masses. Yet developments inside and outside of Mozambique made the first two options unviable.[12] Thus, long-term guerrilla activity became the major strategy of FRELIMO's armed struggle (Isaacman and Isaacman 1983, 88–89; Hanlon 1984, 27).

The evolution of FRELIMO's goals and strategies led to the marginalization of prominent leaders with alternative visions. The conflict escalated after

---

[10] For example, in the Central Committee's report to the Third Congress, the party explains the differences like this: "Within our ranks, people of a capitalist frame of mind openly revealed themselves; and this unleashed a bitter political and ideological struggle inside our organisation. In the first period this took the form of differences of opinion. In reality, these differences masked the fundamental contradiction that we contained: class antagonism" (Frelimo 1978, 6).

[11] See also Cahen (2006). It is true that there was an important regional dimension to the conflict within FRELIMO. However, Bowen (2000, 7) demonstrates that the rural modern merchant elite who the Makonde leader N'kavandame represented was not unique to Cabo Delgado. Wealthier peasants in the central and southern provinces had similar interests to become small capitalist farmers.

[12] Urban uprisings had failed in Angola's capital Luanda in 1961, FRELIMO's underground network had been crushed in Lourenço Marques ("Maputo" after 1976), and spontaneous short-term insurrection had failed in Tete province.

decisions made at the 1968 Second Congress reflected what FRELIMO termed the "revolutionary line." Lázaro N'kavandame, the leader of the Makonde in Cabo Delgado, from where many liberation fighters originated, defected to the Portuguese in 1968. He was identified by Frelimo as representing the "reactionary line." Moreover, Uria Simango, who had hoped to become president at the Second Congress, was expelled from the movement in 1970 after the assassination of FRELIMO leader Eduardo Mondlane in Dar es Salaam in February 1969 (Cabrita 2000, chapter 11; Cahen 2008a).[13] Those with "revolutionary" visions consolidated their power after Mondlane's death, but conflicts continued to be suppressed rather than resolved. In 1970, Samora Machel, a representative of the "revolutionary line," became FRELIMO president and Marcelino dos Santos vice-president.[14]

These internal conflicts resurfaced at independence. The Lusaka Accord granted FRELIMO a preferential position in postindependent Mozambique as the "sole and legitimate representative of the Mozambican people." Immediately after the signing of the accords, about 250 right-wing white settlers took over the radio station and newspaper in Lourenço Marques and sought to declare independence unilaterally (Hall and Young 1997, 45). Uria Simango, who had formed a new political party after returning to Mozambique in 1974, and others called for elections during which FRELIMO would have to compete with opposition parties at independence (Cabrita 2000, 80). However, the turmoil only lasted for a few days. In coordination with the Portuguese, Rhodesians and South Africans, FRELIMO suppressed the revolt, arrested opposition leaders and sent them to reeducation camps in Niassa and Cabo Delgado provinces (Cabrita 2000, 81–84).[15]

[13] The circumstances under which Mondlane died are still not completely resolved. The parcel bomb that killed Mondlane in Dar es Salaam is believed to have been built by PIDE. However, rival FRELIMO leaders were probably involved in the planning of the assassination. Frelimo considered Mondlane's death as the culmination point of the conflict between the "two lines." Frelimo later accused Uria Simango of conspiring with the Portuguese secret service in the planning of the assassination (Frelimo 1978, 11–12). See also Cabrita (2000, 59–60) and Hall and Young (1997, 18). Uria Simango was expelled because he failed to openly attack N'kavandame, who was accused of being involved in the assassination, and because he criticized FRELIMO's internal struggles and socialist direction after Mondlane's death (Cabrita 2000, 64). Simango addressed the accusations in a pamphlet that he released in November 1969, *Gloomy Situation in FRELIMO*, Dar es Salaam.

[14] Representatives of the "reactionary line" – in particular, the Makonde from Cabo Delgado who had supported the early liberation struggle – backed FRELIMO in the last years of the liberation struggle. However, this was not because they came to share the same ideological views. Rather, the Makonde realized that FRELIMO was winning against the Portuguese (De Bragança and Depelchin 1986, 174). As Cahen (1999, 45) argues, the Makonde's goal was not necessarily national independence, but a right to the land, and thus they followed whoever would wage the war to achieve this aim.

[15] On the various opposition movements and how they fused with each other or supported each other during the transition period, see Robinson (2006, 92–94). Frelimo executed some of the dissidents, including Uria Simango, Joana Simeão, Mateus Gwendjere, and Lázaro N'kavandame,

4.1.3 Origins and Consequences of Frelimo Policy after Independence

Frelimo's policies that sought to restructure society and the economy after independence are often cited as a source of discontent among the population and support for Renamo.[16] As the "revolutionary" camp came to dominate FRELIMO, the movement officially adopted the objective of a socialist, anticolonialist, and antifascist revolution and the liberation of *all* of Mozambique (Hanlon 1984, 34).[17] In the "liberated" zones in the northern provinces of Cabo Delgado and Niassa, FRELIMO put these ideas into practice and educated the peasants politically, formed communal villages with collective agriculture, and provided rudimentary education and health services to the villagers (Hanlon 1984, 29). Antiracism, anti-tribalism, and the negation of the very existence of ethnic groups shaped the policies to achieve national unity (Isaacman and Isaacman 1983, 112–13; Cahen 2000, 168). FRELIMO structures replaced the existing traditional leadership, as the movement considered the *regulados* (chieftaincies), which had been the main pillar of the colonial local administrative system, collaborators of the Portuguese.

The newly introduced economic and social policies right after independence had important consequences for the economy. FRELIMO's antiracist stance implied that it did not seek to alienate the white population. However, the nationalization of education, medicine, law, and funeral services a month after independence led to the flight of many white settlers out of fear for their businesses and personal well-being. Businesses were left behind without functioning equipment or trained managers, which shattered whole economic sectors (Hanlon 1984, 46–49).

To stop the erosion of the economy and promote unity of the Mozambican people, FRELIMO created transitional Dynamizing Groups

---

without trial in 1983. President Machel was concerned that Renamo's advances in Niassa province would free the dissidents and thus ordered to kill them (Robinson 2006, 164). Portugal, Rhodesia, and South Africa supported FRELIMO in the oppression of opposition movements, as they sought to ensure peace and stability in region. South Africa thus opted for accepting black majority rule in Angola and Mozambique in exchange for the safeguarding of the apartheid regime (Cabrita 2000, 80).

[16] FRELIMO's policies to restructure society evolved during the liberation struggle, but, as indicated above, they became more pronounced after Mondlane's death. This is why many Renamo supporters have portrayed Mondlane as the black nationalist who was betrayed by the subsequent radicalization of the movement and still honor Mondlande as the great Mozambican liberation leader and democrat (Serapião 1985). However, interviews with Mondlane paint a more complicated picture, as he acknowledges the benefits of a socialist restructuring of society after independence. See an interview published by de Bragança and Wallerstein (1982, 121), cited in Robinson (2006, 25n18).

[17] There is considerable debate over how far Frelimo's policies can be considered socialist or not. For two opposite poles of the debate, see Cahen (1993) and Saul (2005). For a critique of the debate between "revisionists" and "Frelimo sympathizers," see Dinerman (2006), the exchange between Cahen (2008b) and Dinerman (2009), and below.

(Grupos Dinamizadores, GD). These groups, consisting of eight to ten people in every village, neighborhood, and workplace, were intended to provide political education and motivation to the population. The GDs were crucial in those regions that had remained untouched by FRELIMO political activity during the liberation struggle (Isaacman and Isaacman 1983, 106–7). They served as party cells, administrators, local leaders, and providers of public services at the same time: "More than anything else, it was the GDs that introduced Mozambique to Frelimo and to 'people's democracy,' and it was the GDs that kept the country running" (Hanlon 1984, 49).[18] The mass organizations for workers, women, and youth, introduced before and after the party's Third Congress in 1977, took over many of the GDs' activities. In the late 1970s, Frelimo eliminated the GDs in the countryside and completely replaced them with the new party structures (Isaacman and Isaacman 1983, 124).

The party's Third Congress in 1977 marked Frelimo's official turn to Marxist-Leninist ideology, which had important implications for how the movement defined its own role vis-à-vis Mozambique's citizens. At the congress, the party transformed itself from a mass movement into a vanguard party that served as the main body overseeing state and society (Hanlon 1984, 138). The restructuring of the economy included the "socialization of the countryside," which meant the construction of communal villages, agricultural cooperatives, and the creation of productive state farms from abandoned settler plantations and estates (Isaacman and Isaacman 1983, 148). Beyond these economic transformations, Frelimo aimed at creating a "new man" to overcome the "viciousness" of colonial society and the capitalist bourgeoisie. In this vein, Frelimo abolished the remnants of the system of traditional leadership and prohibited the exercise of all forms of religion – "obscurantism" in Frelimo's official language. Cahen (2006) sees in these economic, social, and political transformations the pursuit of an authoritarian modernization project that pursued national unity by creating a "new man" completely separated from African peasant society. Sumich (2013, 100) emphasizes the exclusionary nature of this new conception of citizenship, as only those who joined "the wider collective under Frelimo's leadership" became "true" citizens. All others were declared "enemies of the people" (Machava 2011). Such "enemies" became targets of campaigns such as *Operação Produção* (Operation Production) and were sent to reeducation camps to ensure that all members of society contributed their labor to the collective good (Machava 2018).

As part of the economic and social policies, the construction of communal villages was Frelimo's most ambitious and interventionist project

---

[18] See Cahen (1985) for a critical analysis of Frelimo's "people's democracy" and the limits of its implementation.

in rural areas. It gave rise to a scholarly debate on the degree to which its implementation contributed to peasants' alienation from Frelimo and their inclination to support Renamo, mainly because of the contradiction between Frelimo's ambitions and the realities of their implementation. The construction of communal villages reflected the party's various economic, political, and social aims.[19] Communal villages sought to modernize the countryside by resettling the previously dispersed population, thereby improving access to health care and education and increasing productivity by collectively producing cash crops.[20] The involvement of peasants in various revolutionary institutions provided spaces for their political indoctrination (Hanlon 1984, 122; Isaacman and Isaacman 1983, 152–53). All in all, the organization of all residents into communal villages extended the state's reach into the periphery and made society "legible," similarly to such processes in Tanzania and other countries (Scott 1998). It facilitated close control over citizens to recognize and identify deviant behavior, which proved useful when internal and external security threats increased in the 1980s.

Recognizing the far-reaching interventionist nature of communal villages, many communities did not support building them, or even resisted building them outright. Nampula province saw the construction of a large number of communal villages (Isaacman and Isaacman 1983, 153). However, as Hanlon (1984, 128) notes, "most villages result[ed] from war and natural disaster and involve[d] a high degree of compulsion." Most villages in Nampula were created when the war reached the province, mostly by the army (Dinerman 2006, 22; Minter 1994). In Cabo Delgado, Niassa, and Tete, Frelimo superimposed the villages on the structure of colonial strategic hamlets and settled refugees from Malawi and Tanzania in these villages (Isaacman and Isaacman 1983, 153). In Gaza, Frelimo settled victims of the 1977 floods in communal villages (Roesch 1992).

Several reasons explain why support among the population for communal villages was low. Productivity in the new villages was low, which decreased their appeal.[21] Peasants resisted changing their forms of production in the long

---

[19] FRELIMO had experimented with communal villages in the "liberated zones" in Cabo Delgado and Niassa.

[20] Mozambique is a sparsely populated country. According to the census in 1970, the population density was twenty-six people per square mile/ten people per square kilometer. In 1980, the population density was thirty-nine people per square mile/fifteen people per square kilometer.

[21] The strategies Frelimo used to create communal villages prioritized housing over farming, and thus the land around the villages was often not well suited for agricultural production (Hanlon 1984, 128). In my interviews, community residents frequently complained about the communal villages' bad quality of agricultural land. In Mecubúri district in Nampula, for example, a clan that had resettled to a communal village surrounded by infertile land moved to a more fertile area after complaints to the district administrator. See interview with community leader (2011-11-17-Lm15), November 17, 2011, Issipe, Mecubúri, Nampula.

term to suit being organized into agricultural cooperatives (Isaacman and Isaacman 1983, 155–56). Moreover, traditional leaders and capitalist farmers rejected resettlement. The communal villages also lacked the necessary technical and financial support, as state farms and urban projects received more government resources than communal villages and peasant farming (Hanlon 1984, 123–24; Hermele 1986). Thus, rather than strengthening the peasant sector, Frelimo's policies alienated the middle peasants and failed to adequately support poor peasants (Bowen 2000; Hanlon 1984).[22]

As a consequence, contradictions arose between the ideal of the communal villages and its implementation. The highly idealistic, bureaucratic, and technocratic idea of the communal villages did not correspond with the everyday needs of the people (Cahen 1987, 51). Peasants had to leave their ancestral land and travel too far to reach their individual plots. While it could be argued that the project was driven by good humanist intentions, its implementation chiefly served the state's aim of ensuring social control (Geffray 1990, 35–36). In fact, communal villages became highly organized and vigilante groups and militias helped control the population, which contributed to the goal of forming "true" and compliant citizens (cf. Sumich 2013). Resettlement to the villages was increasingly conducted by force, which further decreased the villages' appeal (Bowen 2000, 15; Minter 1994).

These contradictions prompted a debate among scholars on the degree to which villagization fueled the war on the local level. Most prominent is Christian Geffray's (1990) study of the Erati district in Nampula province, in which he argues that Renamo destroyed villages and sent residents to their previous homes to generate popular support. However, other analysts argue that different policies were more relevant in generating Renamo support. For example, Frelimo's reliance on mechanized state farms rather than family agriculture and the failure to rebuild a trading network for peasants' surplus production created discontent (Fauvet 1990). Still others argue that Renamo's success is largely due to external support from Rhodesia and South Africa (Minter 1994). The following section explores these different arguments in more detail.

4.2 THE FORMATION AND EXPANSION OF RENAMO

There is considerable debate over the origins of the rebel movement Renamo, and in particular over the balance between external influences and internal circumstances that contributed to Renamo's emergence. The historical evidence

---

[22] Moreover, the party made no attempts at mobilizing the important section of the middle peasantry, but rather sidelined them by advising them to hand their means of production to farmers' cooperatives (Bowen 2000, 9). At the same time, however, state support for poor peasants was limited and the cooperatives relied on the means of production and skills of the wealthier peasants.

shows that both were necessary to bring about an armed opposition movement. However, when analyzing Renamo's early history, it becomes clear that external support was more important for the early phases, while internal support was essential for later phases of the war. Significant support from Rhodesia facilitated the formation of Renamo, and Apartheid South Africa ensured the organization's survival beyond Rhodesian independence in 1980. Popular support within Mozambique became crucial in the mid-1980s when Renamo expanded to the northern provinces.

4.2.1 Regional Dynamics and Discontent among Mozambicans Abroad

The formation of Renamo was closely linked to regional political dynamics, in particular to Rhodesian counterinsurgency operations during the country's liberation struggle.[23] During the Mozambican war of independence between 1964 and 1974, FRELIMO-infiltrated areas within Mozambique provided neighboring liberation movements such as ZANLA sanctuary and ground for operations. Upon gaining independence, Mozambique continued supporting ZANLA and imposed sanctions on Rhodesia.[24] Renamo's roots lay in the local armed units that Rhodesia had formed and supported within Mozambique to counter the Mozambican support of Zimbabwean rebel activity (Vines 1991, 10).[25] The Rhodesian military and intelligence agency began its suppression of opposition activities in Mozambique long before Mozambique's independence.[26] In November 1973, the Rhodesian army, in cooperation with the

---

[23] For an introduction into Renamo's origin, aims, and regional and international support network, see Vines (1991).

[24] The Frelimo government closed the borders and denied Rhodesia access to the ports of Beira and Maputo in March 1976 (Vines 1991, 15–16).

[25] Robinson (2006, 191n101) points to an important disagreement between the chief of the Rhodesian intelligence service, Ken Flower (1987), and the researcher João Cabrita (2000) regarding the formation of Renamo. This disagreement reflects the major controversy about the history of the war – the extent to which Renamo's formation had domestic roots. In his book, Flower describes the continuity between the first counterinsurgent units formed by Rhodesia and the formation of Renamo. Cabrita, in contrast, argues that the first Renamo leader, André Matsangaíssa, who defected to Rhodesia in 1976, suggested to the Rhodesians to form Renamo. I agree with Robinson (2006, 102) that it is likely that the Rhodesians already had the idea of forming Renamo when Matsangaíssa defected in 1976. As Cahen points out (personal communication), Flower's and Cabrita's views are not entirely contradictory and the fact remains that there was no Mozambican rebel group operating before 1976. See below for a more detailed discussion of this issue.

[26] The Rhodesians supported the Portuguese military, advising them on the formation of local counterinsurgent groups. The Rhodesians did not have much confidence in the Portuguese response to FRELIMO's activities. Rhodesia preferred local alternatives to Portuguese troops. Rhodesian authorities began collaborating with the Portuguese to form African scouts in the mid-1960s. In March 1972, the Rhodesian Special Air Service attacked Matimbe, the FRELIMO base near Gungwe mountains, since it assumed that ZANLA was operating out of FRELIMO bases. From 1972 onward, the Rhodesian authorities advised the Portuguese on the creation of

Rhodesian Central Intelligence Organization (CIO), formed a special cross-border strike force of about 1,800 men, the Selous Scouts. This group attacked ZANLA camps inside Mozambique shortly thereafter (Minter 1994, 124).[27] Rhodesia continued to attack ZANLA camps even after Mozambican independence in 1975.[28]

Recruiting among exiled Mozambicans, the Rhodesians slowly built an organization that could operate independently against their enemies, so that the government could plausibly deny involvement in Mozambique's internal affairs. Instead of limiting its operations to those against ZANLA, the new organization would direct its attacks against those that *supported* the Zimbabwean liberation movements – the Mozambican government.[29] The CIO started a radio program – *Voz da África Livre* (Voice of Free Africa) – in July 1976 in cooperation with exiled Mozambicans.[30] The program aimed to reach those who had stayed in Mozambique and were stripped of the right to vote or sent to reeducation camps in northern Mozambique.[31]

Renamo was prepared to conduct its operations more autonomously soon after Mozambican independence. Its first independent operations occurred in December 1978, after the liberation war in Rhodesia had intensified (Robinson

counterinsurgent militias – the *flechas* made up of Africans who would support the security service and inform on FRELIMO activity. The Portuguese created the first *flechas* in Angola, where they were almost entirely composed of ex-combatants from the People's Movement for the Liberation of Angola (Movimento Popular de Libertação de Angola, MPLA). However, they did not begin to operate on the ground in Mozambique before 1974 (Coelho 2002, 141, 145–46). The Portuguese also formed all-African counterinsurgent units, the Special Groups (Grupos Especiais, GEs), which mainly operated in central Mozambique. For an overview of African involvement in Portuguese counterinsurgency campaigns in Mozambique, Angola, and Guinea-Bissau, see Coelho (2002).

[27] Ron Reid-Daly (1999), who had founded the Selous Scouts on the model of the Portuguese *flechas*, wrote a memoir about the story behind the formation and operation of the special troops.

[28] For an overview of attacks on ZANLA camps, largely conducted by Selous Scouts in 1976, see Robinson (2006, 99–101).

[29] For this new organization, the Rhodesian agencies recruited many of those who had emigrated during the transition period to Rhodesia – former PIDE agents, soldiers (among them many Africans) and white Portuguese settlers (Hanlon 1984, 219–20). Among those first recruits were many of Renamo's later leaders. Orlando Cristina, a former PIDE agent who had infiltrated FRELIMO in Dar es Salaam, later became Renamo secretary-general. Renamo's first president from 1977 onward, André Matsangaíssa, was a former FRELIMO commander who fled a reeducation camp that he had been sent to for theft. Evo Fernandes, who had PIDE links, became the first European spokesperson in Lisbon.

[30] The station had broadcasts in English, Portuguese, Swahili, and local languages. It was run by Orlando Cristina and aimed to imitate ZANLA's anti-Rhodesian radio station Voice of Zimbabwe, which broadcast via the Mozambican radio station Radio Moçambique (Vines 1991, 143n16; Cabrita 2000, 139–43).

[31] Frelimo called these individuals the "compromised" – all those that had supported the colonial regime voluntarily. President Samora Machel only rehabilitated the "compromised" and returned full rights to them in 1982 (Hanlon 1984, chapter 16).

2006, 105–6).[32] By 1979, Renamo operated from within Mozambique, from camps close to the Rhodesian border, and its activities concentrated on Manica and Sofala provinces (Hanlon 1984, 221). Attacks in these first years of Renamo activity included ambushes on civilian buses and army vehicles and attacks on Frelimo positions and other military targets.

However, pressure from the Mozambican army and developments within Rhodesia made Renamo's future uncertain. After the Lancaster House talks on the future of Zimbabwe-Rhodesia had opened in London in September 1979, the Mozambican army started an offensive against Renamo's base on top of the Gorongosa mountain in Sofala province. During this offensive, Renamo leader Matsangaíssa was killed. When the Lancaster House agreement was signed and Zimbabwean elections were set for February 1980, the CIO head for Mozambique asked the remaining Renamo men in Zimbabwe where they wanted to go – to South Africa as exiles or to Mozambique; they all chose Mozambique. Renamo troops within Mozambique were sent to the Sitatonga base in southern Manica. However, the Frelimo army captured the Sitatonga base in late June 1980, killing almost 300 men and capturing 300 more, thus largely destroying the Renamo organization (Hanlon 1984, 221).

Despite Frelimo pressure and the end of Rhodesian support, Renamo initially survived thanks to increased South African support. Following an internal power struggle that killed further Renamo troops and commanders, Afonso Dhlakama became the organization's new president. Dhlakama was a former FRELIMO commander who was ousted from the army at the same time as his predecessor, the recently assassinated Matsangaíssa. Renamo secretary-general Orlando Cristina supported Dklakama and ensured South African support for Renamo (Hanlon 1984, 222). The South Africans provided training at a camp in the Transvaal and resumed broadcast of the Renamo radio station. South African support via equipment and weapons enabled Renamo to resume activity in most of the sparsely populated areas of Manica and Sofala provinces by 1981 (Hanlon 1984, 225).[33]

---

[32] There is no consensus on the exact start date of the war between Frelimo and Renamo. Various civil war datasets use different dates. For example, the UCDP/PRIO Armed Conflict Dataset, which is based on the definition of an armed conflict as one with more than twenty-five battle-related deaths per year, defines 1977 as the start date (Gleditsch et al. 2002; Themnér and Wallensteen 2012; Themnér 2012). The Correlates of War Intra-state War Dataset uses a definition of civil war as a threshold of 1,000 battle-related combatant deaths and codes the Mozambican war as starting on October 21, 1979 (Singer and Small 1994). Elbadawi and Sambanis (2002) code 1976 as the start year, and their definition of civil war is based on 1,000 deaths over the duration of the war.

[33] South African involvement in Mozambique had begun much earlier than 1980, going back to October 1977, when South African soldiers supported the Rhodesian counterinsurgency in Gaza province (Robinson 2006, 104). By 1979, South Africa also supported Renamo directly with weapons and supplies, and Renamo had political representations in Johannesburg (Robinson 2006, 113). South Africa had prepared in detail for a more active role in Mozambique and the support of Renamo before the Lancaster House conference. Intelligence reports show how South

4.2.2 Renamo's Expansion across Mozambique

Starting out as a small counterinsurgent force, Renamo grew substantively with South African support.[34] Membership within Renamo increased from 76 in September 1977 to more than 900 by the end of 1978 (Cabrita 2000, 149, 154). When South Africa became Renamo's main external supporter in early 1980, the organization had about 2,000 fighters (Robinson 2006, 122), growing to 7,000 in December 1980 and 10,000 in February 1981 (Johnson, Martin, and Nyerere 1986, 19). Cahen (2019, 144) estimates a troop size of 12,300 by the end of 1984.

In the early 1980s, the war spread from the center to the southern and northern regions, affecting approximately one-third of the country by December 1982 (see Table 4.1 for an overview of important events).[35] In 1981, Renamo's area of operation was limited to the territory between the Beira corridor to the north and the Save River to the south. In July 1981, a contingent of 300 men crossed into Inhambane province further south (Cabrita 2000, 192–94). By December 1981, another contingent headed by the commander Calisto Meque had advanced to northern Manica province close to Tete province (Cabrita 2000, 199). During the first half of 1982, Renamo reestablished its headquarters in the Gorongosa mountains in northern Sofala, because the Frelimo army had destroyed Renamo's base in Chicarre in southern Manica close to the Zimbabwean border. While a Renamo offensive in the Limpopo valley in the south aiming to cut the capital Maputo off from the rest of the country failed in late 1982,[36] the creation of

African agencies made short- and long-term plans to influence the political and economic situation in Mozambique via propaganda, manipulating ethnic divisions, and attacks on logistical infrastructure and economic targets in 1979. In contrast to the Rhodesians, however, the South Africans did not want any operations to be traceable to South Africa. While the Lancaster House talks were ongoing, South Africa discussed a political/economic and a military policy option, of which the military option ultimately prevailed. The political/economic policy option aimed for close economic cooperation so that the states in the region would completely depend on South Africa and not go to war. The military option aimed at economic and political destabilization that would eventually lead to the overthrow of rival governments. See Robinson (2006, 115–17, 119).

[34] Renamo was not the only opposition group after independence. There were opposition groups based in Cabo Delgado, Zambézia, and Lisbon, conducting mostly propaganda and low-level military activity. However, none of these groups gained the support and grew in the same manner as Renamo. The most significant of these groups for this study is the Mozambique Revolutionary Party (Partido Revolucionário de Moçambique, PRM), also known as the *África Livre* movement. It was based in Zambézia and united with Renamo and then later split again from Renamo. See Robinson (2006, 109–10) and Chichava (2007, 401–2).

[35] Joseph Hanlon, "Mozambicans Learn to Live with the Silent War," *The Guardian*, December 30, 1982, 5.

[36] Robinson (2006, 157), emphasizing South Africa's influence on Renamo activity, suggests that the Limpopo valley offensive failed because South Africa decided not to provide the necessary support to take Maputo. This decision was due to their preference of using

camps in Malawi in August 1982 proved successful for the extension of the northern fronts to Tete and Zambézia provinces (Hanlon 1984, 226).[37] However, Mozambican Foreign Minister Joaquim Chissano's successful initiative to end Malawian support to the rebels and the army's capture of the main rebel base in Zambézia curtailed Renamo activity in the north (Hanlon 1984, 226–27).

In response, Renamo started another offensive to move north in early 1983, finally reaching all northern provinces by early 1984. The organization sought to secure supply routes by land, air, and sea.[38] Renamo also reactivated the Malawi bases and spread across Zambézia and into Nampula and Niassa provinces. About 350–500 men entered Nampula in April 1983 from the Renamo base near the Namuli mountains in Zambézia province (Cabrita 2000, 218; Do Rosário 2009, 305).[39] In August 1983, a contingent of 150 men from the Milange base in Zambézia crossed into Niassa province and established a base there. In May 1984, Renamo reached Cabo Delgado. By mid-1984, the war had reached all ten provinces of Mozambique.

4.2.3 Renamo's Goals and Strategies

Rhodesian and South African support shaped Renamo's goals and strategies from the beginning, albeit in slightly different directions (Hanlon 1984, 227–28). Rhodesia's interest in Renamo tended to focus on the gathering of intelligence on the Zimbabwean liberation movements. Thus, the Rhodesians had to foster a relatively good relationship with the local population and only conducted small-scale attacks. South Africa, in contrast, was more interested in destabilization and the destruction of economic targets. It therefore did not require such close cooperation with the local population.

Renamo as a tool of foreign policy, which implied destabilizing rather than overthrowing the Mozambican government.

[37] Renamo's crossing into Zambézia was facilitated by the organization's fusion with the Zambézia-based opposition group, the PRM (Chichava 2007, 405–7). In a letter to the former FRELIMO guerrilla and PRM's leader, Gimo Phiri, Orlando Cristina argued for the unification of the opposition groups to ensure the country's future (Chichava 2007, 405–6). On August 11, 1982, Renamo crossed the Zambezi River near Caia with about 500 men and joined the PRM in Zambézia. Gimo Phiri became vice-president of Renamo. See Chapter 5.

[38] For example, Renamo's crossing into Cabo Delgado may also have been influenced by the potential access to a supply route from Saudi Arabia or Oman via the Comoros Islands to northern Mozambique (Robinson 2006, 179). The sweeping across Zambézia after the end of Malawian support in 1986 was also influenced by the need to access the coast and receive South African shipments.

[39] Renamo units crossed into Ribaué district and advanced east along the Nacala railway. The first Renamo manifestation in Nampula was in May 1983 in Iapala locality in Ribaué district (Viera Pinto 1984, 1, cited in Dinerman 2001, 51).

Nevertheless, there is ample evidence that Renamo's sponsors and leaders never had a unified view of the ultimate goal of Renamo's activities. They did not expect that Renamo would develop its own independent goals, which also changed over time. Even within the Rhodesian intelligence community, aims varied from intelligence gathering, destabilization, to even considering Renamo as an alternative Mozambican government (Robinson 2006, 108). Similarly, among the South African security forces and the Apartheid government, conflict emerged between different objectives, which came into conflict and shaped the changes in South African security policy toward Mozambique in the 1980s.[40]

Renamo's leadership defined its own goals more distinctly after the group's survival was secured through increased South African support, and after the movement sought closer contacts to the population within Mozambique following Zimbabwe's independence (Cahen 2008b, 164). In 1981, the head of Renamo's external relations, Orlando Cristina, and Renamo's European spokesperson, Evo Fernandes, wrote a *Manifesto and Program of Renamo* (Renamo 1988), which clearly positioned Renamo as a pro-West, anticommunist organization. The devised goals included multiparty democracy, private enterprise, and rule of law (Vines 1991, 77). Orlando Cristina and Renamo's president Afonso Dhlakama also conducted a tour through Europe to win international support and credibility in 1980 and 1981. In mid-1982, a National Council was formed as a representative political body.[41]

The implementation of Renamo's objectives on the local level implied a complete reversal of Frelimo's policies. Attacks were targeted at infrastructure and personnel of the Frelimo state: schools and health posts, party secretaries, and members of the GD. Renamo mobilized the people to abandon communal villages and move back to their area of origin. In the surrounding areas of Renamo bases, the rebels reinstated traditional leaders (calling them *mambos* in many areas) to mobilize support from the local population. Within Renamo bases, all types of religion could be practiced without punishment.[42]

---

[40] Robinson (2006) identifies the conflicting positions as the minimalist (economic cooperation and dependence), maximalist (destabilization), and the putschist (government overthrow) position. For an overview of South Africa's foreign policy during the 1980s, see Pfister (2005). For perspectives on the war in Mozambique from a regional standpoint, see, for instance, Davies (1985), Johnson, Martin, and Nyerere (1986, 19), Legum (1988), and Chan (1990).

[41] The council, headed by Afonso Dhlakama and Orlando Cristina, was comprised of twelve men, representing different departments, and later reduced to ten members, one from each region; it was generally considered a weak, basic structure as titles and portfolios changed continuously (Vines 1991, 80–81).

[42] Frelimo had abandoned the system of traditional authorities right after independence, since it accused traditional leaders of having collaborated with the colonial state. Moreover, Frelimo sought to abandon "obscurantism" in society – all types of religion including traditional religion and traditional healing.

However, Renamo's military activities were at odds with its political ideas, which limited its ability to recruit volunteers. Renamo's first recruits came from the Ndau speakers in Manica and Sofala provinces (Vines 1991).[43] The first Renamo leader Matsangaíssa's appeal to traditional symbols granted him the support of the local population.[44] Later, and in other areas, however, Renamo's increasing use of indiscriminate violence and limited attempts of political education made voluntary recruitment difficult. Renamo's main strategy became the abduction of young men, including many children (Hanlon 1984, 229).[45] Military units often brought the new recruits to bases far away from their homes, so that flight was not an option. Leaders provided limited political training for those that could read and write and extensive military training for others. Renamo's promises of immediate economic benefits and future positions of power – and in many cases also threat of punishment – convinced the abducted to stay with the armed group (Vines 1991, 95).

Renamo's limited political structure and efforts of mobilization led analysts to conclude that "Renamo was first and foremost a military organization" (Finnegan 1992, 74). While Renamo's political organization was relatively weak, its military organization was strong. The organization had a centralized military hierarchy, which was supported by South Africa's supply of a sophisticated radio network (Vines 1991, 82). Afonso Dhlakama was the commander-in-chief, assisted by a fifteen-member military council composed of three chiefs-of-staff for the northern, central, and southern zones, ten provincial commanders, and Dhlakama's personal staff. Provinces were subdivided into two to three regional commands. One regional command consisted of a

---

[43] In the beginning, many of the higher ranks within Renamo were Ndau speakers, and Renamo soldiers reported that they had to learn Ndau in certain bases, in particular in Gorongosa. The Ndau were known for their "warrior abilities." The predominance of Ndau in Renamo's leadership led to a debate in how far Renamo was an ethnic movement. Some ethnic tensions emerged within the movement – for example, in Zambézia province between the Ndau commander Calisto Meque and the largely non-Ndau rank and file. However, most observers argue that Renamo diversified its leadership over time and ethnic tensions subsided. The early predominance of Ndau resulted from the location in which Rhodesia recruited fighters for its counterinsurgency force. See Vines (1991, 84–85) and Finnegan (1992, 66). For a critique of the view of Renamo as an ethnic or tribalist movement, see Cahen (2000).

[44] Vines (1991, 74–75) calls the appeal to traditional symbols the "Matsangaíssa myth." To explain Matsangaíssa's death, many people tell the story that the Renamo leader sought the support of a spirit medium (*mhondoro*), which provided him with magical powers that would make him and his followers immune to bullets. When his soldiers did not respect the rules that ensured protection, the Frelimo military managed to kill Matsangaíssa and many members of his group.

[45] At the time of their abduction, 4,334 Renamo soldiers (19.7 percent of total ex-Renamo fighters) and 3,073 government soldiers were aged between ten and fourteen and can be considered child soldiers (Barnes 1997, 17).

brigade, which consisted of several battalions (about 250 men), companies (100–150 men), platoons (30 men), and sections (10 men).[46]

The construction of Renamo bases reflected the group's centralized military hierarchy. Casa Banana in the Gorongosa district of Sofala province was Renamo's headquarters until the Zimbabwean recapture of the base on August 28, 1985. Bases were situated in deep forests close to a river for water supply, and huts were dispersed under trees. Many control posts limited access to the center of the base where the main commander stayed. There was a clear separation between Renamo soldiers and the population. The civilian population did not have access to the actual base, but lived in concentric circles around it, thus serving as a disguise for the base and as a "human shield" (Vines 1991, 91; Geffray 1990).[47] In these areas, the population was closely controlled by the locally recruited police force, the mujeeba, that was armed with machetes and knives. The mujeeba worked closely together with mambos to collect food and intelligence for the main base, and at times also went on missions with the armed force (Gersony 1988, 24; Vines 1991, 92–93).

The areas in which Renamo established military bases were part of the organization's "control zones." Control zones were one of three strategic areas that Gersony (1988) identified in a study of the refugee situation and Renamo's human rights violations during the war.[48] Gersony identified the following strategic areas: tax zones, control zones, and destruction zones. Tax zones were areas in which Renamo soldiers collected food contributions from the population and abducted women to rape them. Control zones were areas in which the population was involved in food production for Renamo soldiers and assisted in the transport of supplies to the bases. In tax and control zones, Renamo did not – or only in a very limited manner – supply any services in exchange for food, goods, and services received. Destruction zones included villages that experienced frequent Renamo attacks until they were completely destroyed and their residents had fled.[49]

---

[46] The structure below the regional commanders is not as clear as the higher command and there might have been regional variation (Vines 1991, 81).

[47] Vines (1991, 92–93) notes that this version of a base is a regional variation of Renamo's bases in the north, and in southern regions, where bases were more mobile, combatants lived further away from the population.

[48] The "Gersony Report," as it is often referred to, was one of the first studies conducted to estimate the number of deaths caused by the war. The findings of the report, which accused Renamo of large-scale human rights violations, subsequently shaped US policy toward Renamo. While conservative groups had supported Renamo for some years, official US foreign policy toward Mozambique geared in favor of a solution of the conflict after the report's publication. See Vines (1991).

[49] These zones compare to Kalyvas' (2006) zones of territorial control in the following way: Control zones are areas under full control, tax zones are areas under partial control, and destruction zones are areas in which control is contested. In the latter zone, indiscriminate violence is common.

Renamo thus established relations with the population that were largely characterized by the – calculated – use of force. Abductions, mutilations, and executions were widespread in destruction zones and used for punishment in tax and control zones (Gersony 1988). Frelimo and some reporters characterized Renamo as "armed bandits," implying the arbitrary, unpolitical nature of their violence. However, Renamo's use of violence had a clear strategic goal. Renamo sought to communicate the group's willingness to dominate by "spreading fear" and demonstrating its "power to hurt" (Wilson 1992, 533; Hultman 2009). Renamo's use of violence had "ritualistic elements which the perpetrators – who in such circumstances see themselves as some kind of brotherhood socially discrete from the victims – believe provides or imputes value or power into the activity" (Wilson 1992, 531). Violence was always witnessed and "survivors released to tell the horrific tale" (Wilson 1992, 532–33). This strategy cemented Renamo's control (Wilson 1992, 537).

However, many commentators have remarked that the character and purpose of violence varied substantially across Mozambique. Some early analyses of the war emphasized that there was a difference between violence in the northern and violence in the southern regions. Due to the Frelimo strongholds in the south and Renamo's difficulty at maintaining occupied areas, rebel activity was reportedly more brutal in that region than in the north, where Renamo could count on voluntary supporters among the peasant population (Roesch 1992, 464; Finnegan 1992, 72). Areas in which Renamo had attained a certain level of administrative control or areas of total opposition to Renamo did not see high levels of (ritualistic) violence (Wilson 1992, 534).[50] In the northern regions where Renamo's control was less precarious, abduction and forced resettlement of the population to the areas' surrounding bases were more common than atrocities and homicides.

Nevertheless, due to constraints on the availability of information on violent events during the war, there has not been a comprehensive and systematic analysis of patterns of violence across the entire country. Other analysts therefore criticize the neat distinction between the characterization of violence in the northern and southern regions. Morier-Genoud (2018), for example, shows that in the southern province of Inhambane Renamo could benefit from early popular support, as it tapped into preexisting conflicts within and between communities, which presumably shaped the rebels' perpetration of violence. Cahen (2019) shows, relying on internal Renamo documents from the central region of Mozambique, that Renamo commanders took great care in treating "their" local population respectfully, even if they did so in an authoritarian manner.

Overall then, Renamo evolved into a well-organized military organization that used violence against civilians strategically to expand its control over the

---

[50] This confirms the theoretical expectations of Kalyvas' (2006) theory.

population. In central and northern regions, however, Renamo relied more on abduction and resettlement than on atrocities to intimidate the population. Renamo's rule based on fear raised the question whether Renamo could ever benefit from genuine popular support, or whether its success would always depend on external resources.

4.2.4 The Relation between External and Domestic Sources of War

Frelimo's internal conflicts and economic policies after independence and Renamo's destructive military strategy, limited political goals, and dependence on external resources generated an intense debate on the origins of Renamo's success among scholars of Southern African politics. In 1989, Gervase Clarence-Smith published a review of recent books on the failure of Frelimo's socialist project and the consequences for the war in Mozambique. The publication of Clarence-Smith's article triggered a lively dispute over the size of Renamo's popular support base.[51] Clarence-Smith (1989) identifies the villagization program as a major source of opposition to Frelimo's rural policies, which Renamo was able to exploit.

In fierce critiques of Clarence-Smith's analysis, published in the same journal, two observers contest the notion that there was any popular support for Renamo. Minter (1989), relying on Gersony (1988), argues that Renamo's exclusive aim was the forceful extraction of resources. Minter's (1994) later published book strengthened the case for a destabilization war pursued by Apartheid South Africa without an apparent domestic base within Mozambique.[52] Fauvet (1989) claims that there is no correlation between the number of people living in communal villages in a particular province by late 1980 and the subsequent strength of Renamo in that province. Thus, he concludes, the villagization program cannot explain Renamo success in these areas.

In a more nuanced analysis, Roesch (1989) concedes that forced resettlement created disaffection with Frelimo, and Renamo was able to mobilize the support of discontented traditional authorities. However, Roesch maintains that "Frelimo's loss of popular support and the renewed ascendency of traditional authorities would not, by itself, have precipitated the present level of armed conflict" (Roesch 1989, 20). Disenchantment with Renamo's widespread

---

[51] The books that Clarence-Smith reviewed included Cahen's *Mozambique. La révolution implosée*, a special issue of the journal *Politique Africaine, Mozambique. Guerre et nationalismes*, and Peter Meyns' edited volume *Agrargesellschaften im portugiesisch-sprachigen Afrika* (Cahen 1987; Politique Africaine 1988; Meyns 1988). All three volumes analyze failures of Frelimo's policies for the rural peasant population.

[52] In his book, Minter (1994) compares the civil wars in Angola and Mozambique, asking the counterfactual question: If the rebel groups had not received external support, would there have been a war in both countries? He comes to the conclusion that a war in Angola would have been more likely than in Mozambique.

destruction and violence and an increased system of force put in place by Renamo signifies that Renamo is "not the counter-revolutionary mass that Clarence-Smith's review might lead one to believe" (Roesch 1989, 21).

In a defense of the argument that domestic factors fueled the war, Cahen (1989) states that the war transformed itself from a war of aggression into a civil war in the early 1980s. The urban and technocratic character of Frelimo's policies created dissent that the one-party state had made impossible to voice in a peaceful manner. Cahen acknowledges that without Rhodesian and South African support, opposition to Frelimo would not have expressed itself in the most violent form of resistance – war. However, without Renamo's popular support, South Africa could not have created the kind of movement it did. Consequently, an end of South African support would not equal an end to the war.

This debate has shaped the historiography of the war in Mozambique in lasting ways.[53] For instance, it influenced discussions on the correct characterization of the armed conflict as a "civil war" or "war of aggression/destabilization."[54] However, as Cahen (2000, 172) points out, much of the polemic has not been so much about "the nature of the war as with the nature of Renamo." Thus, he argues, while "peasant revolt" may not be the right label for Renamo, the war could still be called a civil war (Cahen 2000, 173). Whether scholars see the primary origin of the war in external aggression or domestic discontent, they generally agree, however, that domestic conflicts fed into the war.

What then facilitated the continuation of war was more an opposition to the Frelimo government than support for Renamo. The major lesson to be drawn from the evidence presented for the respective arguments is that there was considerable variation in the level of Renamo's popular support across regions and over time. My argument is thus not about whether internal or external factors were decisive in fueling Renamo violence, but what explains regional variation in the formation and spread of violent actors. Domestic and localized conflicts influenced patterns of support in various areas (Geffray 1990; Lubkemann 2005). Internal factors played a larger role after South Africa took over the sponsorship of Renamo and the rebel movement demanded more political autonomy. This regional and temporal variation implies that local

---

[53] For example, the debate gave rise to a limited number of studies that focused on the internal characteristics of Renamo and its dynamics of violence (Hall 1990; Young 1990; Vines 1991). More recent publications are also shaped by this debate, even though they focus more on the nature and evolution of Frelimo's political project (Dinerman 2006, 2009; Cahen 2008a).

[54] This discussion emerged primarily between João Cabrita who advocated for "civil war" as the correct label and Paul Fauvet who argued that "civil war" would not take into account the importance of external aggression. See the discussion on the internet discussion network H-Luso-Africa from November and December 2005 under the thread "Civil war vs. Post-independence conflict," www.h-net.org/~lusoafri/. By referring to the Mozambican war as a "civil war" throughout this book, I emphasize the internal dynamics but do not aim to negate external influences.

support for Renamo did not necessarily reflect "genuine" support for the movement's agenda, but rather an expression of discontent with Frelimo or with local conflicts that people sought to solve through their participation in Renamo (Roesch 1989; Chichava 2007; Do Rosário 2009; Morier-Genoud 2018).

4.3 FRELIMO'S RESPONSE TO RENAMO

Although Frelimo had fought a guerrilla war itself during the liberation struggle, the regime was frequently confounded in its response to the threat posed by Renamo. Frelimo realized the seriousness of the threat when it became clear that Apartheid South Africa was providing major support to Renamo. The regime mobilized external support from neighboring countries and internal support from the people for its various state-initiated vigilante groups and militias to supplement the weak army. However, external support and the militarization of society failed in significantly curbing Renamo's violence.

4.3.1 War against Internal and External Enemies

Efforts to counter the threat posed by Renamo began in earnest in 1981, framed as a response to the aggression by South Africa.[55] The Mozambican government garnered regional support for an offensive to the north and south of Mozambique,[56] and Tanzania, Zambia, and Zimbabwe provided military support starting in March 1982 (Robinson 2006, 142).[57] Renamo escaped southeast through Gaza province to northern Maputo province; Gaza and Maputo became important areas of Renamo activity and clashes with the army in early 1983 (Robinson 2006, 155) (see map in Figure 4.1). However, Renamo also pushed north, reaching Zambézia in 1982 and Nampula in 1983 (Cahen 2018).

Alarmed by increased Renamo activity in early 1983 and its inability to curb the violence, the Mozambican government reached out to South Africa. Frelimo initiated the first of several talks that would lead to the N'komati Accords with South Africa in March 1984.[58] The main aim of the accord was to end the respective government's (in-)direct assistance to opposition movements in the

---

[55] "Mozambique: Frelimo Draws the Battleline," *Africa (London)* (116), April 1981, 38–39.

[56] With this support, Frelimo prepared for a major offensive northward through Inhambane and southward through Manica and Sofala province in mid-1982. Cabrita (2000, 206–10) suggests that Renamo's expansion into Tete and Zambézia in August 1982 might also have been a strategy to force redeployment of the Frelimo army and lift the pressure off Manica, Sofala, and Inhambane.

[57] Tanzanian troops helped to protect the border to Zimbabwe in Manica province, and Zimbabwean troops were stationed along the Beira corridor. Mozambican troops also received training from Portugal (Robinson 2006, 143).

[58] Mozambique and South Africa signed the *Agreement on Non-Aggression and Good Neighbourliness between the Government of the People's Republic of Mozambique and the*

other country, though Renamo and the ANC were not directly named in the accord.[59] Samora Machel also tried to convince many of the western states to grant support to the Mozambican government and deny any support to Renamo. While the talks advanced, both the Mozambican and the South African governments continued their respective military activity. Frelimo had major successes against Renamo in southern Mozambique – particularly in Inhambane and Gaza provinces – in late 1983. South Africa prepared a potential end of support for Renamo and stepped up the delivery of military supplies.[60]

Yet the N'komati Accord did not bring peace. Renamo increased the number of attacks, in particular around Maputo and the border to Malawi in Tete, Nampula, and Niassa provinces (Robinson 2006, 177–78). The war continued in all three Mozambican regions.[61] While in 1984 and 1985 Renamo activity focused on the south and north, Frelimo's counterinsurgency campaign prepared a major assault on Renamo's main bases in Gorongosa in the central region of Sofala province.[62] In August 1985, Frelimo attacked Renamo headquarters in Gorongosa, with support from Zimbabwean paratroopers.[63]

Frelimo's offensive in central Mozambique led to a fierce response by Renamo and a subsequent intensification of the war in Zambézia province. In mid-1986, Renamo was on the defensive. Though the rebels had recaptured

---

Republic of South Africa on March 16, 1984. For a reprint of the accord see Armon, Hendrickson, and Vines (1998, 35–37).

[59] The South Africans agreed to engage in the talks since the destabilization policy in Mozambique and Angola had failed. The South African government realized that they would have to pursue more diplomatic strategies throughout the region (Vines 1991, 20; Robinson 2006, 172).

[60] The South African defense forces prepared Renamo in such a way as to ensure a long-lasting war of economic destruction and destabilization in order to secure their interests in the region after a nonaggression pact (Robinson 2006, 175–76).

[61] Peace talks between delegations sent by Frelimo and Renamo to Pretoria in South Africa after the N'komati Accord did not result in a ceasefire as planned, as the Renamo delegation pulled out of the talks in October 1984 (Vines 1991, 23). This was probably due to conflicts among the South African elites, during which the "maximalists" – those that supported further destabilization in Mozambique – prevailed over the "minimalists" – those that preferred a settlement and close economic relations to the neighbor states (Robinson 2006, 188–89). Conflicts about the objectives within Renamo and influences of Renamo's international support network, in particular in Portugal, might also have played a role (Vines 1991, 24; Robinson 2006, 190).

[62] Frelimo was relatively successful in Zambézia, and Sofala and Manica did not see much Renamo activity in the latter half of 1984. In early 1985, Renamo attacked targets in Tete and Nampula province and on the border between Zambézia and Sofala provinces (Robinson 2006, 191, 200).

[63] The base at Maringué was captured on August 23, 1985, and the headquarters of Casa Banana on August 28, which resulted in the capture of the "Gorongosa documents" – desk diaries that detailed the headquarter operations and confirmed continued South African support (Robinson 2006, 206, 209). Cahen's collection of internal Renamo documents shows, however, that South African support was sparser than is suggested by the documents Robinson relies on for his analysis (Cahen 2018, 2019).

their main base Casa Banana in February 1986, Zimbabwean troops supporting the Mozambican government retook it a few months later. Frelimo prevailed in Nampula, Manica, Sofala, and the Limpopo valley, and the military
put an end to the "virtual siege" of Maputo (Robinson 2006, 213–14, 217).
However, support from Malawi and the channeling of South African supplies
through Malawi facilitated the start of the Renamo offensive across Zambézia
in July and August 1986. When Malawi came under diplomatic pressure from
Zambia, Zimbabwe, and Tanzania for its support of Renamo, it expelled
Renamo troops, which increased rebel activity in Zambézia province after
October 1986 (Munslow 1988, 30).

After President Samora Machel's death in October 1986, the new president
Joaquim Chissano stepped up military pressure on Renamo again and tried to
win the war. Machel died in an airplane crash on his return from South Africa
on October 19, 1986 under mysterious circumstances (Fauvet and Mosse
2003).[64] The subsequent government offensive under Chissano's leadership in
Zambézia province in late 1986 and early 1987 and the end of Malawian
support for Renamo put the rebels on the defensive.[65] In the south, Renamo
perpetrated the infamous Homoíne massacre in Inhambane province on July
18, 1987, where more than 400 people died during the attack and the subsequent fighting (Finnegan 1992, 182; Armando 2018; Morier-Genoud 2018).[66]

In sum, although Frelimo's response to Renamo looked promising in the
short term, government advances were not sustainable. Renamo's two major
offensives – in the Limpopo valley in 1982 and across Zambézia in 1986 – led
to Frelimo counteroffensives in central Mozambique in 1985 and Zambézia in
late 1986 and 1987. However, the Frelimo army was not able to hold all the
towns and localities it recaptured from Renamo. The increased level of atrocities in the south and other Renamo operations in the central and northern
regions strengthened Renamo's position. This led to a military stalemate in
1988; the Mozambican government realized that the war could only be ended
by a negotiated settlement.[67]

---

[64] The circumstances of the plane crash gave rise to many theories that Machel's death was not an
accident. In addition to South Africa, individuals within Frelimo had an interest in Machel's
death after he had announced a restructuring of the army, was in favor of a negotiated settlement
and expressed concerns about the economic liberalization of the country. Among those who
were most critical of Machel's policies were nationalist military commanders who benefited from
their status in the army, the war economy, and economic liberalization. See Robinson (2006) and
Fauvet and Mosse (2003).

[65] Tanzanian and Zimbabwean troops and Special Forces supported the operations in Zambézia
and Sofala provinces.

[66] "South Africa, Mozambique Renew Ties," *Facts on File World News Digest*, October 2, 1987.

[67] Karl Maier, "The Military Mix," *Africa Report* (July–August), 1988, 56.

4.3.2 Challenges to Frelimo's Counterinsurgency Strategy

In the mid-1980s, it became clear that Frelimo's campaign against the "enemies of the revolution" and the strategy to delegitimize any opposition in independent Mozambique had failed. The government attempted to minimize Renamo's and other opposition groups' threat to domestic stability and denied that internal factors contributed to the unrest (Cahen 2000, 164). It also refused to admit that opposition groups had any support from the population. From the very beginning of armed activity after independence, Frelimo officials referred to the perpetrators as "armed bandits" to downplay their political relevance. In archival documents, government agencies also spoke of "marginals" that were involved in enemy activity.[68] Frelimo mobilized the whole population to be vigilant about these "marginals" and organized people into state-initiated vigilante groups and militias. When that strategy proved unsuccessful, the army further undermined the government's stance by engaging in human rights violations such as forced recruitment and the forced resettlement of the population.

Although the Mozambican state military grew out of a guerrilla army that fought the independence war, its response to Renamo's guerrilla war was surprisingly inept. The military was not prepared for counterinsurgency. In fact, the army achieved most military successes in the mid- to late 1980s with support from foreign forces. Moreover, the party had severe difficulties in controlling the army. For instance, the chief of staff, Colonel-General Mabote, was accused of being involved in an attempted coup against Samora Machel, and thus was expelled from the country in 1986.[69] Widespread corruption within the army throughout the war contributed to its ineffectiveness (Robinson 2006, chapter 7).[70]

One of the major difficulties proved to be the mobilization and retention of a motivated and capable fighting force. In 1986, for example, intelligence reports stated that soldiers had low morale and low pay, and there was a lack of

---

[68] República Popular de Moçambique, Ministério da Defesa Nacional, Comando do 1° Batalhão de Infantaria Zambézia, Comando Provincial de Milícias Populares de Zambézia, Moçambique, *Transcrição da carta-circular no. 469/SMP/EMG/80*, August 5, 1980 (AGZ, Quelimane).

[69] Mabote was also accused of being involved in a coup attempt against President Chissano in 1991 at a time when the peace negotiations with Renamo had advanced. "Mozambique: Confusion at Home, Silence Abroad," *Africa Confidential* 32 (14), July 12, 1991, 6.

[70] During the liberation struggle, party and army were one. This changed with independence, when Frelimo separated the party from the army and formed the Popular Forces for the Liberation of Mozambique (Forças Populares de Libertação de Moçambique, FPLM) on September 25, 1975 (Pachter 1982, 605). With the new constitution in 1990, the armed forces were officially renamed the Mozambican Armed Forces (Forças Armadas de Moçambique, FAM), though both "FPLM" and "FAM" were used interchangeably before. The military force that integrated Frelimo and Renamo's armies in 1994 is called the Armed Forces for the Defense of Mozambique (Forças Armadas de Defesa de Moçambique, FADM).

planning and logistics.[71] Since 1978, Mozambique had had compulsory military service, but many districts reported that youths dodged the draft due to difficult conditions in the army and the lack of food and supplies.[72] At the point of the intelligence reports, most soldiers were recruited by force. Soldiers abducted youths on their way to school and brought them to training camps far away from their homes (cf. Schafer 2007, 78–79). This operation was known as *operação tira camisa* (operation shirt removal): Soldiers forced new recruits to take off their clothes and shaved their heads so that it would be easy to recognize them when they fled.[73] New recruits were thus treated like prisoners. As one former Frelimo combatant told me, "We were recruited like thieves."[74] Notably, many of these recruits were under the age of eighteen, which demonstrates that not only Renamo made use of child soldiers.[75] Due to limited access to supplies and low morale, soldiers frequently attacked relief convoys and pillaged goods. Some army commandos also provided Renamo with supplies and information (Cabrita 2000, 259–60).

The government recognized that the military was inadequately prepared for counterinsurgency, but an effort to restructure the army after Samora Machel's death in 1986 did not bring the expected, lasting change on the battlefield. The party considered the army's initial training for conventional warfare and its rapid growth prompted by the fast-changing situation on the ground as the main challenges in its response to Renamo. These factors combined to inhibit proper organization, training, and logistics.[76] The restructuring was supposed to address these shortcomings, and thus in 1987, Chissano replaced most of the provincial commanders and retired 122 officers, mostly veterans from the liberation struggle.[77]

[71] "Mozambique: In Desperation," *Africa Confidential* 27 (10), May 7, 1986, 7–8.

[72] República de Moçambique, Província de Nampula, Administração do Distrito de Mecubúri, *Relatório das actividades do mês Fevereiro/91*, February 28, 1991 (Archive of the Government of Nampula, Provincial Secretariat, Nampula [AGN]).

[73] Interview with former Frelimo combatant (2012-03-08-Fm14), Quelimane, Zambézia, March 8, 2012.

[74] Interview with former Naparama combatant (2011-09-22-Nm16), Nicoadala, Zambézia, September 22, 2011.

[75] According to data from nationwide surveys of ex-combatants during the demobilization process conducted by the United Nations Operation in Mozambique (Operação das Nações Unidas em Moçambique, ONUMOZ), 23 percent of Frelimo combatants and 41 percent of Renamo combatants were recruited below the of age of eighteen (Barnes 1997, 17; cited in Schafer 2007, 80), or 8 percent and 27 percent, respectively, under the age of sixteen, which has been the legal age of recruitment in Mozambique since 1986 (Cahen 2019).

[76] "People's Assembly Reviews 1988," *Mozambiquefile* (January), 1989, 8.

[77] Robinson (2006, 269) argues that the reshuffle of the military did not seek to make the military more efficient, but served to curb the influence of pro-negotiation Machel loyalists and black nationalists. Others argue, however, that Chissano continued a reform already initiated by Samora Machel that sought to replace the elder officers with younger ones (Fauvet and Mosse 2003, 177–78).

The restructuring did not prevent Renamo from successfully launching its offensives across the central region of Mozambique. This led Frelimo in the late 1980s to increasingly rely on Special Forces, such as the Russian-trained Red Berets (Boina Vermelha).[78] In 1987–88, the Red Berets, together with 3,000 Tanzanian troops, supported the government's response to Renamo's offensive in Zambézia province. By March/April 1989, the government had regained control of all the district towns in Zambézia province.[79] Tanzanian soldiers remained stationed in the towns to defend them. Renamo combatants withdrew from northern Zambézia to Nampula province, where violence along the national highway subsequently increased.

In addition to relying on Special Forces, Frelimo increasingly delegated security tasks to state-initiated militias, but their involvement in the war did not bring peace but further deteriorated security.

4.3.3 Frelimo's System of Territorial Defense

A crucial part of the reorganization of the army after 1986 was the creation of a "system of territorial defense and security," a scheme that gave an important role to state-initiated militias.[80] This was not an entirely new institution, as it "dates back to a militia that linked peasants and guerrilla fighters in the war for independence" (Pachter 1982, 608).[81] FRELIMO built on citizen involvement in community patrols and intelligence gathering in its liberated zones before independence, and across Mozambique after. People were organized into vigilante groups (grupos vigilantes) and popular militias (milícias populares) – state-initiated militias that had the task to control the movement of the population. The government signaled its commitment to continuing its independence war strategies by appointing provincial military commanders – veterans from the liberation struggle – to provinces where they were from in March 1982.

In its initial conception, the idea of organizing people into militias was foremost a political and ideological instrument of organizing the masses in support of the state, first in light of internal and later in light of external threats. Warning of "internal enemies," President Samora Machel emphasized the importance of delegating security tasks to the population to safeguard the revolution right after independence (Frelimo 1978, 58). After South Africa took over the role of Renamo's main sponsor, Frelimo expanded the militia and vigilante programs to address threats from external enemies – South Africa supporting Renamo (Hanlon 1984, 232). In 1981, President Machel sharpened his rhetoric and called the people to arms to defend the sovereignty of the young nation: "Sharpen your hoes and picks to break the heads of Boers. Prepare

---

[78] The Red Berets received eight months of military training as an assault force.
[79] Karl Maier, "The Battle for Zambézia," *Africa Report* (March–April), 1989, 14.
[80] "People's Assembly Reviews 1988," *Mozambiquefile* (January), 1989, 8.
[81] Cf. Joseph Hanlon, "Call to Arms in Mozambique," *The Guardian*, September 28, 1982, 7.

yourselves with all types of arms so that no aggressor leaves our country alive."[82] The popular militias thus took on the task of military defense, primarily in those provinces and districts close to the Rhodesian/Zimbabwean border (Alexander 1997, 4). The new statute and program of the party Frelimo approved by the party's Fourth Congress in 1984 formalized this approach and defined the task of the popular militias as supporting the defense and security organs in the defense of territorial integrity against the "internal enemy" and against aggressions by "imperialism's counter-revolutionary forces." It also assigns militias the task to ensure public order more generally.[83]

As a former guerilla movement, Frelimo recognized the importance of the local population for supporting rebels and thus saw in the militia and vigilante program a way to ensure the loyalty of the population. The militarization of society culminated in the late 1980s, when the minister of defense at the time, Alberto Chipande, "argued that the war effort was not merely the FPLM's [army] responsibility, but that all sectors of economic life, and Mozambican citizens in general should play a full role in defence."[84] The minister recalled that during the independence struggle everyone in liberated zones contributed to the victory over Portuguese forces: "'Today as well we must give a popular character to our war,' he urged."[85] These remarks demonstrate that the Mozambican government increasingly saw the war with Renamo as one over people.

Beyond these political-ideological considerations, the training of locals to support the limited number of armed forces served three major, practical purposes: the collection of intelligence, the multiplication of armed forces, and the expansion of control to rural areas. First, the war against the Renamo guerrilla movement necessitated detailed intelligence and close control of the population, which the army and local administration were unable to ensure alone. Organizing community residents with access to local information and a motivation to protect their own neighborhoods seemed a promising way to answer the challenge posed by Renamo (Finnegan 1992, 211). Moreover, in some regions, militias supplemented or even replaced the military. The dire situation of the Frelimo military made army recruitment difficult. Logistical shortcomings caused the army to be severely undersupplied, forcing troops to either grow their own crops or live off the surrounding population.[86] Lastly, militias extended Frelimo's meagre military presence to the countryside.

---

[82] "Mozambique: Frelimo Draws the Battleline," *Africa (London)* (116), April 1981, 38.

[83] The program was published in "Estatutos e programa do partido Frelimo," *Tempo (Maputo)* (670), August 14, 1983, 31–34.

[84] "People's Assembly Reviews 1988," *Mozambiquefile* (January), 1989, 8.

[85] "People's Assembly Reviews 1988," *Mozambiquefile* (January), 1989, 8.

[86] See, for example, República de Moçambique, Província de Nampula, Administração do Distrito de Mecubúri, *Síntese da reunião do Conselho Alargado dos Oficiais do Comando Militar Distrital de Mecubúri*, January 26, 1991 (AGN, Nampula).

The state army concentrated on the district towns and on strategic localities, but most areas outside of the district towns had little, if any, military presence.

Contrary to these expectations, the state-initiated militias did not solve the government's military challenges. The local administration faced major challenges in mobilizing community residents for the state-initiated militias. In the districts under study for this book, militias rarely received uniforms and weapons, and they were typically not paid. Desertion rates were high, the government had to resort to forced recruitment, and the population often complained about militias' ill-treatment of the people they were supposed to protect (Finnegan 1992; Alexander 1997). The decentralization of security became a major problem as the increased supply of weapons to the population contributed to banditry and warlordism (Finnegan 1992, 232).[87] In 1991, the Minister of the Interior recognized that the distribution of weapons to the population had not been well controlled, and thus many people were in possession of illegal weapons.[88]

As the war became a war over people, both Renamo and Frelimo sought to control the population by forcibly resettling people into areas under their control. Together with the army, state-initiated militias were involved in the forced resettlement of the population, which further diminished people's trust in them. With the help of these militias, Frelimo "recuperated" the people in Renamo-held territories and brought them to government-held areas. These people were settled in accommodation centers, named after people's locale of origin (cf. Igreja 2007, 132) and organized in a manner similar to communal villages. The centers had a central party structure and all activities were closely controlled by state-initiated militias. Again, this strategy was taken from Frelimo's playbook of the independence struggle. Thaler (2012, 552) finds that the most common type of Frelimo violence against civilians during the war of liberation was abduction to assemble people away from Portuguese control and effectively indoctrinate them. Frelimo's strategy of population resettlement was to adopt the Portuguese counterinsurgent strategy of building *aldeamentos* – strategic resettlement villages – to concentrate and closely monitor the population. Forced population resettlement became particularly important for the Frelimo government when the peace process advanced in the late 1980s, as peace implied the holding of multiparty elections that Frelimo needed to win.[89]

---

[87] Clayton (1999, 153) estimates that the government distributed about 1.5 million AK-47 rifles to the civilian population over the course of the war (in a country of twelve million inhabitants in 1980), though this is just an estimate and it remains unclear what it is based on. As the Soviet Union had replaced the AK-47 with the new, lighter AK-74 at the time of the Mozambican war, a large number of surplus rifles could be shipped to its allies. Clayton speculates that about six million rifles might have been shipped to Mozambique.

[88] "Distribuição de armas não foi bem controlada reconhece ministro do interior," *Notícias*, May 28, 1991. For a more detailed analysis of militias in Nicoadala district, Zambézia province, see Chapter 7.

[89] Karl Maier, "The Quiet Revolution," *Africa Report* (November–December), 1990, 41.

However, the introduction of the territorial defense system in 1986–87 only brought temporary success. Renamo consolidated its elite forces in October 1988. The Tanzanian troops that supported the government withdrew in December 1988, which made it difficult for the Frelimo army to hold the newly recaptured towns. The government also faced new challenges in the south. In early 1988, the areas the hardest hit were Gaza and Maputo. Renamo's apparent goal was to cut off Maputo from the hinterland and "create a reputation for Dhlakama as 'Savimbi-style' personality with an organized force,"[90] referring to Angola's rebel leader Jonas Savimbi.[91]

In sum, although Frelimo attempted to learn from its own experiences as a guerrilla movement and built on the close control of the population, its counter-insurgency strategy remained inadequate and poorly executed. The forced recruitment of army soldiers and state-initiated militias together with the forced resettlement of the population into communal villages alienated the population. Territorial gains remained temporary, as Renamo regularly regrouped and staged successful counteroffensives. By 1988, the south was under severe pressure. Frelimo considered the war as having reached a military stalemate and seemed to give up on finding a military solution to the conflict. Attempts at creating economic incentives to end the war through the adoption, in January 1987, of an IMF-sponsored structural adjustment program (Economic Rehabilitation Program/Programa de Restruturação Econômica, PRE) did not solve, but rather added to, Frelimo's problems.

4.4 COMMUNITY RESPONSES TO THE WAR

The population was disenchanted with Frelimo's response to Renamo. The failure of Frelimo's counterinsurgency strategy and the lack of military support in the rural areas provoked community responses to the war that resulted in many different armed and unarmed forms of defense.

4.4.1 Sources of Resistance

As is usually the case in irregular civil wars, the population was the main supporter of the war, providing food, supplies, and intelligence to the armed organizations on either side, and was thus also the main target for intimidation, exploitation, and violence. Recognizing the population as a crucial resource for

---

[90] "Mozambique: Pretoria Has the Key," *Africa Confidential* 29 (5), May 13, 1988, 4.

[91] Based on the experience with Angola, South Africa tried to limit Dhlakama's independent personality and ensure that Renamo remained dependent on South African support. When the leader of the National Union for the Total Independence of Angola (*União Nacional para a Independência Total de Angola*, UNITA), Jonas Savimbi, developed an independent profile and was able to receive direct support from the United States, South Africa lost control over him (Robinson 2006, 151).

which they competed, neither side exclusively relied on political indoctrination to convince civilians to support them. They also forcibly recruited combatants and civilian supporters, perpetrated indiscriminate and collective violence against civilians, and forcibly resettled community residents into areas under their control in order to ensure people's loyalty.

Many people came to believe that the war itself was about the population (Cahen, Morier-Genoud, and Do Rosário 2018b).[92] Civilians frequently shifted identities and opted for supporting the side that provided protection at a particular moment (Bertelsen 2009, 222; Legrand 1993). As a consequence, people found themselves between two forces. Due to quickly shifting loyalties and the risk that civilians could serve as informers to the other side, both Renamo and Frelimo considered control over people as a major objective of their operations. As one Renamo combatant I interviewed put it: "The combat was about the people. To have the majority of the population meant to have more security."[93] The goal to control people took on a punitive character and translated into the control of "bodies through herding, coercing, or kidnapping people" (Bertelsen 2009, 222).

Community residents I spoke with saw themselves as the war's main victims who lacked agency. They cited a well-known Swahili and Mozambican proverb, "When two elephants fight, it is the grass that suffers," comparing themselves to the grass that suffers beneath fighting elephants.[94] In a similar way, the Mozambican writer Mia Couto, in his novel *Terra Sonâmbula (Sleepwalking Land)*, characterized the civilian population's situation during the war as one in which the people were the ground for one side, and the carpet for the other: "My son, the bandits' job is to kill. The soldiers' job is to avoid dying. For one side we're the ground, for the other we're the carpet" (Couto 1996, 23). This victim narrative represented civilians as marginalized and without agency. In my conversations, I frequently heard statements like "war is war" or "soldier is soldier," which expressed passive acceptance of the ineluctable violent rules of war.[95] Civilians saw themselves as defenseless spectators, fleeing from their homes into the bush or the mountains in case of an attack: "We were like the children of the household, we only observed what happened."[96] Respondents felt they were helpless in the face of violence.

From this victim narrative emerged a second narrative of the need to transform passivity into activity. When recalling the war situation of the mid- to late 1980s, community residents explained that they were getting "tired of war"

---

[92] Interview with civilian (2012-05-02-f13), Namarrói, Zambézia, May 2, 2012.
[93] Interview with former Renamo combatant (2012-03-08-Rm15), Nicoadala, Zambézia, March 8, 2013.
[94] Interview with community leader (2011-09-27-Lm4), Nicoadala, Zambézia, September 27, 2011.
[95] Interview with religious leader (2011-09-06-Pm1), Nicoadala, Zambézia, September 6, 2011.
[96] Interview with civilian (2011-09-14-f1), Nicoadala, Zambézia, September 14, 2011.

and were looking for ways to end their suffering.[97] They developed both unarmed and armed strategies to defend themselves against what they felt to be an arbitrary war, and by doing so built on preexisting social conventions. In a society in which traditional religion remained strong despite Frelimo's efforts to eradicate all "obscure" beliefs, traditional healers played a large part in these efforts and initiated a range of protective strategies for both Renamo and Frelimo forces, as well as the civilian population.

Communities' reliance on social conventions needs to be understood in the context of the spiritual dimension of the war. In his fascinating study of "cults and counter-cults of violence," Wilson (1992) analyzes how Renamo enlisted the help of spirit mediums in its bases, creating a "myth of invincibility" that was later countered by the community-initiated militia Naparama. References to the spirit world helped Renamo connect to peasants by making its use of power "meaningful," however horrendous its violence was (Wilson 1992, 535). Several important Renamo commanders in Zambézia province were famous for their spiritual powers, and thus shaped events on the battlefield accordingly. Renamo military commanders even declared a "war of the spirits," which represented the fight against Frelimo's repression of all forms of religion (Roesch 1992).

However, "the 'war of the spirits' was later to turn against Renamo" (Wilson 1992, 548), and Renamo's advantage in the realm of spiritual power came to an end in the mid- to late 1980s. Traditional leaders and healers allied with Renamo at first because, as previously mentioned, Frelimo had prohibited the activity of traditional healers right after independence. However, people who initially supported Renamo became alienated by their violent tactics (Wilson 1992, 548).[98] In order to protect themselves from the rebels' spiritual power, community residents engaged in similar strategies to counter Renamo's "cult of violence." At the same time, Frelimo adjusted its stance toward tradition, religion, and culture and began tolerating – but not endorsing – traditional healers' activities, hence the proliferation of traditional healers that offered their assistance to communities and individuals within the military.[99]

The Naparama militia belongs to the community initiatives that made use of such conventions for developing armed strategies of protection.

---

[97] Interviews with former Naparama combatant (2011-09-14-Nm9), Nicoadala, Zambézia, September 14, 2011, and with community leader (2011-09-23-Lm3a), Nicoadala, Zambézia, September 23, 2011.

[98] It is difficult to ascertain how many of such "switches" of traditional healers and spirit mediums actually took place. However, there is a notable increase in the activity of traditional healers for the purpose of defense against Renamo in Zambézia and Nampula provinces in the mid-1980s. See Chapters 5–7 for a more detailed discussion of these aspects of the war in these provinces.

[99] I explore the relationship between Frelimo and traditional authorities and healers in more detail below.

4.4.2 The Rise of the Naparama[100]

In the context of the "war over people" and the spiritual dimension of war, the Naparama, an armed movement led by the traditional healer Manuel António in Zambézia and other healers and community leaders in Nampula, dramatically influenced the dynamics of war in these provinces. No other self-defense mechanisms that had emerged before resulted in anything like the rapid social and military successes Naparama achieved. The first appearance of Naparama was in the border region between Nampula and Zambézia provinces, but it quickly spread across the region. The movement gained control over two-thirds of the northern territory within a short amount of time, becoming "one of the most important military and political factors in contemporary Mozambique" (Wilson 1992, 561).[101]

Due to the militia's legendary character, which built on the fierce reputation of its leader and the seemingly "magical" successes against Renamo, it is difficult to ascertain how large the group actually was. News reports from the time estimate that the number of Naparama recruits jumped from 400 in July 1990 to 20,000 in September 1991.[102] António himself claimed to have about 14,000 fighters in May 1991.[103] After the war, in 1994, news reports spoke of 9,000 Naparama who had assembled in the district of Nicoadala in Zambézia province.[104] However, the journalist Gil Lauriciano, who covered the war in Zambézia extensively, estimates that the group did not have more than 2,000 members.[105] My interviews with former Naparama members indicate that many districts had about 200 Naparama, which only included those in the main district town. As a result, I estimate the size to be about 4,000–6,000 members across both provinces, Zambézia and Nampula.[106] The spiritual roots

---

[100] This section is just an overview and short introduction to Naparama in Zambézia and Nampula provinces. I conduct a detailed analysis of the formation of the group and its evolution in Chapter 5–7. For a summary of Naparama's history, organization, and leadership struggles, see Jentzsch (2018b).

[101] Although Naparama was important for the war in the central and northern regions, there are few studies focusing on the Naparama militia. Exceptions are the excellent studies by Wilson (1992) and Pereira (1999a). Various ethnographic and journalistic accounts of the war refer to Naparama but do not study the group in depth (Finnegan 1992; Nordstrom 1997; Dinerman 2006).

[102] Karl Maier, "Renamo Flee at Sight of Rag-Tag Army," *Independent*, July 27, 1990, 12; "Mozambique: Renamo Under Pressure," *Africa Confidential* 32 (18), September 13, 1991, 4–5.

[103] Rachel Waterhouse, "Antonio's Triumph of the Spirits," *Africa South (Harare)* (May), 1991, 14.

[104] "Naparama Irregulars Start Handing over Weapons to Police," *Radio Mozambique (Maputo)*, August 5, 1994.

[105] Gil Lauriciano, personal communication, July 2010.

[106] There were also some Naparama in districts in Niassa and Cabo Delgado close to the border to Nampula, but few accounts exist. In 2011, the Naparama leadership claimed to have registered

of Naparama lay in the belief that a potion prepared with roots and leaves would make people, through vaccination, immune to bullets. Naparama's combatants only fought with weapons of cold steel – *armas brancas* (white weapons) – spears, arrows, machetes, and knives. Their behavior was codified with a strict set of rules that, when respected, was believed to maintain the vaccine's effectiveness. The rules referred to the militia members' behavior at home, such as prohibiting certain foods, and to their behavior on the battlefield, such as the rule not to retreat. Deaths during battle were usually attributed to violations of these rules.

Building on the strength it could generate as a "traditional" fighting force, Naparama put major pressure on Renamo in Nampula and Zambézia provinces. In 1988 and 1989, it became clear that the Frelimo government had difficulties holding the areas liberated during the military offensive from late 1986 onward. Naparama filled an important gap, helping to defend camps for the displaced, as well as district towns and surrounding areas, and liberating more areas from Renamo control. This put Renamo under pressure during the advancing peace negotiations. As a consequence of the Naparama offensive in 1990, Dhlakama refused to send his negotiation team to the third round of meetings in September 1990.[107] During Renamo's counteroffensive in 1991, the main goal was to recapture lost territory before signing a peace agreement in the politically important province of Zambézia.[108] This new Renamo offensive led to the killing of Zambézia's Naparama leader, Manuel António, in late 1991.

Naparama's success against Renamo must be understood in the context of the spiritual dimension of war and the militia's frightful appearance in combat. Rumors of Naparama's unusual way of fighting explain much of their (initial) effectiveness in battle. Renamo units often fled when they heard Naparama forces approach, as they had heard about the militia's alleged magical powers. Thus, Naparama rarely engaged in direct confrontation with Renamo combatants. Moreover, Naparama forces approached en masse – singing, in an upright position in one single line, instructed to never retreat.[109] This unusual combat behavior scared Renamo combatants, who came to believe that their own

---

4,438 former Naparama in four districts: Inhassunge, Nicoadala, Namacurra, and Mopeia (Interview with former Naparama combatants (2011-08-23-Gr-Nm1), Quelimane, Zambézia, August 23, 2011). As a comparison, Renamo was estimated to have about 20,000 combatants and the UN mission to Mozambique ONUMOZ registered 24,649. The actual size of the government army was unknown for a long time but is estimated at about 30,000 and ONUMOZ registered 67,042 (UN Security Council 1994). FRELIMO's liberation army had about 10,000 fighters.

[107] "Mozambique: A Chance for Peace?" *Africa Confidential* 31 (21), October 26, 1990, 7.

[108] "Mozambique: Confusion at Home, Silence Abroad," *Africa Confidential* 32 (14), July 12, 1991, 7.

[109] I owe this point to the Mozambican journalist Gil Lauriciano who pointed out that when Naparama advanced, they made a lot of noise, which scared the Renamo combatants.

weapons were useless against the traditional force. Lastly, many Renamo combatants were very young and not well trained, so they often missed their targets. This could easily be interpreted as being caused by the power of Naparama's medicine, which was thought to divert bullets fired by Renamo.

In the memory of many community residents I spoke with in the two provinces, the work of Naparama remains positive and significant since the displaced were able to return to their houses and take up work on their fields again. However, some also remark that Naparama contributed to the violence (Wilson 1992, 574; Nordstrom 1997, 94), and this happened in two ways. First, there is archival evidence in government reports of individual Naparama, or even units, who went rogue.[110] Naparama became involved in violence against civilians, looting goods and also deliberately killing civilians they suspected of working with Renamo, in particular during operations that sought to recuperate people to government-held areas. Second, Naparama became the main target for Renamo counter-operations, increasing the number of attacks after Renamo's initial retreat.

The movement seemed to disappear as rapidly as it had emerged. As a consequence of the Renamo counteroffensive and António's death, Naparama's activities slowed down in 1992 and ended with the peace accord. The group disbanded when the peace accord was signed. However, in Inhassunge, former Naparama were accused of being involved in the pillage of warehouses and atrocities against the population, and in Nicoadala, former Naparama fighters protested being left out of the demobilization process and demanded the same benefits that Renamo soldiers were to receive.[111] Although violent protest quickly subsided, Naparama in the Nicoadala district continued to organize themselves, and they demand recognition for their wartime contribution to this day. In the other areas of the two provinces, however, Naparama groups dissolved completely, though the memory of their activities is still strong.

4.4.3 A Threat to Frelimo's Scientific Socialism?

Although the Frelimo government was at first skeptical of the emerging Naparama movement, it soon tolerated and at times even supported the militia. The community initiatives that emerged as a response to Renamo's violence

---

[110] See, for example, República Popular de Moçambique, Província da Zambézia, Administração do Distrito de Pebane, *Boletim Informativo do mês de Novembro/90*, December 2, 1990 (AGZ, Quelimane).

[111] "Mutinying Troops in Quelimane Threaten to Shell City, Seize Airport," *Radio Mozambique (Maputo)*, August 3, 1994; República de Moçambique, Província de Zambézia, Direcção Provincial de Apoio e Controlo, *Comportamento e actuação dos elementos das armas brancas (Naparamas) nos distritos de Nicoadala e Inhassunge*, February 22, 1993 (AGZ, Quelimane).

challenged one of the major foundations of the postindependent self-proclaimed socialist state:

Both Mungoi[112] and [Manuel] António [and his peasant army Naparama] championed traditional African power and culture, and threw political will back onto people, their communities, and the chiefly traditions that governed these – as threatening to the scientific-Marxist government of Frelimo as it was to the Renamo rebels. (Nordstrom 1997, 150)

Frelimo's toleration of Naparama's activities could be explained by the party's slow abandonment of socialist ideology and the resulting "softening" of Frelimo's stance toward traditional power in the late 1980s (cf. Thaler 2012). However, on the local level, Naparama was not threatening because of its use of traditional sources of power *per se*, but because of the potential challenge it presented to government authority.[113] In fact, when local Frelimo officials were convinced that Naparama forces were loyal to the government and could support its war effort and maybe even upset the military stalemate, they supported Naparama's recruitment efforts. This occurred particularly in areas in which the local government did not have a good relationship with the local army contingent due to the army's abuses of the population and disrespect for government officials, and where strong community support for Naparama existed.[114]

Frelimo's uneasiness toward community initiatives to achieve peace is best exemplified by its response to the peace zone of the spirit of Mungoi. The peace zone emerged in southern Mozambique in Gaza province when a traditional healer convinced Renamo not to attack the village. Provincial and district party elites were weary of the new phenomenon, as it showed considerable defiance to government authority by forcing the military to enter the village unarmed (Maier 1998, 61–62). Moreover, Frelimo officials were highly suspicious and attributed the peace zone's success to Mungoi's collaboration with Renamo, and after a meeting with party officials at the seat of the district capital, the local Frelimo commander sought to kill the person that claimed it had personified the spirit (Maier 1998, 63). However, instead of strengthening Renamo, Mungoi weakened the rebel group. In June 1989, twenty-seven Renamo combatants surrendered to Mungoi. When a local critical journalist reported about these incidents, the intelligence service arrested and interrogated him, and then put him in jail for several months (Maier 1998, 65).

---

[112] The spirit of Mungoi created a peace zone in southern Mozambique, which Renamo promised not to attack. I provide more details on this peace zone below and in Chapter 5.

[113] One could even argue that Frelimo embraced the "spiritual war" on the local level by developing relationships with traditional healers to protect its force. See Wilson (1992).

[114] As was the case, for example, in an administrative post in Pebane (Zambézia). República Popular de Moçambique, Província da Zambézia, Administração do Distrito de Pebane, Direcção Provincial de Apoio e Controlo Zambézia, Quelimane, *Síntese da visita do 1° Secretário e Administrador do districto ao Posto Administrativo de Mulela*, November 29, 1990 (AGZ, Quelimane).

As with Mungoi, many Frelimo officials were deeply skeptical about the emergence of Naparama. Observing events in war-torn Angola, where two insurgent movements were fighting against the government, government and party officials feared that Naparama would evolve into a second insurgent force. Moreover, the local administration was concerned that Naparama would make financial and material demands or seek compensation during the war or afterwards. Before António could work in Mocuba district, for example, he had to promise the local administration that his goal was not money or political power, but only the protection of the population.[115]

To some extent, the decision to tolerate Naparama and even cooperate with the militia in certain districts was based on pragmatic calculations to further local power interests, not a change in the official party ideology. Similar to the local party structure's attitude toward traditional authorities, its handling of traditional healing practices showed remarkable continuity throughout the postindependence period. As Dinerman (2006) argues, Frelimo's policy of detribalization had been compromised due to the limited capacity of the state and the "reciprocal assimilation" of traditional and local government elites. In Namapa, the district in which Dinerman primarily conducted her field research, the state's divergence between official and actual policy demonstrated

the proclivity of the state and party representatives to conveniently overlook the role of official institutions in reproducing obscurantist practices – and even, as in this case, facilitating their geographic spread – while, at one and the same time, capitalizing on the consequences of these past actions to further ruling political interests in the present. (Dinerman 2006, 22)

This pragmatic stance is further confirmed by the fact that Frelimo officials on the provincial and national level never officially acknowledged the cooperation with Naparama in certain districts, although the party abandoned all references to Marxism-Leninism at its party congress in 1989 and changed its attitude toward traditional authorities and healers in the early 1990s. Due to this strict denial of Frelimo–Naparama cooperation on the national level, Naparama was not considered a party in the conflict during the peace negotiations between Frelimo and Renamo, and the militia members were therefore not able to benefit from demobilization programs.[116]

4.5 THE SLOW PATH TO PEACE

After Mozambique and South Africa had signed the N'komati Accord in March 1984, increased attempts were made for a solution to the conflict between Frelimo and Renamo. When negotiations for a ceasefire failed in October

---

[115] Interview with former Naparama leader (2012-06-06-Nm46), Lugela, Zambézia, June 6, 2012.
[116] I analyze the various relationships that evolved between Frelimo and Naparama on the district-level in more detail in Chapters 5 and 6.

1984, President Machel granted the Mozambican Christian Council (Conselho Cristão de Moçambique, CCM) permission to start a secret dialogue with Renamo. In 1988, the CCM announced the creation of a Commission for Peace and Reconciliation, consisting of representatives of the CCM and the Catholic Church (Vines 1991).[117]

The peace process made major advances toward a negotiated settlement in 1989. First, Mozambique improved its relationship with South Africa. Frelimo also developed a plan of twelve principles for peace, in which it outlined the necessary principles for negotiations.[118] Renamo accepted Frelimo's initiative for dialogue at its first congress in June 1989 in Gorongosa (Vines 1991, 122).[119] At the Fifth Frelimo Congress in July 1989, the Frelimo leadership received a mandate from the delegates to seek a negotiated solution. Chissano agreed to direct consultations with Renamo and named Robert Mugabe of Zimbabwe and Daniel arap Moi of Kenya as mediators. The congress also marked an "ideological turnaround," as the party dropped its commitment to Marxism-Leninism.[120] The new multiparty constitution was approved in November 1990 and took effect the following December.

However, the peace process was constantly jeopardized by the military actions of both parties. In July 1989, Frelimo launched a major offensive against Renamo headquarters in Gorongosa, during which Renamo president Dhlakama was almost captured. In early 1990, the army together with Zimbabwean troops stepped up pressure in Gorongosa and Sofala. In mid-1990, operations resumed in Tete, Sofala, Manica, and Zambézia provinces, which forced Renamo president Dhlakama to move his headquarters north to Ila de Inhamgoma between the Zambezi and Shire Rivers. In Zambézia, Frelimo (with support from Naparama) regained control over hundreds of thousands of people after five years of Renamo dominance, pursuing a scorched earth policy by burning huts and bombing villages.[121]

Military action became intertwined with developments at the negotiation table. The first round of peace negotiations, hosted by the Catholic Community of Sant'Egidio in Rome, took place in July 1990. Anticipating the talks and a ceasefire that would immobilize forces, Renamo withdrew units in June from the north and sent them south to Gorongosa (Robinson 2006, 318). The army offensives in the Fall of 1990 in Sofala, Manica, Tete, and Zambézia provinces

---

[117] Frelimo's attempt to gain power over Renamo by approving an amnesty law in late 1987 did not succeed. Between 1988 and 1990, more men joined Renamo than officially surrendered to the government (about 4,000) (Gerhard Liesegang, "Der Bürgerkrieg in Mosambik ca. 1980–1992. Abläufe und struktureller Wandel des Landes," Unpublished manuscript, Maputo, 1995, cited in Seibert 2003, 266).

[118] See a reproduction of the plan in Vines (1991, appendix 3).

[119] "Mozambique: Renamo Congress Bids for Peace," *Africa Confidential* 30 (14), July 7, 1989, 1–2.

[120] Karl Maier, "A Program for Peace," *Africa Report* (September–October), 1989, 56.

[121] "Mozambique: The Kenyan Obstacle," *Africa Confidential* 31 (11), June 1, 1990, 4–5.

sought to bring as much of the population as possible under Frelimo control, as the Rome talks set multiparty elections for 1991.[122]

A partial ceasefire signed on December 1, 1990 by Frelimo and Renamo did not bring peace any closer. The agreement limited the activities of Zimbabwean troops to the Beira and Limpopo corridors. In exchange, Renamo was to refrain from attacks against targets in the corridors (Vines 1991, 130). The agreement also allowed the International Red Cross access to both sides and required both Renamo and Frelimo to end the forceful resettlement of the population. Yet mutual accusations of a violation of the terms of the ceasefire created further aggression. Renewed Renamo attacks in Sofala and Manica in February signaled that Renamo was filling the vacuum created by the withdrawal of Zimbabwean troops to the corridors.[123] Apparently, Renamo's strategy aimed at slowing down the peace process to extract more concessions from Frelimo during the negotiations, such as government portfolios.[124] In anticipation of elections, Renamo also sought to gain the upper hand on the battlefield, as the rebels tried to mobilize the people and recapture lost territory in Zambézia and Gorongosa (Meldrum 1991, 65).[125]

Though Frelimo was able to strike major successes in 1990 and early 1991 in Zambézia and Nampula due to Naparama activities, the situation deteriorated in late 1991. In June 1991, the Chissano government discovered that party leaders and marginalized army generals who were discontent with Chissano's program of reform and negotiation with Renamo were plotting a coup.[126] Later that year, Renamo launched an offensive against Naparama in Zambézia. The situation also deteriorated in Nampula, Niassa, Inhambane, Gaza, and Maputo.

The peace negotiations continued in 1992, reaching their twelfth and final round in June 1992. With international pressure on Renamo, the General Peace Agreement was signed on October 4, 1992. The United Nations approved a peacekeeping mission to ensure the ceasefire and sent 8,000 troops to Mozambique on ONUMOZ (Boutros-Ghali 1995). Renamo and Frelimo troops began to assemble in demobilization centers in early 1993, but formal demobilization did not start until March 1994.[127] Elections were held October 27–29, 1994. Frelimo won the parliamentary elections with a narrow margin. In the presidential elections, Chissano achieved 53 percent of the vote and

---

[122] Karl Maier, "The Quiet Revolution," *Africa Report* (November–December), 1990, 41.

[123] "Mozambique: Setback to Peace," *Africa Confidential* 32 (4), February 22, 1991, 4.

[124] "Mozambique: Renamo Takes the War Path," *Africa Confidential* 32 (6), March 22, 1991, 1–3.

[125] "Mozambique: Renamo Takes the War Path," *Africa Confidential* 32 (6), March 22, 1991, 1–3; Andrew Meldrum, "Railway of Refuge," *Africa Report* (May–June), 1991, 65.

[126] "Mozambique: Confusion at Home, Silence Abroad," *Africa Confidential* 32 (14), July 12, 1991, 6–7.

[127] On the process and meaning of reintegration for Renamo veterans since the war's end in Maringue, the important center of Renamo activity in Sofala province, see Wiegink (2020).

Dhlakama 33 percent (Mazula 1997). Observers considered the elections free and fair, but Renamo alleged fraud and threatened to boycott parliamentary sessions.

4.6 CONCLUSION

This chapter analyzes the origins and evolution of the war in Mozambique, the relevant actors involved, and their relation to the population. Throughout the chapter, I made three major arguments. First, both actors sought control over people rather than territory. When Frelimo or Renamo (re-)occupied district towns and rural areas, residents fled as they were fearful of being accused of having supported the other side and killed. This led Renamo and Frelimo to forcibly resettle the population into areas under their control, as they lived off what people produced and sought to control the movement of the population. Second, the focus of the war on the population led to a militarization of society, as Frelimo and Renamo enlisted civilians to control each other. Frelimo did so through state-initiated militias; Renamo built on the support of mambos and mujeeba. Third, the focus on the people for intimidation and violence provoked the emergence of community defense initiatives, such as Naparama. The spiritual dimension of war explains why community-initiated militias using social conventions such as Naparama could have the effect it did on the dynamics of war.

Overall, the chapter demonstrates that the debate on the balance between external and internal sources of the conflict becomes less central to our understanding of the war when local dynamics and fluid loyalties are taken into account (cf. Cahen, Morier-Genoud, and Do Rosário 2018b). As discussed above, the label "civil war" for Mozambique's war is contested among scholars of Mozambique and Mozambicans due to diverging views on whether Renamo could rely on a social base within Mozambique. In southern Mozambique – Frelimo's stronghold – people speak of the war as one of "destabilization" due to South Africa's apparent aim to destabilize, but not overthrow the Frelimo government. In central and northern Mozambique, people refer to the "sixteen-year war." Respondents often spoke of a "war between brothers" to demarcate the difference between the liberation struggle and the war that ensued after independence.

Taking into account local dynamics shows that Frelimo's conflictual history and policies to restructure society and economy alienated important sections of the population and made them more amenable to support Renamo. However, instead of genuinely supporting the rebels' goals, peasants collaborated with Renamo to solve local conflicts or improve their position in local politics (cf. Lubkemann 2005; Morier-Genoud 2018). Moreover, popular support waned when Renamo combatants increased their use of indiscriminate violence. The same was true for Frelimo. Popular support did not necessarily reflect an affirmation of Frelimo policies, and support diminished when

Frelimo was unable to effectively counter Renamo's violence. As a consequence, the local population quickly supported a new armed movement initially independent of Renamo and Frelimo that promised an end to the violence.

The following chapters analyze the causal processes of Naparama's formation and diffusion in detail, first, by exploring the trajectory of the Naparama movement as a whole in Zambézia and Nampula provinces over time; second, by comparing the diffusion of Naparama forces to two adjacent districts in Zambézia province; and lastly, by identifying the mechanisms that made the mobilization of militia members such a successful process.

5

People Tired of War

The Timing of Community-Initiated Militia Formation

When I asked a former militia member in Nicoadala district how the Naparama leader Manuel António convinced people to join the movement, he seemed surprised about the question. In his view, the Naparama leader did not have to do anything specific to persuade youths to be initiated into the movement. Community residents repeatedly told me that when Naparama formed, they welcomed the opportunity to contribute to ending the war: "We were tired [of the war]! So we joined [Naparama] voluntarily."[1] Potential members did not need particular incentives to join, but volunteered to become militia members: "[Naparama] didn't receive anything. The people revolted. They were tired of the war, so they preferred volunteering, confronting those who were waging war and ending it."[2]

With the notion of "being tired of war," my respondents suggested that the conflict was "ripe" for a community response. Community residents expressed a sense of urgency to respond to the dynamics of the war by forming militias. They perceived the war as "intense" and "hot"; because of frequent attacks, they could not sit down "even for five minutes," as they constantly had to flee their homes.[3] Working their land had become impossible, and peasant farmers had become dependent on relief goods.[4] Seeing only the suffering, they did not

[1] Interview with former Naparama combatant (2011-09-14-Nm9), Nicoadala, Zambézia, September 14, 2011.

[2] Interview with local government representative (2011-09-15-Gm1), Nicoadala, Zambézia, September 15, 2011.

[3] Interview with local leader (2011-09-27-Lm4), Nicoadala, Zambézia, September 27, 2011; Interview with former Naparama combatant (2011-09-28-Nf1), Nicoadala, Zambézia, September 28, 2011; Interview with former Naparama combatant (2011-09-19-Nm11), Nicoadala, Zambézia, September 19, 2011.

[4] Interview with local leader (2011-09-23-Lm3a), Nicoadala, Zambézia, September 23, 2011.

understand why the war had to be fought "between brothers" or what could be gained by winning it.[5]

Indeed, in the late 1980s, the war reached a point at which elites on both sides perceived that a military victory was out of sight and that continued fighting was costly. Slowly, a "mutually hurting stalemate" (Zartman 1989) emerged on the national level, which prepared the way for negotiations.[6] Community residents, however, reluctant to wait for their leaders to end the war, requested immediate change. Why was the time ripe to form a militia? Why did community residents opt for armed defense against insurgent violence at that particular time?

In this chapter, I show that the strategic context of a military stalemate on the local level helped form community-initiated militias. I apply the concept of a "community-empowering stalemate," introduced in Chapter 2, to show that the military stalemate had two important consequences. First, its violent character made community residents vulnerable and war-weary, as neither side of the conflict was able to protect them. Second, the stalemate implied that a significantly weakened government was incapable of fighting back another armed group in addition to the rebels and thus tolerated the grassroots formation of militias. Local administrations welcomed the militia as a force multiplier, particularly in areas in which the state armed forces had a weak presence. So the community-initiated Naparama militia that originated in the late 1980s in Zambézia and Nampula provinces after a large counteroffensive by Frelimo failed to stop Renamo advances and to restore stability. The militia offered its services to communities and local administrations at a crucial point during the war. In the following, I discuss the emergence of the stalemate in Zambézia and Nampula provinces and then show how it helped form the Naparama militia, first from the perspective of the civilian population and then from the perspective of the local state.

5.1 THE EMERGENCE OF A COMMUNITY-EMPOWERING STALEMATE

While the Mozambican civil war took place mostly in the center and south of the country between 1976 and 1982, Zambézia and Nampula became important battle grounds from 1982 to 1983 and onward. After Zimbabwe's independence in 1980, Apartheid South Africa became Renamo's main external

---

[5] Interview with religious leader (2011-09-06-Pm1), Nicoadala, Zambézia, September 6, 2011.

[6] In 1988, a bishop from the Catholic church managed to meet Renamo leader Afonso Dhlakama in Gorongosa, beginning a slow and tentative process of preparing negotiations between Renamo and Frelimo (Serapião 2004, 384). The peace negotiations began in July 1990 and ended with the signing of the General Peace Accords on October 4, 1992. Thus, at the elite level, a moment of ripeness slowly emerged, as both Frelimo and Renamo leaders came to realize that their own victory was unlikely.

supporter and the rebels further developed political objectives in addition to the military goal of destabilizing Mozambique (see Chapter 4). To achieve these political aims, Zambézia and Nampula became strategically important as they were the most populous provinces in the country and centers of agricultural production. At the time of the war, each province had about three million inhabitants, out of the country's fifteen million. Zambézia was the source of over 50 percent of Mozambique's sugar, tea, copra, and coconut production.[7] Nampula province produced more than 50 percent of the cotton grown in Mozambique. The Nacala corridor that crosses through Nampula province links Malawi to the port of Nacala, one of the best deepwater harbors on the East African coast at the time.[8]

Due to the provinces' political and economic significance, Renamo made inroads into Zambézia in August 1982 (Legrand 1993, 91–92) and Nampula in April 1983 (Do Rosário 2009, 305). When crossing the Zambezi River, Renamo merged with an armed group that had been operating in a limited capacity in eastern Zambézia from 1976 to 1982, the PRM (Hall 1990, 40). The PRM had its origins in a nationalist organization of the 1960s, the Rumbezi African National Union (UNAR), which sought to reestablish an independent state – Rombézia – between two rivers, Rovuma in the north and Zambezi in the center of Mozambique (Legrand 1993, 89; Coelho and Vines 1992, 32).[9] UNAR's area of activity had been Milange in eastern Zambézia, so the PRM benefited from high levels of support in that region.[10] The PRM had tactics similar to Renamo's and targeted the symbols of the Frelimo state: local government officials, teachers, health workers, and state infrastructure such as schools, health posts, administrative buildings, and

---

[7] Karl Maier, "The Battle for Zambézia," *Africa Report* (March–April), 1989, 14.

[8] "Chissano Encourages Local Solutions in Nampula," *Mozambiquefile* (November), 1988, 15.

[9] As discussed in Chapter 5, the PRM was known as Africa Livre (Free África). However, as its former leader Gimo Phiri explained in an interview with the Mozambican researcher Sérgio Chichava, África Livre as a movement never existed. Instead, África Livre referred to all the movements that fought against Frelimo. Actually, it was a radio station set up by Rhodesia, which spread anti-Frelimo propaganda (Chichava 2007, 400–01). Nevertheless, in popular recollection – and even by the members of this movement – the PRM is still remembered as África Livre. See interview with former members of África Livre and current Renamo party members (2012-05-21-Gr-Rm1), Namarrói, Zambézia, May 21, 2012.

[10] The center of activity of the PRM/África Livre was Milange and Gurué, but the movement was also present in Lugela, Namarrói, Morrumbala, and Mopeia in Zambézia; Mutarara in Tete province; and Mecanhelas in Niassa province (Chichava 2007, 402). Vines (1991, 114) argues that the construction of protected settlements in Milange led people to join the PRM/África Livre. However, the PRM never appeared as an alternative to the government, and thus rather than supporting the PRM en masse, Zambézia's population chose more traditional forms of resistance, such as refusing to work in nationalized plantations and minimizing contact with the state (Legrand 1993, 91). Opposition also took the form of rumors that the state pursued citizens at night to suck their blood; this phenomenon (called "chupa-sangue") has reemerged throughout the history of Zambézia in times of rapid social change (Chichava 2007).

communal villages (Chichava 2007, 403). The movement disrupted political life in Milange to such an extent that Frelimo forced people into communal villages to better control them.[11] The PRM's alliance with Renamo did not last long, however. Due to conflicts about goals and strategy, the PRM left Renamo in 1987, and later aligned itself with Frelimo.

In the years following its unification with the PRM in 1982, Renamo targeted state and economic infrastructure, set up camps in rural areas, and pillaged people's belongings in the villages surrounding rebel bases. Zambézia proved "ideal for large-scale rebel operations" (Finnegan 1992, 71) due to the local political weakness of Frelimo, the porous border to Malawi, and high forestation.[12] Indeed, in conversations with Lisa Hultman, Renamo leader Afonso Dhlakama and Raul Domingos, Renamo chief of general staff during the war, explained that it was easier to operate in the northern and central provinces than in the south due to its hilly forests and availability of water (Hultman 2009, 831). Renamo established its first bases in Zambézia in the Morrumbala district and in the Namuli mountains near Gurué (Cabrita 2000, 202–3). The major bases were located in Morrumbala (Alfazema) and Mocuba districts (Namanjavira and Muaquiua) (see map in Figure 5.1). Frelimo estimated that after Renamo's offensive across the province, 6,000 rebels (of a force of 18,000–20,000) were stationed in Zambézia.[13]

Both Zambézia and Nampula provinces experienced an escalation of violence in late 1986 when Malawi expelled several thousand Renamo combatants from its territory.[14] This was part of an ongoing negotiation between the governments of Mozambique, South Africa and Malawi. When the rebels occupied several district towns along the border to Malawi and in Zambézia and Nampula, the Frelimo government feared that the rebels would take control over the north and cut the country in half along the Zambezi valley, to the South of Zambézia province (see map in Figure 5.1).[15]

---

[11] The armed forces describe these missions as "busca e captura" – "search and capture" operations. See República Popular de Moçambique, Ministério da Defesa Nacional, Comando do 1° Batalhão da 7° Brigada de Infantaria Motorizada em Mocuba, *Relatório*, July 30, 1982 (AGZ, Quelimane).

[12] Election results from 1994 confirm that overall Renamo's popular base was strong in both provinces. Renamo strongholds included the central and northern provinces (Manica, Sofala, Tete, Zambézia, and Nampula) with exception of Cabo Delgado and Niassa, the fronts during FRELIMO's struggle for liberation. In these five provinces, Renamo gained 82.4 percent of the vote (Cahen 2000, 173). Closer analysis shows, however, that many communities in Nampula and Zambézia were divided and Renamo did not achieve results comparable to Frelimo's two-thirds majority in many districts in the southern provinces (Cahen 2000, 177).

[13] Alexandre Luís, "Ainda a face dos bandidos armados," *Tempo (Maputo)* (930), August 7, 1988, 18.

[14] "Mozambique: Pandora's Boxes," *Africa Confidential* 27 (23), November 12, 1986, 1–3.

[15] William Finnegan, "A Reporter at Large. I – The Emergency," *The New Yorker*, May 22, 1989, 62. This concern is also expressed in a report by the Provincial Frelimo Party committee summarizing the military and political situation in Zambézia since 1983 in preparation for the

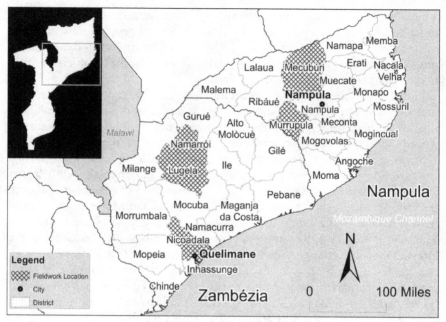

FIGURE 5.1. Map of district boundaries in Nampula and Zambézia provinces in
Mozambique indicating fieldwork sites
Note: Cartography by Sofia Jorges

After Mozambique's president Samora Machel died in a plane crash in South
Africa in 1986, the new government under Joaquim Chissano rejected a nego-
tiated settlement and sought to win the war (Seibert 2003, 271). In late
1986 and early 1987, the Mozambican military, together with allied forces
from Zimbabwe and Tanzania, began a counteroffensive in Zambézia province. The beginning of the offensive was marked by the creation of the
Advanced Command Post and General Headquarters (Posto de Comando
Avançado, PCA) – a joint command of all defense and security forces – in
Quelimane in November 1986.[16] With the help of the PCA and 3,000
Tanzanian soldiers, Frelimo recaptured significant parts of territory and reset-
tled the population into Frelimo-held areas. In January 1987, the first aid

IV provincial party congress, Frente de Libertação de Moçambique/Frelimo, Comité Provincial
da Zambézia, *Relatório do comité provincial à IV conferência provincial do partido*, December
6, 1989 (AGZ, Quelimane).
[16] República de Moçambique, Governo da Província da Zambézia, *Relatório*, July 21, 1987 (AGZ,
Quelimane). The PCA existed until July 7, 1987 (Cabá 1998, 47).

convoys reached Alta Zambézia and formerly isolated districts were reconnected to Quelimane.[17]

Although Frelimo's counteroffensive in 1986 and 1987 returned all district towns to Frelimo control by July 1988, it was not decisive in the war in Zambézia and did not create enduring stability.[18] Local stalemates emerged in which the government could regain control over the district towns, but many localities remained occupied by Renamo forces and the outskirts of the district towns experienced frequent skirmishes. The radius of action in the district towns remained limited between five and ten miles, and towns and villages suffered from frequent attacks.[19] Renamo also continued occupying district towns, but it did not hold them much longer than a few days. While the Renamo occupations in various districts in 1985 and 1987 lasted between 300 and 600 days, from 1988 onward, rebel control of towns was much shorter (with the exception of Lugela district) (see Table 5.1).

The local stalemates that arose were violent ones, resembling a war of attrition. The military situation in Alto Molócuè, the district in Zambézia province that first experienced Naparama activity, was characterized by frequent rebel attacks "with no end in sight" (Pereira 1999a, 58). In the late 1980s, Renamo occupied all rural areas, while Frelimo controlled the main town and the top of the Nauela mountain. Pereira describes this situation as the "conflict's peak" in the district, at which the conflict appeared "saturated" (Pereira 1999a, 60). Neither Frelimo nor Renamo was able to make significant advances at that particular time in the war.

During these local military stalemates, both Frelimo and Renamo combatants committed indiscriminate violence against civilians in the areas under the adversary's control. The number of violent incidents rose in 1987–89 (Figures 5.2–5.4).[20] The armed groups considered civilians in contested areas potential enemy collaborators, and thus legitimate targets of violence (Pereira 1999a, 48). Furthermore, due to the lack of material and ammunition, Frelimo and Renamo both preferred attacking the population in the zones under the

---

[17] Gil Lauriciano, "Zambézia. Ligeiras melhorias na situação militar," *Tempo (Maputo)* (853), February 15, 1987, 10–11; Benjamim Faduco, "Visita Presidential. Paz desponta na Zambézia e em Sofala," *Tempo (Maputo)* (862), April 19, 1987, 8–15.

[18] The counteroffensive forced Renamo forces to retreat to the south where they perpetrated one of the largest massacres of the war, the massacre in Homoíne in Inhambane province (Seibert 2003; Morier-Genoud 2018; Armando 2018). See Chapter 4.

[19] See, for example, República Popular de Moçambique, Província da Zambézia, Gabinete do Administrador do Distrito de Lugela, *Relatório, período de 1 a 3 de Julho, ano de 1988*, August 2, 1988 (AGZ, Quelimane); República Popular de Moçambique, Província da Zambézia, Administração do Distrito de Pebane, *Relatório referente aos meses de Abril/Maio/Junho/Julho de 1989*, August 1, 1989 (AGZ, Quelimane).

[20] The types of violence included in my own dataset include battles between rebel and government forces, and violence against civilians. For details about the coding of my own dataset, see the Appendix.

TABLE 5.1. *Number of days of Renamo occupation of district towns in Zambézia province*

District		Date Occupied by Renamo	Date Reoccupied by Frelimo	Days under Renamo Occupation
1985	Mopeia	August 6, 1985	March 7, 1987	578
	Morrumbala	August 20, 1985	April 28, 1987	616
	Gilé	October 3, 1985		
1986	Namacurra	February 1986	February 1986	3
	Milange	September 26, 1986	June 2, 1988	615
	Maganja da Costa	September 27, 1986		
	Namarrói	October 1986	October 1986	3
	Gilé	October 28, 1986	July 10, 1988	621
	Namarrói	December 29, 1986	December 16, 1987	352
1987	Pebane	September 25, 1987	September 26, 1987	1
1988	Lugela	August 17, 1988	December 2, 1988	107
	Gurué	November 27, 1988	November 30, 1988	3
1989	Ile	February 16, 1989	February 23, 1989	7
	Mopeia	June 27, 1989	July 6, 1989	9
	Mopeia	November 15, 1989	November 20, 1989	5
1991	Namarrói	December 1991	December 1991	3
1992	Lugela	October 19, 1992	November 21, 1992	33

Note: This table is compiled by the author and the evidence is drawn from archival documents, newspaper reports, and interviews. It is not a complete list of Renamo occupation of district capitals in Zambézia, as the exact dates and length of occupation are difficult to determine in many cases. It only serves an illustrative purpose.

adversary's control over fighting direct battles. The war in Zambézia is thus often described as a "war of avoidance" (Legrand 1993, 98).

The tendency toward indiscriminate violence can be traced on both sides, linking them to the dynamics of war. Although Renamo initially enjoyed some popular support in rural areas, rebel forces increasingly targeted civilians indiscriminately, particularly in those areas they did not control. Many respondents in the districts of Nicoadala, Lugela, and Namarrói told me a similar story: during the first phase of the war, Renamo units selectively targeted Frelimo representatives such as party and state officials, teachers, and health workers. The rebels abducted civilians to transport pillaged goods to Renamo bases or to train youths as combatants, but usually did not kill them. They also mobilized people in the areas they controlled to support them with food and information and set up political administrations in collaboration with local chiefs.[21]

---

[21] Pereira (1999a) finds similar evidence for the district of Alto Molócuè, also in Zambézia province.

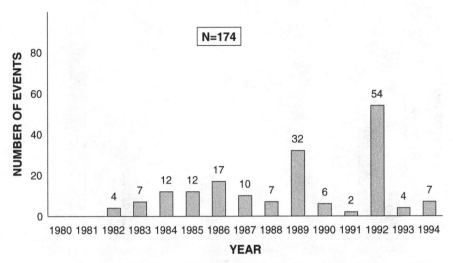

FIGURE 5.2. Number of incidents of violence against civilians in Zambézia province, 1980–94, based on newspaper sources

Note: This graph is based on data from Weinstein (2007). The types of violent events in Weinstein's dataset include killing, mutilation, kidnapping, detention, injury, arson, rape, looting, and forced displacement. The events are coded from the reporting by the national newspaper *Notícias* (Weinstein 2007). I thank Jeremy Weinstein for kindly sharing his dataset.

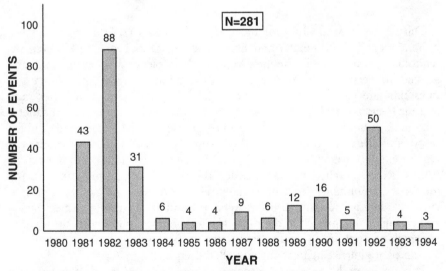

FIGURE 5.3. Number of incidents of violence against civilians in Zambézia province, 1980–94, based on government reports

Note: This graph is based on data coded from provincial and district government reports collected during fieldwork. The events include direct and indirect lethal forms of violence against civilians. See the Appendix for details on the data and coding.

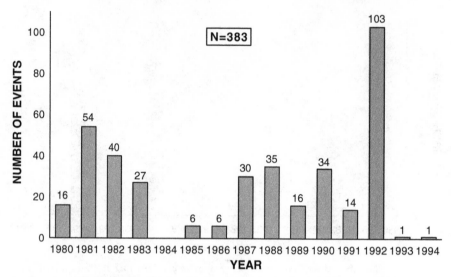

FIGURE 5.4. Number of battles between government and rebel forces in Zambézia
Province, 1980–94, based on government reports
Note: This graph is based on data coded from provincial and district government reports
collected during fieldwork. The events include direct confrontations between government and rebel
forces with and without changes in territorial control. See the Appendix for details on the data
and coding.

During the second phase of the war, respondents reported that violence
became more indiscriminate, and Renamo combatants began to kill civilians
without any official ties to Frelimo. Much of this violence was instrumental and
seemed to serve logistical purposes. Most analysts agree that Renamo's
indiscriminate violence could not be explained by indiscipline of lower rank
and file (Gersony 1988; Hall 1990; Seibert 2003). Without significant sanctuaries in neighboring countries, Renamo had to rely on the local population for
resources such as food and labor (Hall 1990, 52–53). In order to ensure the
regular supply of new recruits and provide sufficient material resources to its
troops, Renamo relied on violence for the purpose of intimidation. In my
interviews, community residents usually referred to Renamo as "they," implicitly including in the same category Renamo combatants, roving armed bands,
and criminals that existed at the time. The use of a pronoun masks the identity
and goals of a particular group, underlining the perception of the indiscriminate
character of violence against civilians (Bertelsen 2009, 219).

It is not entirely clear why Renamo shifted from more selective to more
indiscriminate forms of violence, but it seems to be linked to the loss of popular
support and the government's counterinsurgent campaign. In the Maringué
district in the central province of Sofala, for example, civilians became

disenchanted with Renamo's coercive style of rule in the late 1980s and with-held provisions from the combatants (Pereira 1999b, 49). Though Renamo formed governance structures, they usually remained rudimentary and provided few services. The loss of support, in turn, triggered coercive recruitment and terrorizing forms of violence such as mutilations in order to pressure civilians into obedience (Pereira 1999b, 49–50). The evolution of violence in Sofala appears to mirror the situation in Zambézia province. In Zambézia, violence against civilians rose when Calisto Meque took over Renamo's northern command in 1986 (Robinson 2006, 265–66). Meque was a powerful and widely feared personality, known for his brutal treatment of the population. The rebels targeted civilians not only in Frelimo-held areas, but also in areas under their own control and enforced a coercive governance structure. Though Renamo had to accept certain setbacks as a consequence of Frelimo's counterinsurgency campaign, the rebels ruled based on a system of fear in about 80 percent of the province until 1990 (Legrand 1993, 98).

While it is usually acknowledged that Renamo committed more violence against civilians than Frelimo, the government's army also targeted civilians indiscriminately. The security and defense forces responded to Renamo's 1986 offensive with a scorched-earth tactic to displace the population from Renamo-controlled territory (Legrand 1993, 95–96), which amounted to political cleansing (cf. Steele 2017). The head of the newly created PCA was General Hama Thai, and General Lagos Lidimo was named Chief of Staff, "one of the most feared men in the army, having earned a reputation for ruthlessness and effectiveness as provincial commander in Zambézia in 1987–1988."[22] Thus, Frelimo soldiers identified the PCA with strict discipline: all soldiers who defied orders and deserted were shot.[23]

In sum, the Frelimo government was able to avert Renamo's attempt to cut the country in half along the Zambezi River. However, Frelimo only regained control over the district towns; the countryside remained under Renamo influence and occupation. From there, rebels initiated frequent attacks on Frelimo strongholds. Such violent stalemates help community-initiated militias to form.

5.2 CIVILIAN RESPONSES AND NAPARAMA'S FORMATION

The Naparama militia emerged toward the end of Frelimo's counteroffensive, presumably in late 1988. The population responded to the local military stalemates in various ways to protect itself and find a way out of the war, a process that culminated in forming the militia.

Zambézia's population suffered severely from the consequences of war. Civilians were most vulnerable in contested areas, as a resident of a rural area

---

[22] "Mozambique: The Kenyan Obstacle," *Africa Confidential* 31 (11), June 29, 1990, 5.
[23] Interview with former Frelimo combatant (2012-05-04-Fm18), Namarrói, Zambézia, May 4, 2012.

in Nampula province explained: "We patrolled the bush, we stayed for two to three days [at a certain location] and then moved. We were afraid of both, the army and Renamo."[24] In addition to the violence, the coastal areas of Nampula and the central areas of Zambézia were affected by famines in the late 1980s. Drought, poor harvest, and theft of relief goods by local officials, soldiers, and civilians led to hunger and mass starvation.[25] In early 1987, the situation in Zambézia was the worst in the country, with 105,000 people affected by hunger.[26]

Though early on in the war the Frelimo government began to mobilize people to join popular militias and vigilante groups to help the war effort, civilians seem to have been rather passive victims in these early years. A resident of Nicoadala contrasted the involvement of the population in the war after the Naparama militia had emerged with people's passivity before: "[When] the people came to experience the war [first-hand] and confronted the enemy, [the war] became a people's war, whereas [before] when it was only Frelimo, the army confronted the enemy, and the people fled."[27]

In fact, before the Naparama militia formed, most people had responded to the violence by fleeing from their homes. At the time of Naparama's emergence, 500,000 people in Zambézia province were displaced or affected by the war and 100,000 refugees had fled to neighboring Malawi.[28] The Frelimo government even actively encouraged displacement and sent civilian collaborators to Renamo-held areas to convince people to move to Frelimo-held areas. Many seemed to have resettled voluntarily into communal villages or centers for the displaced under government control. Local government reports from the Alto Molócuè district, for example, frequently refer to the mobilization efforts by militias and vigilantes in enemy areas and state the number of people who arrived in Frelimo-held zones.[29]

However, the displaced in camps no longer had access to their fields and were dependent on limited relief aid supplies. That is why displacement often took on a temporary, and frequently a collective, character. Many respondents described to me how they left their village in the late afternoons:

---

[24] Interview with male civilian (2011-11-24-m19), Murrupula-Namilasse, Nampula, November 24, 2011.

[25] "Mass Starvation in Memba," *Mozambiquefile* (March), 1989, 4–5; "Memba Death Toll Still Rising," *Mozambiquefile* (April), 1989, 8–9.

[26] "Milhares de víctimas da fome e da guerra," *Tempo (Maputo)* (847), January 4, 1987, 23.

[27] Interview with local leader (2011-09-11-Lm3a), Nicoadala, Zambézia, September 11, 2011.

[28] Fernando Manuel, "Para compreender o presente," *Tempo (Maputo)* (993), October 22, 1989, 7. Across Mozambique in late 1989, one-third of the country's 15 million people were threatened by famine, 100,000 had been killed, more than 1 million people had fled the country, and 2 million were displaced within Mozambique. Karl Maier, "A Program for Peace," *Africa Report* (September–October), 1989, 58.

[29] See, for example, República Popular de Moçambique, Província da Zambézia, Administração do Distrito de Alto Molócuè, *Relatório mensal do mês de Agosto*, September 10, 1989 (AGZ, Quelimane).

"[We] organized five to six families and went to sleep in the bush, in the morning [we] returned home. But courageous men got up during the night and [checked on] the house, since there were also others who came behind [Renamo] as bandits – not armed bandits – who broke into the houses."[30] It was common for villagers to sleep and even cook in the surrounding areas of the village as long as the danger of attacks was high. This also shows that residents sought to stay close enough to their houses to keep an eye on their belongings and defend them against rebels and criminals.

Apart from displacement, civilians found different ways to protect themselves from the consequences of war, including various forms of what Arjona (2019, 231) calls "cooperative" and "non-cooperative" behavior toward the armed group in control. Many civilians in Renamo-held areas cooperated with the rebels and abided by their rules, supported them with food, or even joined the rebels as combatants. But others, both in rebel- and in government-held areas, engaged in noncooperative behavior, such as informing the Frelimo authorities about rebel activity and conducting violent and nonviolent resistance against rebel rule and violence.[31] For example, when fleeing into the mountains in the Namarrói district, villagers developed elaborate techniques to defend themselves in their hideout and control the movement of people:

[W]e built a trap on the mountain. Many people arrived on the mountain through one single entrance. We placed stones by the entrance, and when the enemy was coming, we let the stones roll down [the mountain path], and this method let us save this area [from the enemy].[32]

The pastor who told me this story explained that people were motivated to organize such resistance because they were "tired of being kidnapped, killed, and [their] property being burned; people began to search for ways to survive, and they asked themselves whether the war would [ever] end or not, as [they believed that] the people were the ones who would end it." Community residents believed that they could not rely on the protection from the warring sides but had to organize their own forms of protection.

The most elaborate collective form of nonviolent resistance was peace zones, areas in which people were able to convince Renamo and Frelimo forces not to attack. These zones emerged in Zambézia with support from the Catholic Church and Jehovah's Witnesses, and under the guidance of certain chiefs (Wilson 1992). However, peace zones provided limited relief from the hardship of being removed from one's areas of origin. Peace zones were static and did not extend from one area to another. Thus, people were not protected in their home

---

[30] Interview with local government representative (2011-09-15-Gm1), Nicoadala, Zambézia, September 15, 2011.
[31] This latter behavior can also be described as "voice," in contrast to "support" or "flight" (Barter 2014).
[32] Interview with religious leader (2012-05-01-Pm9), Namarrói, Zambézia, May 1, 2012.

area, but had to move into such peace zones to be spared rebel violence.[33] Moreover, in the cases of the religious peace zones, membership was limited to those belonging to the religious community.

In contrast, those who violently resisted defended villagers in their home areas, which helped to maintain or even expand territorial control by the Mozambican government. Thus, the local and provincial administration (implicitly and explicitly) encouraged civilian violent resistance, and from the mid-1980s onward, society slowly militarized. In Marea, a locality in Namarrói district in Zambézia province, community residents used spears and machetes to defend those who had fled into the mountains.[34] A newspaper report from 1986 estimates that more than 10,000 civilians had armed themselves with spears and knives.[35] This development was not unique to Zambézia. In Nampula province, in the Nahipa locality of the Mecubúri district, the grupo decidido (the committed group), a group of civilians armed with spears and knives patrolling at night, emerged before the arrival of Naparama, mainly to respond to robberies and general lawlessness.[36] Everyone was called to defend their community, as this comment from a reader of a local magazine published by the Catholic Diocese in Nampula shows: "In my neighborhood, there is no mechanic, no professor, no one who is boss of any business. There is only one job: militiaman."[37]

What triggered communities to opt for violent forms of resistance? We should expect civilians to join and support the stronger side in search of protection (Kalyvas and Kocher 2007). However, in this type of local military stalemate, there was no side that was clearly stronger than the other.

---

[33] The activities of traditional authorities and the creation of peace zones did not only have a military dimension but also an economic one. Peace zones provided "major opportunities for trade and production in an environment of scarcity" (Wilson 1992, 556). Opportunities emerged not just for the community that would be able to engage in trading and farming, but also for the traditional authorities. For example, Mungoi asked for presents or work in exchange for liberating family members from Renamo-held areas. Traditional war medicines were not provided for free but sold to communities and individuals. This mixture of military, economic, and social effects of the "counter-cults of violence" had significant implications for the evolution of these movements until the end of the war (Wilson 1992, 555). Jane Perlez, "Spared by Rebels? The Spirit Says that'll Be $2," *The New York Times*, August 24, 1990.

[34] Interview with religious leader (2012-05-01-Pm9), Namarrói, Zambézia, May 1, 2012.

[35] Gil Lauriciano, "Resistência popular cresce na Zambézia. Dez mil pessoas armadas com zagaias," *Notícias*, November 22, 1986. Lemia (2001, 46) tells the story of small groups of twelve men, the Anakabudula, that were independent of the army and defended the entrance to the district town of Namacurra from 1986 to 1990. But these groups soon began to engage in arbitrary violence after which they lost the support of the population.

[36] Some interlocutors stated that the initiative for the group came from the local administration; nevertheless, the group attracted many youths and took on the character of a community-based group. See interviews with former Naparama combatants (2011-10-26-Nm29), Nahipa, Mecubúri, Nampula, October 26, 2011; (2011-10-22-Nm27), Mecubúri, Nampula, October 22, 2011. For a more detailed discussion of Mecubúri and the grupo decidido, see Chapter 6.

[37] "Sim à paz," *Vida Nova* (January–February), 1991, 19.

In Renamo-held areas, logistical problems and the fact that the population served as a human shield for the rebels provided few benefits to those who did not have any political motivations to join or support the rebels. In Frelimo-held areas, the army's inability to protect civilians against frequent Renamo attacks pointed to its weakness in dealing with the rebel threat. In the Alto Molócuè district, shortly before the Naparama militia emerged, "everything pointed to the fact that the government of Frelimo had lost control of the situation" (Pereira 1999a, 59). The violent nature of the stalemate required community residents to act. Villagers did not expect any effective response by the state, and thus sought to respond to the experience of the violence and loss of family members themselves. The leader of the above-mentioned grupo decidido in the Mecubúri district, for example, decided to organize the group in order to avenge his mother's death at the hands of the rebels, a motivation that would also prove important for late joiners of the Naparama militia (see Chapter 7).[38] In that sense, we can speak of a *community-empowering stalemate*; its violent nature required and enabled civilians to act.

Violent resistance against rebel violence was not necessarily an expression of ideological support for Frelimo. The relevance of mechanisms such as revenge fits with Kalyvas' (2006, 97–101) expectation that the formation of (pro-government) militias does not necessarily need to be an expression of loyalty or ideological support for the government. In fact, both Zambézia and Nampula provinces have a long history of opposition to Frelimo due to the provinces' historical marginalization and Frelimo's failure to mobilize the population for the party's cause (Legrand 1993, 88; Chichava 2007; Do Rosário 2009). Thus, Renamo could exploit local grievances and benefit from higher levels of popular support by peasants in the north than in Mozambique's south.

Several factors account for the "rebellious" character (Chichava 2007) of Zambézia and strong opposition in Nampula. Frelimo's party and state elite has been dominated by southerners; the independence movement's penetration of both provinces during the liberation struggle was slow and ineffectual or – in the case of Nampula province – completely absent (cf. Legrand 1993, 88); and the peasant population opposed Frelimo's policies after independence.[39] In Nampula, the construction of communal villages and the abolishment of traditional authorities sparked popular discontent (Geffray 1990). In Zambézia, it was the disrespect for traditional values more generally, which

---

[38] Interview with former Naparama combatant (2011-10-16-Nm25), Mecuburi, Nampula, October 16, 2011.

[39] According to Legrand (1993, 89–90), Zambézia's early resistance was due to the following factors, among others: the continuation of a plantation-based agriculture by nationalizing Zambézia's colonial plantations; Frelimo's hostility toward religion in a Catholic-dominated society; the resettlement of the population into protected settlements in the border region to Malawi; and Frelimo's hostility toward traditional authorities.

had been the basis for life in the province, that provoked opposition (O'Laughlin 1992, 115; Ranger 1985, 189).[40]

The Naparama militia built on the initial civilian responses to the military stalemate and the "tradition of rebellion," but offered distinct offensive tactics, which increased the effectiveness of civilian protection and defense. The militia's leader in Zambézia, Manuel António from the Namuno district of Mozambique's northernmost province Cabo Delgado, was a charismatic young leader who claimed to possess special powers and to have received a calling to liberate the Mozambican people from the suffering of war. He was responsible for the formation of Naparama in a few districts in Nampula as well as districts across Zambézia.[41] The story he told community residents, journalists, and scholars was that he had died of measles as a child, had been buried, and then was resurrected after seven days (Nordstrom 1997, 58).[42] He maintained to have then spent six months in the mountains, where he received a divine mission from Jesus Christ and learned of a medicine to turn bullets into water.[43] António mobilized the first peasants in the Ribáuè district of Nampula province in late 1988 and then entered Zambézia in early 1989.[44] In Ribáuè district, António mobilized several men who then accompanied him on his travels as his personal guard.[45]

---

[40] Even during the colonial era, the Portuguese colonial government faced much opposition in Zambézia; Isaacman and Isaacman (1976) speak therefore of a "tradition of resistance" in the Zambezi valley. For the historical roots of opposition in Nampula province, see Do Rosário (2009).

[41] Interviews with former Naparama combatants (2011-09-19-Nm11), Nicoadala, Zambézia, September 19, 2011; (2011-09-20-Fm2-N), Nicoadala, Zambézia, September 20, 2011.

[42] Rachel Waterhouse, "Antonio's Triumph of the Spirits," *Africa South (Harare)* (May), 1991, 14.

[43] Carolyne Nordstrom, who visited areas of Naparama activity during the war, reports that the medicine presumably came from a "powerful and venerated spirit leader and healer who lived in the remote bush of Nampula province" (Nordstrom 1997, 69–70). This spirit leader presumably was the elder Zinco from the village of Méti in Lalaua district, as several respondents mentioned that António had reached other districts in Nampula coming from Méti. See interview with civilian (2011-11-29-m23), Chinga, Murrupula, Nampula, November 29, 2011; Interview with former Naparama combatant (2011-09-20-Fm2-N), Nicoadala, Zambézia, September 20, 2011. Dinerman (2006, 7) assumes that Zinco created his own Parama vaccine independently of António and then created a group of Naparama combatants in Namapa district in 1990 with the help of the district administrator who was previously the head of the local administration in Lalaua. From the evidence that I collected, however, it is very likely that António learned about the medicine from Zinco.

[44] Rachel Waterhouse, "Antonio's Triumph of the Spirits," *Africa South (Harare)* (May), 1991, 14. See also interview with former Naparama combatant (2011-09-20-Fm2-N), Nicoadala, Zambézia, September 20, 2011; Interview with civilian (2011-11-29-m23), Chinga, Murrupula, Nampula, November 29, 2011; Interview with former Renamo combatant (2011-10-15-Rm2), Mecubúri, Nampula, October 15, 2011.

[45] Among them was Manuel Sabonete, who took over the leadership after António's death in late 1991. See interview with Naparama combatant (2011-09-30-Nm20), Nicoadala, Zambézia, September 30, 2011. In my conversation with him, Manuel Sabonete claimed that António and his first group of Naparama from Ribaué also mobilized people in Muecate and Lalaua

The elaborate story of the birth of the movement was an attempt to legitimize António's formation of an otherwise illegitimate armed group that could potentially challenge the Mozambican government. In the Makua-Lomwe culture that dominates the region in which António began to work, ancestral spirits live in cemeteries, the wilderness, rivers, and mountains (Lerma Martínez 2008, 207). António's claimed stay in the cemetery and mountains was therefore significant for receiving magical powers from ancestral spirits.[46] In addition to building on traditional religion, the Naparama leader relied on references to Christianity, such as portraying himself as a messenger of Jesus Christ and using the bible in ceremonies. Combining traditional and Christian religion resonated within Zambézian communities for whom traditional leadership and religion and Catholicism were important cornerstones of their society.

The militia's reliance on religious idioms fits well with a context in Mozambique in which the population develops severe grievances, but all political activity seems suspicious to the rulers (Machava 2011; Bertelsen 2016). Margaret Hall (1990) suggests that leaders tend to rely on a religious framework to mobilize communities when a clear political ideology driving protest is lacking and political activity is suppressed. Across Africa, "inherently political peasant grievances have been channelled within a religious idiom. Traditional forms of belief particularly lend themselves to this form of protest, because of the usually strong association between the spiritual realm and the land" (Hall 1990, 47–48). As Hall argues, this is how Renamo came to both support religious practice (within its own organization and within the communities it controlled) and reinstate traditional chiefs.

It is unsurprising, therefore, that the Naparama leader appealed to the beliefs and values important for the communities in which he was active.[47] The close link between Naparama to the communities was frequently expressed in my conversations with community residents and former Naparama combatants. Respondents stated that the primary task of the Naparama militia was to

---

districts, but I was not able to confirm this information. Interview (2011-09-30-Nm20), September 30, 2011, Nicoadala, Zambézia.

[46] The exact story varies in different accounts. In Nordstrom's account, António received this mission on Mount Namuli in Gurué district in the border area between Nampula and Zambézia provinces (Nordstrom 1997, 58). Other accounts, however, state that he learned about traditional medicine in the mountains in his province of origin, Cabo Delgado (Interview with former Naparama combatant [2011-09-30-Nm20], Nicoadala, Zambézia, September 30, 2011). Since Mount Namuli is the legendary origin of the Makua and Lomwe people, the story of receiving the mission in a place as culturally significant for the potential recipients of his services as the Namuli Mountain served as a powerful legitimation for António's work.

[47] This tactic can be considered in another way, which is more closely tied to the dynamics of the war and the use of traditional religion by Renamo combatants. I analyze this dynamic in Chapter 4.

"defend the population."[48] Former Naparama combatants claimed that they were the main – or even only – armed group that could successfully fight back Renamo and "save our sons, belongings, and family members."[49] A former Naparama combatant confirmed, "we fought for the cause of the people."[50]

Community residents were enthusiastic about Naparama because the militia's belief system resonated with them and the militia achieved concrete results for the local population. After years of displacement, Naparama allowed the displaced to finally return home.[51] António recruited young men living in impoverished refugee camps around government-controlled hamlets "with a promise of a means to restore their dignity" (Maier 1998, 67). Most of the Naparama combatants in Nicoadala district, for example, came from among the displaced:

Where did Manuel António mobilize the people to initiate them into Naparama combatants?

That was in the village [for the displaced]. Because many refugees lived in the village – people tired of the war. So when [Manuel António] Naparama arrived and said he was bringing [this medicine], all of those who were in the village and suffered agreed [to participate], and the headquarters was there in the village.[52]

Naparama's major task was not to kill Renamo combatants and collaborators, but rather to capture them and their weapons and "recuperate" the population from Renamo-held areas:

We didn't go [on missions] to kill. If a [Renamo combatant] was shooting over there and no more bullets were left in the magazine, we said "drop your weapon." Really – you are here and he is where that mango tree is [*demonstrating the proximity between himself and the Renamo combatant*], [we said] "drop your weapon." So he approached to fight with his bare hands – "let's go, brother." We, this movement, from the beginning to the end, it was all about recuperating [population]. It was not about killing. We recuperated people, even [when they were] armed. We captured weapons. Then we took the people [and the weapons] and presented them to the government.[53]

[48] Interview with former Frelimo combatant (2011-09-13-Fm1), Nicoadala, Zambézia, September 13, 2011.

[49] Interview with former Naparama combatants (2011-11-30-Gr-Nm2), Nampula, November 30, 2011.

[50] Interview with former Naparama combatants (2011-10-22-Nm27), Mecubúri, Nampula, October 22, 2011.

[51] Karl Maier, "Triumph of Spears over Guns Brings Refugees Home," *Independent*, February 23, 1990.

[52] Interview with former Naparama combatant (2011-09-09-Nm1), Nicoadala, Zambézia, September 9, 2011.

[53] Interview with former Naparama combatant (2011-09-30-Nm18), Nicoadala, Zambézia, September 30, 2011.

The militia's activities were largely successful. The British journalist Karl Maier estimated in February 1990 that Naparama had succeeded in returning over 100,000 displaced people to their homes.[54]

In sum, Naparama provided a viable alternative to passivity for the community residents affected and displaced by the war, and a strategically effective response to the military stalemate. Communities were empowered as the warring sides could not make any significant military advances, leaving room for a third force to emerge to try and improve the odds of a government victory.

5.3 HOW FRELIMO CAME TO TOLERATE NAPARAMA ACTIVITY

The success of forming the Naparama militia hinged on the government response to a potential third armed force. Frelimo's reaction to the local military stalemates was twofold. First, the government focused on defending the status quo and its control over most district towns. Second, however, due to military and political weakness, its response became one of political and military inertia. Numerous reports written by local administrations and sent to the provincial headquarters of the directorate responsible to support local government at the time pointed to the dilemma in which local administrations found themselves. District towns received large numbers of displaced people that they sought to protect. However, the towns' military capabilities were weak, as pointed out in several local government reports like the following describing the situation in Zambézia's Lugela district in July 1988:

The defense and security forces in this district face lots of difficulties with the fulfillment of their missions, either due to the decrease in human resources or due to some of those responsible not fulfilling their responsibilities. As a consequence, the radius of our activities is limited to 5 km and it is most unfortunate that people are kidnapped from the district town without an adequate response from our side.[55]

Lugela's district administrator explicitly warned in his report that the stalemate could tip toward the rebels if the government would not provide an adequate level of security to the population. Although 5,000 people returned to government-held territory in June and July 1988, he feared that some would return to rebel-held zones because they were targets of violence in the government-held areas: "If we delay any further, the people will drink the politics of the enemy and it could be very difficult to recuperate [them]."[56] In fact, the report expressed concern that the population who used to live under

[54] Karl Maier, "Triumph of Spears over Guns Brings Refugees Home," *Independent*, February 23, 1990.

[55] República Popular de Moçambique, Província da Zambézia, Gabinete do Administrador do Distrito de Lugela, *Relatório, período de 1 a 3 de Julho, ano de 1988*, August 2, 1988 (AGZ, Quelimane).

[56] República Popular de Moçambique, Província da Zambézia, Gabinete do Administrador do Distrito de Lugela, *Relatório, período de 1 a 3 de Julho, ano de 1988*, August 2, 1988 (AGZ, Quelimane).

Renamo control was politically indoctrinated, had gotten used to living under rules of banditry and had come to adopt an ethos of "not obeying anyone." Speaking to the legitimacy of the administrator's concerns, about two weeks after writing this report, Lugela's district town was attacked and occupied by Renamo, lasting until December 1988.

Lugela district's situation was one of the worst in the entire province, but it is exemplary of the pressure under which local administrators found themselves. Like Lugela's district administrator, many administrators frequently requested military reinforcements for their districts, which they did not receive. Due to the limited number of troops available, Frelimo's response was to create a "system of territorial security and defense," which included the recruitment and training of village youths.

Given the strategy to involve the population in their own defense, Frelimo elites should have been highly enthusiastic about the newly formed Naparama as an auxiliary force. However, Frelimo's official attitude was characterized by skepticism, for two main reasons. First, the roots of Naparama's power went against Frelimo's socialist stance against all things traditional (see Chapter 4). An official endorsement of Naparama or official collaboration with the militia would have contradicted the core of Frelimo's ideology. Second, Frelimo was wary of Naparama's true objectives during and potentially after the war. The government did not want to risk losing even more control over the war through outsourcing violence. Frelimo elites were concerned that a third armed force had emerged, which would, alongside Renamo, mount a challenge to the state. They did not trust Naparama sufficiently to grant them the agency needed to fight Renamo.

While the first reason was more of a concern for the provincial and national party leadership, the second reason was an immediate concern for the local administrations. Naparama initially formed without their knowledge, raising suspicions about their true objectives. In the first district of Naparama activity in Zambézia, Alto Molócuè, for example, António did not introduce himself to the local administrator when he arrived in the district town (Pereira 1999a, 83). Similarly, in Nampula province, the Naparama unit in the Murrupula district formed without the knowledge of the local administration. What happened subsequently in Murrupula shows how suspicious Frelimo was of the militia. When Murrupula's district administrator learned about the new armed group, he contacted the party provincial headquarters in Nampula city for advice.[57] The provincial governor asked the "department of ideological work" to conduct a study and they sent a delegation of party officials to meet with the Naparama leadership in Murrupula. As the head of the delegation explained to me, the Frelimo leadership feared that the war in Mozambique could

---

[57] Interview with former Naparama combatant (2011-11-03-Nm31), Móthi, Murrupula, Nampula, November 3, 2011.

intensify in the same way as it had in Angola if it allowed a third armed group to operate:

> The government was concerned that, similar to Angola where there was the MPLA, the movement of Holden Roberto and the movement of Savimbi, the same thing would happen here and there would be three movements, Frelimo, Renamo and Naparama struggling for power. . . .

> I went [to Murrupula] because we in the government thought that Naparama was a movement that would seek to govern after the war. We found that Naparama only sought to end the war. They were volunteers and didn't not have any political program.[58]

The investigation into Naparama in the Murrupula district thus concluded that Naparama would not pose a threat to Frelimo, whether over the short or the long term.

Thus, the party's hesitance to rely on the support of the community-initiated militia soon gave way to pragmatic considerations. Local state and military officials realized the value of Naparama's contribution to stability in the short term. In many districts, local officials actively supported the mobilization of youths for militias like Naparama. This created a window of opportunity, which helped form Naparama units in various districts. Local administrations realized that if they wanted civilians to support the war effort, they had to tolerate groups like Naparama. As a provincial government representative told me,

> When the government asked for the population to defend itself, it did not foresee the Naparama, a group well organized. Samora Machel[59] said that Naparama [militias] are bandits and thieves. However, during the colonial period, the Portuguese called Frelimo "turas" [disobedient people; rebels], but they were well organized.[60]

So even though Frelimo was tempted to label Naparama "thieves" to delegitimize them, local government officials were forced to take the militia seriously. Being too weak to defeat Renamo on its own, Frelimo had no choice but to tolerate Naparama. One district administrator pointed out that "all of us were preoccupied with how the war could be stopped."[61] Another local government representative expressed how helpless the local government was:

---

[58] Interview with provincial government representative (2011-10-10-Gm7), Nampula, October 10, 2011.

[59] Samora Machel was Mozambique's first president after independence until 1986 when he died (see Chapter 4); the respondent probably meant Joaquim Chissano, Machel's successor, or just used Machel's name to refer to Frelimo in general.

[60] Interview with provincial government representative (2011-10-10-Gm7), Nampula, October 10, 2011.

[61] Interview with former district administrator (2012-03-29-Gm21), Nampula, March 29, 2012.

Were you worried that Naparama would create a group that would fight against Frelimo?

The war was really bad, so what could we have done?[62]

Thus, as a community leader conveyed, "the government didn't see any alternative to accepting [António's offer] to do the work that he sought to do."[63]

While Frelimo's most common strategy was to tolerate Naparama activity, it sometimes even actively collaborated with the militia. In some instances, Frelimo representatives encouraged local leaders to mobilize youths for Naparama and supported the militia with weapons and supplies. Naparama's successes on the battlefield dispelled Frelimo's initial concerns:

After [Naparama] defeated [Renamo], Frelimo assisted them in the collection of war material – there was support, yes, because Naparama went in front [and the army behind them]. Frelimo didn't like Naparama, but after they had seen the work that Naparama was doing, they liked them.[64]

Thus, the governors of both provinces, Zambézia and Nampula, supported local administrations collaborating with Naparama. Nampula's governor signed a document supporting the work of Naparama in Murrupula.[65] Frelimo encouraged the local party and provincial leadership to develop ways to integrate Naparama into the local security apparatus.[66] In Zambézia as well, the provincial governor "recommended to work with António. We had to welcome him and tell him that he could work in our districts. However, he was not part of the military, he was a civilian."[67]

In emphasizing the "civilian" role of António and Naparama, Frelimo sought to control the militia's activities and ambitions. The district administrators' overall attitude was "to give [Naparama] space, but also to control them."[68] Government representatives reiterated that Naparama was a force of

---

[62] Interview with local government representative (2011-11-02-Gm9), Murrupula, Nampula, November 11, 2011.

[63] Interview with community leader (2011-09-23-Lm3), Nicoadala, Zambézia, September 23, 2011.

[64] Interview with community leader (2011-09-23-Lm3), Nicoadala, Zambézia, September 23, 2011.

[65] Interview with provincial government representative (2011-10-10-Gm7), Nampula, October 10, 2011.

[66] Partido Frelimo, Comité Provincial, Departamento de Trabalho Ideológico, Nampula, *Relatório do levantamento e estudo efectuado sobre o fenómeno "Napharama" no distrito de Murrupula*, November 15, 1990 (personal archive of Ambrósio Albino).

[67] Interview with local government representative (2012-02-25-Gm16), Quelimane, Zambézia, February 25, 2012.

[68] Interview with former district administrator (2012-02-22-Gm15), Quelimane, Zambézia, February 22, 2012.

the people and that militia members were volunteers.[69] In addition to denying Naparama any political or military character by labeling Naparama members "civilians," Frelimo avoided recognizing – and paying – Naparama as an official auxiliary force. Also, the government maintained that it could not be held accountable for offenses perpetrated by Naparama.[70]

Naparama worked hard to win the trust of the local administrations. Naparama leader António repeatedly highlighted his nonpolitical objectives – for the time of the war and after. His response to the question about his ambitions was always that his only goal was to liberate the Mozambican people.[71] He stated that he did not seek political power and was a loyal Frelimo supporter:

When the war ends, the battle ends. I will plow a field, I will live. They say [about me] that I want to form a party. How?! With what money? ... My father is Frelimo, my mother is Frelimo, I am Frelimo![72]

To counter the government and the army's suspicion, the Naparama units in both Nampula and Zambézia provinces presented themselves as civilians tired of the war who had formed a group that would not challenge the government: "When the government asked, [Naparama] said, 'We are tired of the war. We don't want to stage a protest or anything like that. We want the war to stop.'"[73]

When confronted with the provincial government's investigative delegation, Naparama members in Murrupula insisted that they were civilians whose objectives were merely defensive, not political. Recalling the delegation's visit, Murrupula's Naparama leaders told me that

We met [the members of the provincial government delegation] and we told them that we were civilians, that we were tired [of the war], and that we were not [militarily] trained. We lost many of our belongings, and that's why we prepared ourselves to go and search for our belongings in the bush. ... They asked us whether we wanted to be paid, but we told them that we didn't have a mandate; we had our drugs only to defend ourselves.[74]

[69] Interview with former district administrators (2012-02-22-Gm15), Quelimane, Zambézia, February 22, 2012; (2012-03-29-Gm21), Nampula, March 29, 2012.

[70] While the lack of remuneration did not provoke disagreements during the war, it did create conflicts after the war when former Naparama members demanded the same benefits as the officially demobilized.

[71] Interview with community leader (2011-09-23-Gm4), Nicoadala, Zambézia, September 23, 2011.

[72] Statements by Manuel António, cited in David Borges, "O último dos paramas," *Grande Reportagem* 111 (10), 1992, 52 (translation from Portuguese by author).

[73] Interview with religious leader (2011-09-06-Pm1), Nicoadala, Zambézia, September 6, 2011.

[74] Interview with former Naparama commander (2011-11-03-Nm31), Móthi, Murrupula, Nampula, November 3, 2011.

Naparama combatants in Nicoadala in Zambézia province emphasized that there was no contradiction between Naparama's and Frelimo's goals and that both had the same enemy:

The Naparamas are Mozambican, Frelimo is Mozambican. Renamo knows that [Frelimo] fought for Mozambique and that is why [Frelimo] is [ruling], but [Renamo] does not want [that]. Everyone is joining Frelimo in their sorrow. [Renamo] doesn't want [it].[75]

A journalist who had met António concluded that Naparama did not have political ambitions, but sought to help the people:

They said they neither belonged to Frelimo nor Renamo. They were independent. They did not have political aims, but social aims – to liberate the people. Renamo included many people who were not convinced [by the group's aims], so the aim was to liberate these people.[76]

In sum, Frelimo had significant concerns about the newly formed Naparama. Nevertheless, the challenges the state faced during the war against Renamo forced the Frelimo leadership to tolerate and even actively encourage local administrations to mobilize Naparama units in Zambézia and Nampula provinces. The need for additional defensive capacity and the helplessness of the local administrations created a window of opportunity for Naparama to form.

5.4 CONCLUSION

Naparama formed because of the distinct dynamics of war in Zambézia and Nampula provinces. Military stalemates on the local level encouraged communities to form militias. This strategic situation shaped community incentives to form armed groups rather than flee or rely on Frelimo's army to protect them from insurgent violence. The stalemate also shaped Frelimo's incentives to tolerate militia activity. Naparama's offensive tactics promised a more effective response to the threat posed by Renamo. Frelimo's changing attitude toward traditional forms of power facilitated the formation of the Naparama militia, as it created a window of opportunity for an additional armed group to fight the insurgents.

This implies that had the military situation been more beneficial for Frelimo, the population and the local state and military elites would not have had to rely on an auxiliary force. At the same time, had Frelimo been losing and its areas of control been taken over by Renamo then the formation of a militia would not have been possible – at least not a militia inclined to support the incumbent.

---

[75] Interview with former Naparama combatant (2011-09-19-Nm11), Nicoadala, Zambézia, September 19, 2011.
[76] Interview with journalist (2012-03-12-Jm3), Quelimane, Zambézia, March 12, 2012.

Some level of control over territory and population is necessary to form militias that work alongside the incumbent.

Having defined the conditions under which civilians take the initiative to form militias, I will now turn to an aspect that distinguished the Naparama militia from the other civilian initiatives that responded to the war: its rapid diffusion from one district to another.

6

The Diffusion of Repertoires of Collective Action

The Location of Community-Initiated Militia Formation

Stories and rumors about Naparama's successes across the region featured prominently in the narratives I heard about the militia. Naparama commanders and initiators in Murrupula, the center of Naparama activity in Nampula province, told me that people came to their district to receive the Parama vaccine because they had heard that the "war did not reach [Murrupula]."[1] They suggested that residents from surrounding districts sought to form their own militia groups because they saw how Naparama was able to ward off the rebels in Murrupula. The same dynamic evolved in neighboring Zambézia. After learning about Naparama's effective response to the violence in adjacent districts, local residents wanted to form a group of their own. Zambézia's Naparama leader Manuel António went "on foot if necessary, to 'wherever the people call me to help'."[2] And when Naparama forces sought to mobilize new followers in new places, they pointed to the stories of past successes: "[When] we reached Namacurra, we convinced people that the group that had come and retaken the town was [us, Naparama], so we [said we] want to [mobilize] more men."[3] Thus, much of the growth of Naparama was due to *diffusion*, the spread of rumors and stories, followed by the spread of a new form of collective action across community boundaries.

The core argument of this chapter is that militias tend to emerge in places that border on communities where militias already exist. This occurs through two mechanisms: (1) *learning* and (2) *migration*. Communities hear about and learn from each other's experiences through the sharing of information.

---

[1] Interview with former Naparama combatant (2011-11-03-Nm32), Murrupula, Nampula, November 3, 2011.
[2] Rachel Waterhouse, "Antonio's Triumph of the Spirits," *Africa South (Harare)* (May), 1991, 15.
[3] Interview with former Naparama combatant (2011-09-19-Nm11), Nicoadala, Zambézia, September 19, 2011.

Knowledge about what happens in other communities during upheaval and war is often distributed through rumors and storytelling (Greenhill and Oppenheim 2017), in particular when communities are linked through social networks, such as ethnicity (Larson and Lewis 2017). Ethnic, ideological, cultural, and historical bonds between communities facilitate the spread of information, and thus the diffusion of collective action repertoires, in particular when these bonds are reinforced by population movements and the (temporary) migration of community residents and local elites between these communities.

Although rumors and storytelling facilitate the militias' ability to spread to neighboring communities, they are not enough to sustain this diffusion. The sustained diffusion of community-initiated militias – that is, their integration into the local security apparatus as well as their ability to influence war dynamics – depends on conditions that I seek to identify and explore in this chapter. I suggest that militias integrate into local institutions when social, political, and military elites are relatively unified. Relative unity among elites has two main consequences. First, it prevents community-initiated militias from becoming the private army of an elite. And second, community residents and local elites have more trust in the ability of the militia to curb violence, and hence they support the new institution, ensuring its survival.

Using the methods of controlled comparisons and process tracing, I develop these arguments with an analysis of militia diffusion to two adjacent districts with similar geographic, demographic, and war-related characteristics in the Zambézia province of the central region of Mozambique. While the Naparama militia virtually replaced the state military in one district, the newly founded force quickly fell apart in an adjacent district. I then explore my argument further with a third case of Naparama diffusion to a district in Nampula province. The case studies show that migration and learning were the mechanisms that facilitated the initial militia diffusion, but that diffusion was only sustained because elite conflicts were absent and community residents and local elites had faith in the militia to improve the local security situation.

6.1 MILITIA DIFFUSION IN ZAMBÉZIA AND NAMPULA PROVINCES

Much of the initial spread of the Naparama militia was driven by the travels of the main Naparama leaders who offered their services to communities, either on their own initiative or on the initiative of community residents requesting the militia leaders' services. Naparama had two main leaders, one in Zambézia and one in Nampula province, and each was responsible for forming units across their province.

Coming from Nampula, António entered Zambézia province in 1989 in the Alto Ligonha area in Gilé district and first worked in Alto Molócuè district (see map in Figure 6.1) (Pereira 1999a, 82). In Alto Molócuè, António began

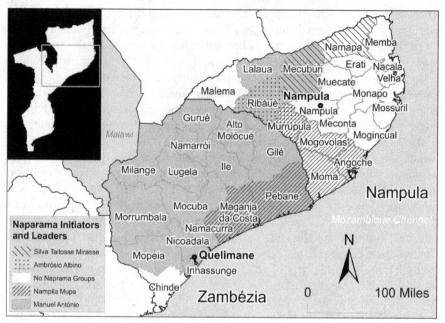

FIGURE 6.1. Map of initiators and the diffusion of Naparama militias across Zambézia and Nampula provinces

Note: This map presents an overview of Naparama leaders and the districts in which they formed Naparama units in the period between 1988 and 1992. (Cartography by Sofia Jorges)

offering his services to bus travelers seeking protection for their travels on roads often targeted by Renamo ambushes. He then formed small groups to attack Renamo strongholds in the northern part of the district. From a base in Nampevo, Naparama launched offensives into Mocuba, Ile, and Gilé (Pereira 1999a, 86). The base at Nampevo also served as a launchpad for Naparama's epic attack on Renamo's regional base at Muaquiua. In Nauela, a former Renamo stronghold, Naparama punished the population for supporting Renamo by pillaging their property. Consequently, Naparama lost the support of the population and António had to move further south (Pereira 1999a, 84). The militia then spread, seemingly along the main N1 highway, into the Ile, Gilé, and Mocuba districts.[4] In Mocuba, António established his main headquarters, later moving them to Nicoadala. He also formed Naparama militias in the districts of Pebane, Maganja da Costa, Namacurra, Nicoadala, Lugela, Namarrói, Milange, Gurué, and Inhassunge.

---

[4] Interview with Naparama commanders (2011-09-30-Nm20), Nicoadala, Zambézia, September 30, 2011; and (2011-08-23-Gr-Nm1), Quelimane, August 23, 2011.

In Nampula province, the traditional healer Ambrósio Albino from Nampula city claimed that he and his nephew Silva Taitosse Mirasse had brought the Parama vaccine to Murrupula district, the center of Naparama activity in Nampula. His nephew then responded to requests from communities in Mecubúri and Namapa districts to form militias there. Murrupula's eminent traditional healer, Nampila, became an important Naparama leader in Murrupula and neighboring districts, and mobilized militias in Moma, and presumably also in the coastal districts of Mogovolas and Angoche, at the request of their respective communities. In 1990, communities who had heard about Nampila's work called him to work in Zambézia, in Pebane district close to Nampula province, where he disappeared in 1991 (see overview of Naparama leaders and the districts in which they formed Naparama units in Figure 6.1).[5]

The first part of this chapter tells the story of how the militia spread to two adjacent districts in Zambézia province. In 1990, Zambézia's Naparama leader António arrived in Lugela and Namarrói, two districts that had seen much Renamo activity due to their proximity to rebel sanctuaries in Malawi, the deep forests in which rebels could hide, and residents' historical sympathy for opposition movements. Lugela and Namarrói both lie in Alta Zambézia, a mountainous region at the southern end of the Great Rift Valley populated by the Lomwe ethnic group (see map in Figure 6.2). Lugela and Namarrói districts had about the same number of inhabitants at the beginning of the war – 107,000 and 100,000, respectively, in 1980 – but Lugela had a much lower population density, covering twice the area of Namarrói (2,300 square miles). The districts were prone to political activity by the PRM, or Africa Livre, the opposition movement based in Malawi that united with the rebel group Renamo in 1982 (Vines 1991; Chichava 2007). These districts were also the first to be affected by Renamo's war in Zambézia province.

As outlined below, government reports at the time identified Lugela and Namarrói as among those districts in Zambézia province in which the military, political, and social situation was the most critical. In 1986/1987, Renamo occupied both district towns for many months, and the rebels maintained control over about two-thirds of the area of each district for most of the war. Frelimo's radius of action was reduced to five miles in the towns, and Renamo units frequently attacked the towns and surrounding areas. In both districts, the army contingent was small and the existing troops faced a lack of military supplies. Necessary reinforcements from the military headquarters in

---

[5] The causes of Nampila's disappearance are unclear. Nampila's family accuses António of having killed Nampila in Zambézia province. There is evidence from archival records and my interviews with local government officials that Nampila and António got into conflict in Pebane district in Zambézia, as each accused the other of not having access to the proper medicine. The power struggle supposedly resulted in António's kidnapping and murder of Nampila sometime in 1991. For a more detailed discussion of this intra-movement struggle, see Jentzsch (2018b).

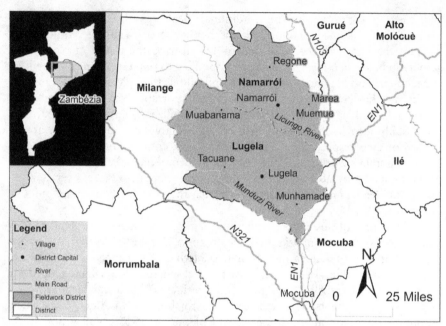

FIGURE 6.2. Map of Lugela and Namarrói in Zambézia province
Note: Cartography by Sofia Jorges

Mocuba – more than forty miles away from each district town – were slow and often arrived too late to effectively respond to Renamo attacks. The population frequently fled to the bush and, particularly in Lugela, suffered from severe hunger. The rebels' strong presence during the war is reflected in the electoral victory of the rebel-turned-opposition-party Renamo in the first multiparty elections in Mozambique in 1994. In Namarrói, Renamo gained 53 percent of the vote for parliament (compared to 30 percent for Frelimo), and in Lugela 56 percent (compared to 33 percent for Frelimo). In all of Zambézia province, Renamo gained 52.5 percent and Frelimo 31.5 percent (Mazula 1995).

Although both districts faced similar challenges, Naparama forces only spread sustainably to Lugela. In Lugela, Naparama constituted a large and influential force, while in Namarrói its size and activities were limited and only survived for a short time in one village. How can this difference in Naparama's formation in the two districts be explained? What accounts for the variation in diffusion processes of community-initiated militias across districts in Zambézia province?

6.2 SUSTAINED DIFFUSION OF NAPARAMA TO LUGELA

6.2.1 The Military Situation in Lugela

Even before Renamo reached Lugela district in 1982, the district had been an area of opposition activity. Starting in the late 1970s, PRM/Africa Livre units created insecurity in the rural areas. Local government reports from Lugela in 1979 link this "enemy activity" to infiltration from across the border in Malawi to the neighboring district of Milange.[6] Milange borders on the administrative post of Muabanama in Lugela, about forty-five miles from the district town of Lugela. Muabanama was the location of the only communal village in the district, and thus a target of frequent attacks by those who opposed Frelimo's policies after independence.[7]

Much of this early violence perpetrated by PRM/Africa Livre targeted the Frelimo state and focused on securing access to resources. The local administration accused "counter-revolutionaries" of mobilizing monetary support from local residents, stealing household goods, plundering health posts and stores, and burning administrative buildings and residences of Frelimo secretaries.[8] On April 20, 1981, armed men murdered Muabanama's administrative head and pillaged administrative buildings, the health post, and the main store.[9]

Renamo attacks from 1982 onward had similar targets as PRM/Africa Livre's – symbols of Frelimo's economic and social policy in the east and north of the district. In the fall of 1982, rebel units attacked and destroyed the Emochá and Madal tea factories and destroyed the bridge over the Munhamade River in the administrative post of Tacuane, about twenty miles to the east of the district town.[10] Renamo occupied the tea factories and surrounding areas shortly thereafter and maintained control of these areas until the end of the war.[11]

[6] República Popular de Moçambique, Província da Zambézia, Gabinete do Administrador do Distrito do Lugela, *Relatório que se refere a Mensagem N° 1/DPAC/980, da Direcção Provincial de Apoio e Controle da Zambézia, de 31.1.980*, June 1, 1980 (AGZ, Quelimane).

[7] Interview with community leader (2012-06-08-Lm24), Lugela, Zambézia, June 8, 2012.

[8] República Popular de Moçambique, Província da Zambézia, Gabinete do Administrador do Distrito do Lugela, *Relatório que se refere a Mensagem N° 1/DPAC/980, da Direcção Provincial de Apoio e Controle da Zambézia, de 31.1.980*, June 1, 1980 (AGZ, Quelimane); República Popular de Moçambique, Província da Zambézia, Gabinete do Administrador do Distrito do Lugela, *Relatório mensal de 15 de Maio a 15 de Junho de 1982*, June 15, 1982 (AGZ, Quelimane); República Popular de Moçambique, Província da Zambézia, Gabinete do Administrador do Distrito do Lugela, *Relatório mensal de 15 de Abril a 15 de Maio de 1982*, May 15, 1982 (AGZ, Quelimane).

[9] República Popular de Moçambique, Ministério da Defesa Nacional, Comando do 1° Batalhão da 7° Brigada de Infantaria Regular em Mocuba, *Exposição sobre o assassinato do administrador da localidade de Muabanama*, n.d. (AGZ, Quelimane).

[10] On the same day of the attack on Emochá on August 28, 1982, Renamo also attacked local stores in nearby Limbué-Mabú and stole goods meant for distribution to local residents. República Popular de Moçambique, Província da Zambézia, Gabinete do Administrador do Distrito do Lugela, *Relatório mensal de 15 Agosto a 15 de Setembro de 1982*, September 14, 1982 (AGZ, Quelimane); Interview with community leaders (2012-06-14-Gr-Lm4), Lugela, Tacuane, Zambézia, June 14, 2012.

[11] República Popular de Moçambique, Província da Zambézia, Gabinete do Administrador do Distrito de Lugela, *Relatório Mensal de 15 de Novembro a 15 de Dezembro de 1982*, December 20, 1982 (AGZ, Quelimane). In February–March 1983, Renamo units attacked and occupied

Renamo pursued both military and political objectives in Lugela. The rebels mobilized the people for their cause and – especially in the beginning – received much support. When the rebels convened community meetings, they declared that Frelimo did not treat residents well and offered them their protection. They also mobilized collaborators, who would join mujeeba, Renamo's main informants and local police.[12] Initially, community residents welcomed the opposition movement and provided the soldiers with food.[13] One of the strategies to gain popular support was to trick people into thinking that Renamo already controlled major towns – for example, by providing rare goods such as salt. In this way, the population felt it did not have a choice but to support the new ruling movement.[14] As in other regions, local chiefs overwhelmingly supported Renamo because it promised that they would regain the power that Frelimo had taken from them at independence.[15]

However, Renamo's military objectives guided their behavior toward civilians more than their political ambitions. Popular support decreased when Renamo started targeting civilians indiscriminately. While the rebels' initial operations focused on the intimidation of Frelimo party and state representatives, indiscriminate violence increased after Renamo abducted and trained youths from the areas under occupation and expanded its military presence in the rural areas.[16] Many of Renamo's abductees were forced to carry pillaged metal to Malawi, where it was sold. Whoever refused was killed.[17]

During Renamo's second military offensive across Zambézia in 1986, the military situation in Lugela worsened significantly and Renamo occupied the district for several months. Rebel units attacked and occupied the district town in March 1986, occupying it four more times until 1988. Whenever Frelimo retook the district town, its radius of action remained limited to about five miles. Access roads to surrounding villages were impassable, and travel to Mocuba, the next large town and location of Frelimo's provincial military headquarters, was only possible on bush paths. Even when Frelimo had regained control of the district town, rebels constantly attacked, and control

---

Tacuane for three days and destroyed all administrative buildings. See República Popular de Moçambique, Província da Zambézia, Gabinete do Administrador do Distrito de Lugela, *Relatório mensal de 15 de Fevereiro a 15 de Março do ano de 1983*, March 15, 1983 (AGZ, Quelimane).

[12] Interview with civilian (2012-06-14, m34), Tacuane, Lugela, Zambézia, June 14, 2012.

[13] Interview with community leaders (2012-06-14-Gr-Lm4), Tacuane, Lugela, Zambézia, June 14, 2012.

[14] Interview with civilian (2012-06-18-m36), Lugela, Zambézia, June 18, 2012.

[15] Interview with civilian (2012-06-18-m36), Lugela, Zambézia, June 18, 2012.

[16] Interview with community leaders (2012-06-14-Gr-Lm4), Tacuane, Lugela, Zambézia, June 14, 2012.

[17] Interviews with civilian and community leaders (2012-06-15-Gr-f2); and (2012-06-15-Gr-Lm5), Tacuane, Lugela, Zambézia, June 15, 2012.

of the town and the surrounding areas changed frequently.[18] As soon as the army was able to organize convoys with supplies from Mocuba, Renamo returned and assaulted the convoys and stole the supplies.[19]

The frequent attacks and change in territorial control meant community residents and government representatives perceived the situation as chaotic. Since they constantly had to flee their homes, the people lived a "nomadic existence."[20] Community residents searched for security as well as food, as several years of low crop yield had led to severe hunger. After the March 1986 rebel attack and occupation, members of the local administration and most of the population fled into the mountains and then to the locality of Namagoa close to Mocuba, where the government set up a camp for the displaced on the grounds of a former Sisal fiber factory.[21] Frelimo actively mobilized people to leave Renamo-held areas and assisted them in resettling to the camp in Namagoa throughout the town's occupation.[22] Namagoa was the only place where people could find some form of relief; the remaining areas of the district became ungoverned and anyone who tried to cross them risked being killed or arrested by Renamo or Frelimo armed forces:

From then on, the war spread, any person could be killed and people were confused; there was no government or anything. Many of us went to Mocuba, following Frelimo. Frelimo was over there, and here was Renamo. When you crossed the Lugela River to Namagoa, you were killed, and from here to there you were arrested. When someone left here to go to Mocuba, he was welcomed and we were given maize, sardines, beans, oil – many things. We were given clothes; men received pants and a coat. But when coming from there to here – [when] I forgot something, my own brother would inform [Renamo] and they would catch you and kill you out of fear that you came to collect intelligence.[23]

The district administration was unable to cope with the situation. The district administrator repeatedly complained in his reports to the provincial government about the lack of military and logistical support from the province.

---

[18] Interview with local government official (2012-02-22-Gm15), Quelimane, Zambézia, February 22, 2012.

[19] Interview with local government official (2012-02-22-Gm15), Quelimane, Zambézia, February 22, 2012; (2012-06-19-Gm27), Lugela, Zambézia, June 19, 2012.

[20] República Popular de Moçambique, Província da Zambézia, Gabinete do Administrador do Distrito de Lugela, *Relatório trimestral (Julho a Setembro/87)*, October 1, 1987 (AGZ, Quelimane); República Popular de Moçambique, Província da Zambézia, Gabinete do Administrador do Distrito de Lugela, *Relatório, período de 1 a 30 de Junho, ano de 1988*, July 15, 1988 (AGZ, Quelimane).

[21] Interviews with: local government official (2012-06-19-Gm27), Lugela, Zambézia, June 19, 2012; former militiaman (2012-06-09-Gr-Mm1), June 9, 2012, Lugela, Zambézia; and former Frelimo combatant (2012-06-12-Fm24), Lugela, Zambézia, June 12, 2012.

[22] Interviews with civilian (2012-06-14-m34) and community leaders (2012-06-14-Gr-Lm4), Tacuane, Lugela, Zambézia, June 14, 2012.

[23] Interview with community leaders (2012-06-14-Gr-Lm4), Tacuane, Lugela, Zambézia, June 14, 2012.

Only one battalion – half of which consisted of newly trained local forces – protected the district.[24] A local government official estimated that 40 percent of the force was either malnourished or wounded and unable to participate in combat.[25] Thus, each time Renamo units approached the town, the district commander had to call for military reinforcement from Mocuba. Moreover, since the military did not have any supplies, it had to live off the population and often did so by force.

Frelimo's grip on power over the district began to slip. Lugela's administrator made it clear in reports that without provincial logistical and military support Frelimo control could no longer be upheld in the district: "If we delay any longer, the population will drink the enemy's politics and their recuperation will be very difficult."[26] As a solution, the district administrator proposed to train local forces as part of the country-wide "territorial security and defense system." The situation only improved from 1990 onward, partly due to a new military commander who committed himself to not leaving the district until the situation had improved.[27]

6.2.2 Initial Diffusion of Naparama to Lugela

As the district administrator recognized, only the local population's involvement in the defense of the town held any promise of improving the security situation. Naparama units formed in the camp for the displaced in Namagoa, presumably in late 1990. By that time, António had moved from Alto Molócuè, a district close to Nampula province, to Mocuba, where he was working closely with the provincial command of the military, headquartered there.[28]

Although the military and local administration later supported mobilization for Naparama forces, they were not involved in the initial diffusion of Naparama to Lugela. António arrived in Namagoa on his own initiative, then introduced himself to the local authorities and requested authorization to mobilize youths to be treated with the Parama vaccine. Joining was voluntary and mobilization occurred in cooperation with lower-level administrative elites such as neighborhood secretaries.[29] Naparama's main task became patrolling

---

[24] Interview with former Frelimo combatant (2012-06-12-Fm24), Lugela, Zambézia, June 12, 2012; Interview with local government official (2012-02-22-Gm15), Quelimane, Zambézia, February 22, 2012.

[25] Interview with local government official (2012-02-22-Gm15), Quelimane, Zambézia, February 22, 2012.

[26] República Popular de Moçambique, Província da Zambézia, Gabinete do Administrador do Distrito de Lugela, *Relatório, período de 1 a 3 de Julho, ano de 1988*, August 2, 1988 (AGZ, Quelimane).

[27] Interview with local government official (2012-06-19-Gm27), Lugela, Zambézia, June 19, 2012.

[28] On the manifestation of Naparama in the Alto Molócuè district, see Pereira (1999a).

[29] Interview with former militiaman (2012-06-09-Gr-Mm1), Lugela, Zambézia, June 9, 2012.

the camp at night.[30] Later, the designated Naparama leader in Namagoa brought his group to Lugela to improve the security situation in the district town once it was retaken by Frelimo.

Community residents welcomed Naparama activities as they were convinced that António would be able to liberate them from the hardships of the war and help them return to their homes.[31] Community residents' narratives reveal the fascination with the Naparama forces:

[Manuel António] Naparama is someone to admire – [he is able to] fight with machete [and] spear. God helped him to help the population.[32]

Naparama! They put in the work, they captured the enemy alive! They didn't retreat. Renamo attempted to shoot them, but they didn't die. Because this was a magical war! That's why they did not have anything to fear, they were not afraid, they went there, captured the enemy, and brought him back together with [his war] material. In those days, Naparama worked [hard]. They [really] worked [hard].[33]

The way community residents were intrigued by the power of Naparama and the group's leader demonstrates that cultural bonds existed between Lugela and the communities in which Naparama previously formed. Community residents believed in António's power to defend the people with nothing but spears and machetes, and they were even convinced that he had divine powers. Individuals in the community understood the cultural references Naparama made, and they believed that Naparama units were able to prevail in a "magical war" with Renamo. Thus, cultural bonds between communities facilitated Naparama's initial diffusion.[34]

Naparama's diffusion was closely linked to stories about their success in one of Renamo's main bases in the Mocuba district. Naparama units formed in Namagoa after António supposedly killed the famous Renamo regional commander Calisto Meque in the Muaquiua rebel base.[35] After Naparama's successful attack on Muaquiua, António asked a Lugela community leader named

---

[30] Interview with former Naparama commander (2012-06-10-Nm46), Lugela, Zambézia, June 10, 2012.

[31] Interview with community leaders (2012-06-14-Gr-Lm4), Tacuane, Lugela, Zambézia, June 14, 2012.

[32] Interview with civilians (2012-06-12-Gr-m1), Lugela, Zambézia, June 12, 2012.

[33] Interview with former Frelimo combatant (2012-06-12-Fm24), Lugela, Zambézia, June 12, 2012.

[34] Ethnic bonds existed between the communities as well, since Lugela is part of the Makua-Lomwe linguistic group area from where Naparama spread.

[35] Interview with former Naparama combatant (2012-06-11-Nm47), Lugela, Zambézia, June 11, 2012. This story traveled all over the province, as my interviews with former Naparama combatants in Nicoadala confirm. Whether Naparama killed Meque is contested, however, as Frelimo claimed to have done so much earlier during a battle in the town of Gilé in July 1988. See Wilson (1992) and "Mozambique: Setback to Peace," *Africa Confidential* 32 (4), 1991; 4.

Namudavale to take a group of Naparama combatants to Lugela.[36] As Namudavale narrated,

So it was at that moment [after the battle of Muaquiua] when Manuel António demanded, "You will take your combatants to your district of Lugela and help the [military] commander who is there." So I brought my 128 men here to the district. When I arrived here, I increased the number of combatants. [António] gave me some of the medicine to vaccinate these men. When I arrived here, I asked for more men. Volunteers showed up, I gave them the vaccine; we went to fight in Mdedereia [and] we entered Mdedereia.[37]

A resident of Namagoa explained how closely he and his community monitored events in the neighboring district of Mocuba, comparing the Mocuba residents' situation to their own:

In the area where [Naparama] emerged, miracles occurred and the population came to live well, while we were in Namagoa and watched the good situation in which the population of Mocuba was in. Since [Mocuba] was a district that was very close [to Namagoa], [we were] talking about Naparama, what they were like, what their work was like.[38]

In sum, the spread of information about Naparama enabled the diffusion of Naparama to Namagoa and subsequently to the town of Lugela. This was made possible by two causal mechanisms. The first was the (temporary) migration of diffusion agents – António and Namudavale – who linked communities with strong ethnic and cultural bonds. Due to these ethnic and cultural bonds, the social conventions underpinning Naparama's power resonated in these communities. In addition, through the demonstration effect of successful missions in other areas – such as the battle of Muaquiua – people learned that they would be better off supporting a new Naparama force in their district.

6.2.3 Sustained Diffusion of Naparama to Lugela

The Naparama militia became an important force in Lugela, meaning that the local administration integrated the militia into the local security apparatus. Naparama collaborated closely with the local administration and the armed forces stationed in the district. The local administration supported the growth of the militia by aiding the Naparama members' mobilization process, and when Naparama moved to the town of Lugela the force reached a size of about

---

[36] Namudavale had gone on several missions together with António in Mocuba's surrounding areas and claimed to have accompanied the Naparama leader to the battle in Muaquiua.

[37] Interview with former Naparama leader (2012-06-10-Nm46), Lugela, Zambézia, June 10, 2012.

[38] Interview with former militiamen (2012-06-09-Gr-Mm1), Lugela, Zambézia, June 9, 2012.

240 men.[39] The recruits stayed in huts at the militia's headquarters and went to their homes during the day when they were not sent on missions.[40]

Naparama's sustained diffusion was facilitated by the militia leader's standing in the community and the faith that people put into the group as a result. Naparama leader Namudavale was a trusted community leader respected by local authorities, and thus elite conflicts did not arise. As a former combatant during the liberation struggle, Namudavale became secretary of the Frelimo party's dynamizing groups after independence. When the district population relocated to the displacement camp in Namagoa, Namudavale organized and distributed food to the people – an important task in times of war when such resources are scarce. Namudavale remained a loyal Frelimo party member throughout the war and beyond, and at the time of our conversation he served as a member of the district party committee.[41]

In order to gain and retain the trust of community residents and local authorities, militias need to prove their service to the community. Namudavale's Naparama forces proved their loyalty by retrieving the population that had been abducted by Renamo. The district administration was worried at first that Naparama would formulate political and/or monetary demands after the war. However, when militia members proved that they were willing to take risks to go to Renamo camps and managed to retrieve people who had been abducted by the rebels, the district administrator decided to tolerate the group's activities:

The government did not support Naparama. However, as the people were seeing good results from Naparama's actions, the government did not organize a force to eradicate Naparama. Because Naparama said over there is an advanced military position or camp – there is a Renamo base. Naparama was prepared to go to these bases. And in some way they brought with them some uncles from these areas. They brought some ladies from these areas back here. Taking them from [Renamo's] base! The disposition of such an individual [António] is welcome. "Ah, that's how [he does things]!" An individual who reached a dangerous place in order to retrieve his uncle. [They] retrieve your wife who had been with the bandit, with Renamo. Even retrieve your wife! From then on, there was no way for the government to prohibit the work of the Naparama.[42]

The militia's success in bringing back abducted family members generated extensive popular support for Naparama. The administration could therefore not prohibit Naparama's operations without alienating community residents.

---

[39] Interview with former Naparama commander (2012-06-10-Nm46), Lugela, Zambézia, June 10, 2012.
[40] Interview with former Naparama combatant (2012-06-15-Nm49), Tacuane, Lugela, Zambézia, June 15, 2012; Interview with community leaders (2012-06-14-Gr-Lm4), Tacuane, Lugela, Zambézia, June 14, 2012.
[41] Interview with former Naparama commander (2012-06-10-Nm46), Lugela, Zambézia, June 10, 2012.
[42] Interview with local government official (2012-06-19-Gm27), Lugela, Zambézia, June 19, 2012.

In fact, the local government came to consider the militia as a last resort to fulfill the people's desire for peace.[43] The situation was thus ripe for the community-initiated militias to form. As a government official pointed out, "[e]ven if Naparama had not appeared, the people would have asked the military for firearms [to defend themselves]."[44] The Naparama leader in Lugela explained to me that people could no longer rely on the army for help; it was a time in which everyone had to defend themselves at their own risk.[45] The militia demonstrated that it was able to take over defending the people and not threaten Frelimo control, and this is what allowed the local administration to make the militia part of the local security apparatus.

A relationship based on mutual trust also evolved between Naparama and the armed forces. When asked about allegations that the military stole relief aid during the war, Namudavale demonstrated great loyalty by strongly denying any such corruption existed within the armed forces. He also emphasized that Naparama and the Frelimo army always conducted joint operations, during which each group remained independent and respected each other:

Were the military headquarters always aware of Naparama operations?

They knew about them, we worked together. The army commander with whom I had spoken even told [the soldiers], "Work with [the Naparama] together as if you were brothers. Wherever you have to go, go there together, work, and return. You just can't command [the Naparama]. Your commander can only command your own men. Though whoever disobeys his own commander, will die." He did not tell us what to do – no, we went together.[46]

Although Naparama had a degree of autonomy, the army monitored their activities closely, and often joined them on missions to Renamo bases or to accompany military convoys to Mocuba.[47] Lugela's Naparama leader lived in the very center of town, close to the army commander, and his assistant

---

[43] Interview with local government official (2012-02-22-Gm15), Quelimane, Zambézia, February 22, 2012.

[44] Interview with local government official (2012-06-19-Gm27), Lugela, Zambézia, June 19, 2012. Recruitment in Lugela was not completely voluntary. One Naparama member reported that he was abducted to become Naparama in the displacement camp when the Naparama leaders went from house to house to recruit new members, and one of the displaced from Lugela in Namagoa also reported that the military and Naparama units abducted new Naparama recruits. Nevertheless, although they could have left Naparama, these new recruits stayed with them to enjoy the force of their protection. See interview with former Naparama combatant (2012-06-15-Nm49), Tacuane, Lugela, June 15, 2012; Interview with civilian (2012-06-18-m36), Lugela, Zambézia, June 18, 2012.

[45] Interview with former Naparama leader (2012-06-10-Nm46), Lugela, Zambézia, June 10, 2012.

[46] Interview with former Naparama commander (2012-06-10-Nm46), Lugela, Zambézia, June 10, 2012.

[47] Interview with former Naparama commander (2012-06-10-Nm46), Lugela, Zambézia, June 10, 2012; Interview with former Naparama combatant (2012-06-15-Nm49), Tacuane, Lugela, Zambézia, June 15, 2012.

controlled activities in the displacement camp by the river, about a mile from the town center.[48] Naparama also collaborated with the popular militias that possessed firearms. Ten militiamen and twenty Naparama combatants were assigned to each administrative unit of the district town, and in the late afternoons all of them were expected at the control post for their nightly patrol.[49]

Former Frelimo combatants confirm the positive relationship between Naparama and the army stationed in Lugela:

We [Naparama and the military] considered ourselves friends, because [Naparama] were also fighting for the same purpose, and that is why there was no difference. In battle we were all military men, no one could say "I'm Naparama, I'm from the Frelimo army," no, we were all soldiers, we were fighting and returned victorious.[50]

This affirmation by Frelimo soldiers of the close collaboration between Frelimo and Naparama is remarkable, as in other districts and at the provincial level, Frelimo representatives usually downplayed their reliance on Naparama forces. Officially, Frelimo could not concede that the party compromised its commitment to a socialist ideology that is hostile to traditional forms of power (Dinerman 2006).[51]

The trust between the militia, the army, and the local government further found expression in the fact that when António died and Naparama's strength seemed to wane, the local administration supplied Naparama with firearms:

So when the government saw that their leader had already died – [that Naparama] were dying – that is when it gave them firearms, saying that [Naparama] could not lose, they were already losing the drugs' force, thus they gave them firearms, saying – epah! – you can now carry firearms. [Naparama] were fighting [Renamo]. It was already the end of that drug. [They were] already dying.[52]

The local government needed Naparama's support and trusted them sufficiently to hand them weapons when they realized that the powers of the Parama vaccine were not as reliable as Naparama claimed them to be.

In sum, the Naparama militia diffused sustainably to Lugela. The community-initiated militia grew quickly in size, was integrated into the local security apparatus, and played a vital part in the protection of the displacement

---

[48] Interview with former Naparama commander (2012-06-10-Nm46), Lugela, Zambézia, June 10, 2012.

[49] Interview with former Naparama commander (2012-06-10-Nm46), Lugela, Zambézia, June 10, 2012.

[50] Interview with former Frelimo combatant (2012-06-12-Fm24), Lugela, Zambézia, June 12, 2012.

[51] For more discussion of Frelimo's changing attitude toward traditional authorities and healers and religion, see Chapter 4.

[52] Interview with former Frelimo combatant (2012-06-12-Fm24), Lugela, Zambézia, June 12, 2012.

camp and later the district town. Diffusion was made possible by the cultural bonds that existed between communities and the success of the movement in other parts of the province. Migrating diffusion agents and local residents' acquired beliefs that Naparama would help them curb the violence convinced community residents to support forming Naparama units in their district. These mechanisms only led to sustained diffusion, however, because the Naparama leader was a trusted community leader who would not challenge Frelimo dominance. As I will explain below, Naparama did not enjoy such support among the people and the administration in the Namarrói district due to ruptures in the relationship among political and military elites.

6.3 LIMITED DIFFUSION OF NAPARAMA TO NAMARRÓI

6.3.1 The Military Situation in Namarrói

Renamo's war reached Namarrói from the neighboring Lugela and Milange districts in September 1982. As in Lugela, respondents and local government reports point to frequent movements of "bandits" – presumably linked to Africa Livre – in the district before September 1982.[53] When Renamo first entered the district in 1982, it soon controlled the district's north, where it established its major regional base (see map in Figure 6.2).[54] The base was located in Nantutu but was then transferred to Maquiringa, an area deep in the forest close to the Regone locality, which remained occupied from 1983–91.[55] The mountain range that crosses the district from east to west became a frontier between Frelimo-held and Renamo-held areas. Frelimo controlled five localities; two remained occupied by Renamo until the end of the war. Renamo attacked the localities under Frelimo control from the northern part of the district and from Lugela district to the south.[56]

As in Lugela, opposition movements initially enjoyed popular support. During the early years of the war, the local population collaborated with

---

[53] The first violent event occurred in Namarrói on June 28, 1982, when Africa Livre units killed three teachers in the locality of Inlugo. República Popular de Moçambique, Província da Zambézia, Gabinete do Administrador do Distrito do Ile, *Mensagem No. 19/A/28*, June 29, 1982 (AGZ, Quelimane). See also Cuahela (1998).

[54] Renamo reached Namarrói on the road linking Munhamade, a locality in Lugela district, to Muémue, a locality on the road between the district town of Namarrói and the adjacent district Ile. From Milange, Renamo entered the area of Regone in the north of Lugela district.

[55] Renamo's first base in the district was located in the area of the chief Nantutu (Cabá 1998, 35). Chief Nantutu remained the head of all the mambos (chiefs collaborating with Renamo), which might explain why in some cases, the base continued to be referred to as Nantutu base. When the base was moved to the area of chief Maquiringa, the actual camp was located about ten miles from Maquiringa in the area of Rumala, named after the local headman.

[56] República Popular de Moçambique, Província da Zambézia, Gabinete do Administrador do Distrito de Namarrói, *Relatório anual de 1985*, February 21, 1986 (AGZ, Quelimane).

Africa Livre and Renamo by identifying representatives of the Frelimo state. This way, opposition forces were able to target state and party officials, professors, and health workers, and destroy critical economic infrastructure.[57] A teacher who was among the targeted explained:

During this time, the population distanced itself from the political cadre, teachers, and nurses. For example, teachers [who were] seeking shelter among the population – they turned [them] away, and they even reported them to Renamo, claiming that they were living [too] well.[58]

Similar to the situation in Lugela, support for Renamo waned when the rebels no longer limited their violence to representatives of the Frelimo state. When Renamo began targeting the population indiscriminately, "a feeling of solidarity among the population and the officials [emerged]. In the beginning [of the war], people thought that after the punishment of the officials, the war would end."[59] Instead, Renamo kept a tight grip on the population living in areas under their control. For example, the rebels received the support of chiefs by promising them benefits and status after the war.[60] But when the chiefs did not comply with the rebels' demands, they were killed, often along with their families and sympathizers, as happened in a neighborhood in the district town in 1986.[61] Mambos and mujeeba collected food from peasants and closely controlled people's movements, and they often did so by force.[62] Renamo also committed several massacres. On February 22, 1983, for instance, between fifty and ninety people were killed in Mualiua, a neighborhood in the district town, after residents had been called from their fields to a meeting.[63] Thus, support for Renamo diminished among the population in Frelimo-held areas.

[57] The first attack on the district town took place on September 25, 1982, when Renamo units destroyed the bridge over the river Mulumasse on the road toward Regone, which cut the district's north off from the south. During Renamo's second attack on Namarrói town in 1983, combatants pillaged and destroyed the state agricultural marketing board's building in the town center. See interviews with former Frelimo combatants (2012-05-04-Fm16); (2012-05-04-Fm17), Namarrói, Zambézia, May 4, 2012.

[58] Interview with a teacher in Namarrói, Zambézia, cited in Cuahela (1998, 56) (translation from Portuguese by author).

[59] Interview with a teacher in Namarrói, Zambézia, cited in Cuahela (1998, 57) (translation from Portuguese by author).

[60] Interview with community leader (2012-05-24-Lm22), Maquiringa, Namarrói, Zambézia, May 24, 2012.

[61] Interview with community leaders (2012-05-15-Gr-Lm1), Namarrói, Zambézia, May 15, 2012.

[62] Interview with community leader (2012-05-24-Lm22), Maquiringa, Namarrói, Zambézia, May 24, 2012.

[63] Interviews with community leader (2012-05-03-Lm19), Namarrói, Zambézia, May 3, 2012, and local government official (2012-05-07-Gm24), Namarrói, Zambézia, May 7, 2012. One of Mualiua's inhabitants, Muango, had joined Renamo because he felt unjustly treated by Frelimo and returned together with a Renamo commander who ordered the massacre. Cabá (1998, 34) states that Muango was a chief who became Renamo commander in 1982 and 1983. According to Cabá's information, forty-four to forty-five people died. The episode is a good

In its response to Renamo's violence, Namarrói's district administration faced two major dilemmas. First, Renamo benefited from a wide network of local informers. Many of Renamo's combatants stationed in the main base in Maquiringa were from Namarrói and their family members served as collaborators at all levels of the Frelimo state and party apparatus. Political sympathy for Renamo was strong across the district. Thus, similarly to Lugela's district administrator who was worried that the population would "drink the enemy's politics," Namarrói's district administrator maintained in a local government report from 1985 that Namarrói needed serious "political-military work and not just simple speeches."[64] Second, as in Lugela town, the armed forces stationed in Namarrói town were weak, as they only consisted of poorly trained and poorly equipped popular militias. Local government reports of the time frequently express concern that the district's small military force lacked weapons and supplies.[65] The armed forces were entirely made up of locals who did not stay at the military barracks due to logistical problems. Most of them were trained as popular militias in 1979 and then retrained to join the military when the war reached Namarrói.

Like Lugela, Namarrói suffered from long-term rebel occupation, during which the population fled to a neighboring district. Frelimo's inability to defend meant that the district town fell to a group of Renamo combatants trained in Kenya on December 29, 1986.[66] Coming from Malawi, Renamo had started a major offensive that would lead to the occupation of many district towns across Zambézia. Most of Namarrói's population fled to Ile, the neighboring district about forty-five miles from the town. The district administration moved its offices to Ile's district town. The armed forces remained stationed in the

example of the fragmentation of war and the settling of local conflicts through civil war violence (see Chapter 4).

[64] República Popular de Moçambique, Província da Zambézia, Gabinete do Administrador do Distrito de Namarrói, *Relatório referente aos meses de Julho a Outubro 1985*, November 14, 1985 (AGZ, Quelimane).

[65] República Popular de Moçambique, Província da Zambézia, Gabinete do Administrador do Distrito de Namarrói, *Relatório referente aos mês de Junho 1985*, July 10, 1985 (AGZ, Quelimane); República Popular de Moçambique, Província da Zambézia, Gabinete do Administrador do Distrito de Namarrói, *Relatório anual de 1985*, February 21, 1986 (AGZ, Quelimane).

[66] The town had experienced a major attack before, on September 15, 1985, which had not led to occupation by Renamo. After the destruction of Renamo's main base at Gorongosa in Sofala province, many troops moved to the Maquiringa base and this enabled the rebels to stage a major attack against the district town. More than one company divided into two groups simultaneously attacked the market and the administrator's residence at opposite ends of the town and destroyed much of the local administration's infrastructure. República Popular de Moçambique, Província da Zambézia, Gabinete do Administrador do Distrito de Namarrói, *Relatório referente aos meses de Julho a Outubro 1985*, November 14, 1985 (AGZ, Quelimane); República Popular de Moçambique, Província da Zambézia, Distrito de Namarrói, Gabinete do Administrador, *Relatório*, September 16, 1985 (AGZ, Quelimane).

Muémue locality to the south of the town on the road linking Namarrói to Ile, but they struggled to defend the remaining three localities under their control.[67]

The security situation in Namarrói remained difficult even after the army had succeeded in retaking the district town after almost a year of occupation. Frelimo forces tried twice, unsuccessfully, to retake the town.[68] Only on December 16, 1987, did the army reoccupy Namarrói with the support of a major reinforcement, helicopters, and MIGs, and a new military commander called Jacinto Rudes, commander of battalion 054. The new commander and the reinforced troop contingent managed to defend the town in the following years. On January 2 and December 21, 1988, Renamo attempted to occupy the town with a large contingent, but both times the rebels were unsuccessful. Subsequently changing their strategy, Renamo units divided into small groups of four to six people and infiltrated areas around the town.[69]

Namarrói experienced some relief after Frelimo attacked and destroyed the main base in Maquiringa (also known as Nantutu) in September 1988: "[The base] was believed by local people to be impregnable until special units of the Mozambican armed forces stormed it in September. The destruction of Nantutu consolidated the Mozambican army's hold on the district."[70] The destruction of the base facilitated the population's return from Ile starting in 1989. The administration settled people into communal wards so they could be supplied with relief aid and their movement controlled. Renamo only staged new attacks when parts of the military contingent left the district, for instance, on December 18, 1991.

While the larger Frelimo troop contingent stationed in the district after retaking the town in 1987 had reduced the rebel threat, Frelimo soldiers increasingly became a threat to the population. Local government reports sent to the provincial government at the time frequently spoke of the bad relationship between the soldiers and the population, and the soldiers and the local government. Soldiers were often drunk, killed civilians arbitrarily, and threatened to kill party and state representatives who criticized their

---

[67] The localities remaining under Frelimo control were in Muémue, Márea, and Mudine, but they were frequently attacked by Renamo units who burnt down the localities' government offices several times. See República Popular de Moçambique, Província da Zambézia, Gabinete do Administrador do Distrito de Namarrói, *Relatório de Janeiro à Março/87*, April 10, 1987 (AGZ, Quelimane); República Popular de Moçambique, Província de Zambézia, Conselho Executivo do Distrito de Namarrói em Ile, *Relatório do primeiro semestre do ano de 1987*, June 30, 1987 (AGZ, Quelimane).

[68] Interview with civilian (2012-05-19-f15), Namarrói, Zambézia, May 19, 2012.

[69] República Popular de Moçambique, Província da Zambézia, Administração do Distrito de Namarrói, *Informação do Governo Distrital sobre as actividades realizados referentes ao meses de Janeiro a Setembro 1989*, October 2, 1989 (AGZ, Quelimane).

[70] "Rebuilding Namarroi," *Mozambiquefile* (December), 1988, 16.

behavior.[71] The state-initiated popular militias were disorganized, if they existed at all. Efficient and capable command was lacking, weapons were in short supply, and desertion was widespread.[72] The few militia units that existed mistreated the population on their patrols in residential areas.[73] The local administration therefore trained locals for new (state-initiated) militias. By the end of 1988, Frelimo had mobilized 1815 men, organized into 137 control posts, who were tasked with regular patrols and the collection of intelligence from strategic areas under Renamo control.[74]

Overall, the military situation in Namarrói resembled the situation in Lugela. Namarrói faced a similar threat as Renamo perpetrated indiscriminate violence against civilians, and Frelimo forces were too weak to adequately respond to the threat in either district. As in Lugela, the local administration in Namarrói organized community residents into (state-initiated) militias, and these became increasingly important to the defense of the town because of the army's unreliability. However, community initiatives to form militias did not have the same level of success in Namarrói as in Lugela.

6.3.2 The Rise and Fall of Naparama in Namarrói

Naparama leader António made a lasting impression on the people when he visited Namarrói and demonstrated the power of his medicine. However, the group he left behind quickly fell apart. Cultural bonds between neighboring communities and Namarrói and migrating diffusion agents facilitated the spread of Naparama to Namarrói. However, the case of Namarrói shows that the lack of opportunity to learn about Naparama's successes and the existence

---

[71] República Popular de Moçambique, Província da Zambézia, Gabinete do Administrador do Distrito de Namarrói, *Relatório referente ao mês de Abril*, May 18, 1987 (AGZ, Quelimane); República Popular de Moçambique, Província de Zambézia, Conselho Executivo do Distrito de Namarrói em Ile, *Relatório do primeiro semestre do ano de 1987*, June 30, 1987 (AGZ, Quelimane). This situation only improved in 1989. The population supported the military units with food and information, which improved the army's effectiveness: "The better the soldier/population relationship becomes, the higher will be [the soldiers'] combat morale," a government report stated in 1989. See República Popular de Moçambique, Província da Zambézia, Administração do Distrito de Namarrói, *Informação do Governo Distrital sobre as actividades realizados referentes ao meses de Janeiro a Setembro 1989*, October 2, 1989 (AGZ, Quelimane).

[72] República Popular de Moçambique, Província da Zambézia, Administração do Distrito de Namarrói, *Informação do Governo Distrital sobre as actividades realizados referentes ao meses de Janeiro a Setembro 1989*, October 2, 1989 (AGZ, Quelimane).

[73] República Popular de Moçambique, Província de Zambézia, Distrito de Namarrói, Conselho Executivo, *Relatório sobre actividades realizadas pelas comissões de trabalho da Assembleia Distrital vinculadas em várias sectores laborais do distrito*, February 15, 1990 (AGZ, Quelimane).

[74] República Popular de Moçambique, Província de Zambézia, Conselho Executivo do Distrito de Namarrói, *Relatório anual de 1988*, April 3, 1989 (AGZ, Quelimane).

of elite conflicts prevented local officials from institutionalizing the community-initiated militia.

Namarrói's residents still vividly remember Naparama leader António's initial visit because the cultural references he used during a public ceremony resonated with the community. When the Naparama leader came to the town in late 1990, he introduced himself to the administration, which then organized a meeting with community residents. The district administrator made it clear to António that his endorsement of António's work did not imply a promise to pay salaries, and he sought to limit Naparama's activities to acts of self-defense.[75] António performed a ceremony in order to demonstrate his powers, during which he re-enacted Christ's resurrection.[76] Many respondents had a distinct memory of this ceremony:

On the day [António] arrived, it was at the [student housing building], here at the secondary school, when he arrived he said, "here I am, I am Naparama." He called together all the people, us as well, in order to meet Naparama and he said, "I am Naparama, whoever doesn't know me, here I am. Today I want to go to [the area] where Renamo is, I will collect everything and I will kill all the Renamo combatants and bring weapons." All the people were there. He dug [a hole] into the ground, went into [the grave] and [others] put sand [on it] and he said, "I died." After some time, he came out and said, "I will go and capture them all." So he vaccinated some youths who were there and volunteered. The vaccination occurred with a machete. He took some medicine and [used] the machete to make cuts [into the person's body], but the machete did not [hurt the person], this was the vaccine. When they were finished, he went at night and captured all of [the rebels], killed them and took their weapons.[77]

Another respondent remembered the performance like this:

The first day I saw Naparama was on a Sunday. The Administrator Mucutueliua had invited many people in order to see how [Naparama] did things, there by the church. We didn't wait long and went to watch. They dug a grave as if it was a cemetery and they started singing and carried [António] over to [the area] where the student housing is today and buried him there. They put a mat [in the grave] and a big rectangular mirror and he started talking. That there are this many troops and that many weapons in the base of Sahia and in the base of Mussisse that many. Everything that was at the base. Then they covered the grave. When he left [the grave], they started to sing and started a fire with big pieces of firewood. He went [to the fire], sat down and started to take piece after piece [out of the fire] and put them on his chest. They brought some leaves and a mortar .... The youth who wanted to join the group came and took a leaf from the mortar and when they took a machete and struck [his] body, they put the leaf [on the wound] and the wound healed right away. The next day, they left and went to test

[75] Interview with local government official (2012-02-25-Gm16), Quelimane, Zambézia, February 25, 2012.
[76] Interviews with civilian (2012-05-19-f15), Namarrói, Zambézia, May 19, 2012, and with Naparama combatant (2012-06-26-Nm53), Namarrói, Zambézia, June 26, 2012.
[77] Interview with civilian (2012-05-01-m24), Namarrói, Zambézia, May 1, 2012.

whether the medicine worked. They advised the new Naparama combatants that who-ever ducked down or retreated [would die]. Even though the enemy had a weapon, you should not withdraw – they even captured [the enemy] and brought the captured men here with their weapons.[78]

The awe with which respondents told these stories and the detailed recollec-tion of the events demonstrate that the cultural references – both to traditional medicine and Christian religion – invoked during the ceremony resonated with the community. As in the Lugela district, the cultural bonds among the com-munities helped spread the violent collective action repertoire. António served as a diffusion agent; he traveled to Namarrói and formed new militia units.

However, cultural bonds and migrating diffusion agents only led to Naparama's initial diffusion. Respondents pointed out that Naparama activity in Namarrói was short-lived:

When [António] left, the day he went to [the district of Morrumbala], [Naparama] did not continue going [on missions]. Also, when [António] died [in December 1991], no one continued with this work.

Did he leave a commander behind?

... Here he had left [someone]. But when [Naparama in Namarrói] heard that [António] had died, they stopped doing their work, and the war ended. It didn't take long [for the war] to end, [during] the time of Naparama.[79]

The strong impressions of António's ceremony contrast with respondents' narratives of Naparama after António had left Namarrói. Several respondents emphasized that António died soon after he had left Namarrói, after which the group fell apart. Even though António only died in December 1991, respond-ents do not have any recollection of major Naparama activity in Namarrói after António's initial visit in late 1990. The little they remember was that the Naparama combatants who were left behind did not form a strong group and disregarded the rules that ensured the medicine's effectiveness:

Did Manuel António leave someone behind who could vaccinate people?

No, when he returned [to where he came from], he just left behind his troops and a commander. He didn't leave behind instructions to continue to vaccinate. Only those who had been treated [with the vaccine] stayed. But when they started to contradict the orders received, they began to suffer, because one time when Renamo men came and attacked, they fled. They were not allowed to eat *feijão jogo* [a certain type of beans], sweet potato leaves, but they started eating it. Then, the [effect of the] drug started to disappear.[80]

This statement implies that the Naparama militia was a weak group of combatants with little discipline, and that the militia soon fell apart. Thus Naparama's diffusion was not sustained.

---

[78] Interview with civilian (2012-05-26-m28), Namarrói, Zambézia, May 26, 2012.
[79] Interview with civilian (2012-05-01-m24), Namarrói, Zambézia, May 1, 2012.
[80] Interview with civilian (2012-05-26-m28), Namarrói, Zambézia, May 26, 2012.

6.3.3 Explaining the Limits of Naparama Diffusion to Namarrói

What explains the failure of sustained diffusion of Naparama to Namarrói? Comparing Naparama's manifestation in Namarrói to that in Lugela, I identify two factors that explain Naparama's different trajectories in the two districts: First, Naparama in Namarrói lacked integration into the local security apparatus because people did not have an opportunity to learn about the positive effects of Naparama's work on security in and around Namarrói. From the perspective of community residents, the security situation was not sufficiently similar to the one people had heard about in other districts where the Naparama militia was active. Second, the district's elites were in conflict with each other, so the Naparama leader came to pose a threat to local authorities rather than providing welcome support. This situation resulted in, at best, lukewarm support for Naparama among the population.

Regarding the first explanatory factor, in contrast to Lugela's residents, Namarrói's population was not convinced that Naparama forces could have a lasting effect on security in Namarrói. Respondents reported that when António left, Naparama combatants died on missions, fled in the face of an attack, or no longer went on missions at all.[81] Residents also pointed to the fact that the war was already at its end when Naparama emerged, and thus, in their memory, Naparama did not operate for a long time.[82] Moreover, the district administrator had made sure that Naparama's activities were limited to patrolling and accompanying military convoys. They reportedly never had any direct encounters with Renamo troops, which further diminished their pertinence to the improvement of the district's security situation.[83] Thus, although people were fascinated with António's personality, they did not experience that his work was crucial in improving their situation.

The perceived limited impact of Naparama on the security situation in Namarrói can be attributed to the timing of the Naparama leader's arrival. At the time, troops in the district had strengthened and reorganized and the district had seen fewer attacks. The former district administrator explained that the security situation did not allow António to demonstrate his powers in battle:

We organized a meeting with the population – I was there, I wanted to know what he will say to the people. He vaccinated some people during this meeting. But he didn't have much impact in Namarrói – he couldn't show what he was able to do since during the

---

[81] Two Naparama died during a mission to accompany a military convoy to Regone. See interview with former Naparama combatant (2012-06-26-Nm53), Namarrói, Zambézia, June 26, 2012.

[82] See also interview with traditional healer (2012-05-06-Hm3), Namarrói, Zambézia, May 6, 2012.

[83] Interviews with community leaders (2012-05-15-Gr-Lm1), Namarrói, Zambézia, May 15, 2012, and Naparama combatant (2012-06-26-Nm53), Namarrói, Zambézia, June 26, 2012.

three days he was there, there was no attack, and so he didn't have the opportunity to show off. In the other districts he had more impact since he could show his work.[84]

Residents remembered the time after the end of the town's occupation as relatively peaceful. In people's memories, the improvement of the security situation was not due to the Naparama's emergence, but to the military commander Rudes who was in charge of the operation to liberate the town from Renamo occupation. Even if people praised what Naparama had done in the region generally, they did not consider the militia's activities to have brought about a significant change to their own district's situation. In contrast, commander Rudes was remembered as a powerful man, as he succeeded to recapture the town in 1987. To underline Rudes' effect on security, Namarrói residents pointed out that when the military commander left the district in 1991, Renamo restarted their attacks, forcing people to flee to the bush.[85] In a way then, the Naparama leader's services were rivaled by those of the military commander, who had demonstrated his effectiveness in a powerful way that could not be repeated by the Naparama leader.

Regarding the second explanatory factor, there was a lack of trust between Naparama and Frelimo elites. Rivalry and mutual distrust prevented the armed forces from cooperating with the militia. The district administrator pointed out that "the military thought [António] was crazy and laughed at him."[86] The Naparama district commander, Makosso, was a Frelimo combatant who had fought during the liberation war in Lugela and Namarrói, but had left the army in disgrace.[87] According to a local government official, before becoming a Naparama commander, Makosso had been discharged from the military due to bad conduct – allegedly killing civilians arbitrarily.[88] Others maintained that he had been a member of a Frelimo death squad.[89] Before António came to Namarrói, Makosso lived without work in his home village Muémue and then made use of the opportunity to become involved in the war as a Naparama commander. He nominated himself for the militia

---

[84] Interview with former district administrator (2012-02-25-Gm16), Quelimane, Zambézia, February 25, 2012.

[85] Interview with civilian (2012-05-21-m29), Namarrói, Zambézia, May 21, 2012. Rudes' fame can also be seen from a letter to the editor published in the national magazine *Tempo* (970), May 14, 1989, in which the author, a Namarrói resident, praises Rudes and his forces for liberating the district.

[86] Interview with local government official (2012-02-25-Gm16), Quelimane, Zambézia, February 25, 2012.

[87] Interview with community leaders (2012-05-22-Gr-Lm2), Namarrói, Zambézia, May 22, 2012.

[88] Interview with local government official (2012-06-26-Gm28), Márea, Namarrói, Zambézia, June 26, 2012.

[89] Interview with traditional healers (2012-05-22-Gr-Hm1), Muémue, Namarrói, Zambézia, May 22, 2012.

leadership, and António delegated the task of recruiting more Naparama combatants to Makosso after his departure.[90]

Naparama combatants did not think highly of the army either. From the militia combatants' perspective, cooperation with the army was undesirable. The way Naparama combatants fought – standing upright in plain sight – was incompatible with the way the army fought: Soldiers "[took cover and] crawled and we did not crawl, [so] we were afraid of them because they could crawl and we would go in front of them, [and then] they [would] shoot [and] hit us."[91] Some Naparama combatants adopted a rather arrogant attitude toward the armed forces:

Although all fought for the same purpose, there was some alienation ... between Naparama combatants and soldiers. They disrespected the soldiers, telling them that they were nothing, that, although they used weapons, they did not succeed in destroying bases, and [Naparama] with spears and machetes was able to do so.[92]

By pointing to their superior power, Naparama combatants claimed to be entitled to the food aid meant for the army.[93] Militia members even held the army responsible for their losses during battle. The rivalry between the army and Naparama culminated in a clash between the two forces in Inlugo in the locality of Mudine after António's death in late 1991, resulting in the death of several Naparama combatants.[94]

The distance between the military and Naparama could also be felt geographically. Presumably due to the strong presence of the armed forces in Namarrói district town and their attitude toward Naparama, the Naparama district commander created the militia's headquarters in the Muémue locality on the road toward Ile.[95] Most of the Naparama combatants – about eight – were stationed in Muémue.[96] Naparama's headquarters were at the opposite end of the locality from those of the small armed force in the same village.

[90] Interview with traditional healers (2012-05-22-Gr-Hm1), Muémue, Namarrói, Zambézia, May 22, 2012.

[91] Interview with Naparama combatant (2012-05-22-Gr-Nm3), Muémue, Namarrói, Zambézia, May 22, 2012.

[92] Interview with former Frelimo combatant (2012-05-18-Fm18), Namarrói, Zambézia, May 18, 2012.

[93] Interview with local government official (2012-06-26-Gm28), Márea, Namarrói, Zambézia, June 26, 2012.

[94] Interview with former Frelimo combatant (2012-05-04-Fm18), Namarrói, Zambézia, May 4, 2012.

[95] The group's activities focused on the road to Lugela since the main threat for the locality came from the Renamo base of Ererune in the Lugela district. See interview with Naparama combatants (2012-05-22-Gr-Nm3), Muémue, Namarrói, Zambézia, May 22, 2012.

[96] Interview with local government official (2012-06-26-Gm28), Márea, Namarrói, Zambézia, June 26, 2012.

The Naparama force in Muémue overpowered the military contingent, which was only one section of twelve men.[97]

Conflict and rivalry were also present between Naparama and Frelimo's administrative apparatus, for example in Muémue. Not long after the formation of the Naparama unit in Muémue, the then-head of the local administration told me that Makosso got into conflict with him because the Naparama commander sought to take control of the locality:

[Naparama] went to Lugela and successfully brought back some women who they captured over there and took them to me. I placed them into families who could provide them with food. So these people stayed and lived [with these families]. While they were living [with these families], the time came when the amnesty law was passed. With the amnesty law, [violence] decreased a little. So when the women saw that the situation had [improved], they wanted to return to Lugela. When these three women with their children were on their way to Lugela, militiamen captured them. They asked, "Where are you going?" – "We are returning home to Lugela." [The militiamen] sent [the women] back [to Muémue]. When they sent them back, they took them to the Naparama. At that time, I was at a meeting in the town. So Naparama started to investigate: "Where did you go?" – "We were returning home." Commander Makosso said, "You wanted to betray us, go and provide [Renamo] with information so that they could attack us." So instead of waiting to inform me, [Makosso] wanted to assassinate these people. [Naparama] had already distributed the children among them. So when I returned from the town and arrived at home, my secretary informed me that these women who had lived in the house of that person no longer lived.[98]

In the absence of the local administration head, Makosso assumed responsibility, ignored the stipulation of the new amnesty law, charged three women with treason and ordered their assassination. When the head of the locality learned that one of the women had survived and returned to Muémue, he sent a nurse for her and brought her clothes. This led the Naparama commander to threaten him:

So when this commander [Makosso] heard about this, he gathered his group to assassinate me, as I had ordered to rescue someone who was betraying him. So this group came, encircled my office, someone came and told me that a group was outside that wanted me to come outside and talk to them. I went outside. I started asking, "What is the problem?" – "Ah, you are a mujeeba because you ordered to rescue a person that we ordered to [kill]."[99]

---

[97] Many militias had left the militia forces to join Naparama, as some militia units had suffered severe losses during earlier Renamo attacks and had joined Naparama because they sought to benefit from better protection. See interview with Naparama combatant (2012-05-22-Gr-Nm3), Muémue, Namarrói, Zambézia, May 22, 2012.

[98] Interview with local government official (2012-06-26-Gm28), Márea, Namarrói, Zambézia, June 26, 2012.

[99] Interview with local government official (2012-06-26-Gm28), Márea, Namarrói, Zambézia, June 26, 2012.

Confronted with this threat, the head of the local administration called the police. The policemen took Makosso with his three men to the district town, where he was arrested and sent to Ile for imprisonment. After this event, Naparama stopped operating in Muémue. This story demonstrates the deep mistrust that existed between the army, the local government, and the Naparama militia, as the local government perceived the militia to rival and threaten Frelimo's control over the district and to help fight elite-level power struggles.

In sum, Naparama activity in Namarrói was erratic and riddled with challenges. Community residents remembered Naparama's activities as short-lived. Two factors prevented Naparama from sustainably diffusing to Namarrói. First, community residents were more impressed by the Frelimo military commander who had liberated the town than by the Naparama leader who did not get the opportunity to demonstrate his powers, so they perceived Naparama's impact on the improvement of security as limited. Second, elite rivalry prevented the militia's institutionalization and its integration into the local security apparatus. The army was relatively well organized and suspicious of Naparama, and the militia leadership entered into conflict with the army and the local administration. Instead of supplementing the army, Naparama sought to rival the army. Instead of expressing its full loyalty to Frelimo, the group sought to replace the Frelimo administration. Instead of remaining a people's movement, it evolved into a personal army of a single commander.

6.3.4 Alternative Explanations

Two alternative explanations for the observed differences of militia diffusion to the two districts in Zambézia province deserve consideration. First, the type of agent might matter for sustained diffusion. Naparama's leader, António, arrived in the Namarrói district on his own accord, and not as a consequence of the dislocation of local residents who brought him to Namarrói. This could have led to a lower level of community support for Naparama and thus to limited diffusion. However, the sustained diffusion of Naparama to Lugela was also not based on the residents' dislocation and demand of a Naparama force and yet militia diffusion was sustained.

A second alternative explanation is that Namarrói's residents may not have believed that cultural practices would aid them in their quest for security. Cultural (and ethnic) bonds were not strong enough to convince Namarrói's residents to include a traditional militia in its collective action repertoire. However, Namarrói is known for its people's spiritual powers, and during the war several traditional healers are said to have contributed to the protection of the town and its inhabitants.[100] In fact, some respondents attributed

---

[100] The name of the district is the name of a powerful régulo who had a wound – "Namarrói" means the one that is wounded – and the liquid from this wound was supposedly used as a medicine to protect his soldiers from violence. For a long time, the régulo resisted against the

Frelimo's success in retaking the town to the help of a traditional healer who had treated soldiers before their mission and advanced in front of them when recapturing the town.[101] Thus, cultural bonds were actually very strong, which was necessary for initial diffusion, but on their own they were not sufficient to enable sustained militia diffusion.

6.4 EXPLORING THE IMPLICATIONS: NAPARAMA DIFFUSION TO MECUBÚRI

If the argument outlined above holds, we should observe similar dynamics in the diffusion processes of the Naparama militia to other districts. I explore whether the arguments developed through the comparison of the two districts in Zambézia province hold in a different case in a different province, that of the diffusion of Naparama from Murrupula to Mecubúri district in Nampula province (see map in Figure 6.3). Naparama in Nampula evolved independently of Naparama in Zambézia province. One of António's confidants, Ambrósio Albino, formed his own militia in the Murrupula district, and Murrupula's traditional healer, Nampila, became an important Naparama leader. Mecubúri faced similar wartime challenges as the two districts discussed above in terms of its remoteness, proximity to Renamo's major bases, and levels of violence. The independent evolution of Naparama in Nampula and the similar wartime conditions thus make Mecubúri an excellent case to explore whether the arguments developed in the comparison of Lugela and Namarrói hold in a different context.

The conditions and mechanisms that account for the divergent trajectories of Naparama in the cases of Lugela and Namarrói districts lead to the following expectations for Mecubúri (see a summary of the argument in Table 6.1): (1) Ethnic and cultural bonds facilitate the spread of collective action repertoires through the mechanism of migration. Diffusion agents strengthen these bonds and community residents react positively to cultural tropes used by these agents; (2) successes in neighboring regions facilitate the diffusion of collective action repertoires through the mechanism of learning. The receiving community considers its security situation as sufficiently similar to that of neighboring communities and expects the community-initiated militia to have the same impact in their community; and (3) the integration

---

Portuguese seeking control over the area, reportedly until he was betrayed by his wife who was alleged to have revealed his secrets to the Portuguese in exchange for power in the local colonial administrative system. Today, Namarrói is also known for its cobra dance. Traditional healers prepare a vaccine that makes men immune to cobra bites and then these men catch a cobra in the forest and dance with it as entertainment at festivals and celebrations.

[101] Interview with former Frelimo combatant (2012-05-04-Fm18), Namarrói, Zambézia, May 4, 2012.

TABLE 6.1. *Overview of factors, mechanisms, and indicators explaining sustained diffusion*

Factor	Mechanism	Indicator
Ethnic and cultural bonds	Migration	Dislocation of diffusion agents and community residents' positive reaction to cultural tropes
Success of militia in neighboring regions	Learning	Community identifies with neighboring communities and considers its security situation as sufficiently similar to that of neighboring communities
Absence of elite rivalry	Trust	High level of cooperation and coordination between Naparama, the local administration, and the armed forces stationed in the district

of Naparama forces into the local security apparatus is facilitated by the absence of elite rivalry, which increases trust among local elites and the community. A high level of cooperation and coordination between Naparama, the local administration, and the armed forces stationed in the district exists.

The following sections first discuss the military situation in Mecubúri, which provide the context for the rise of the Naparama militia, and then analyze the conditions for sustained diffusion of Naparama to Mecubúri.

6.4.1 The Military Situation in Mecubúri

When Renamo entered Nampula province in May 1983, it advanced along the train line from Cuamba to Nampula, which crosses the south of the Mecubúri district. Mecubúri lies fifty miles to the east of the provincial capital Nampula. With major Renamo bases in Murrupula (Namilasse) to the south and Muecate (Namahia) to the north, Mecubúri became a transit area for Renamo units moving between these bases.

As in Lugela and Namarrói districts, Renamo attacks first focused on economically viable areas, the destruction of (state) infrastructure, the kidnapping of people, and the intimidation of party and state representatives. The war reached the district in June 1983, and the district town of Mecubúri in June 1986. Coming from Ribáuè district to the east, Renamo units attacked Tocolo twenty miles to the northwest of the district town in 1983, kidnapped several people, cut Frelimo officials' ears off, and pillaged people's belongings.[102] On June 24, 1983, Renamo units attacked the communal village of Nametil to the northeast of the district town, pillaged and burned houses, and told people to

---

[102] Interview with local government officials and religious leaders (2011-10-15-Gr-G/Pm), Mecubúri, Nampula, October 15, 2011.

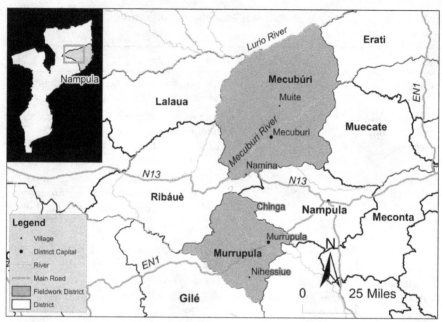

FIGURE 6.3. Map of Mecubúri and Murrupula in Nampula province.
Note: Cartography by Sofia Jorges

return to their ancestral lands.[103] On June 24, 1986, Renamo units coming from Murrupula district attacked the district town of Mecubúri for the first time, pillaging the warehouse and people's belongings.[104]

The district saw some of the worst violence between 1988 and 1990, shortly before Naparama emerged in the area. During this time, the district administrator was killed during an attack on the communal village, Mucheluia.[105] After the military battalion, which had been stationed in the district after Renamo's initial attacks in 1984, had left in July 1989, violence increased significantly.[106] Within a year, the number of displaced people in Mecubúri rose from 2,000 in 6 accommodation centers in December 1988 to almost

---

[103] Interview with former Frelimo combatant (2011-10-26-Fm6/N), Nahipa, Mecubúri, Nampula, October 26, 2011.

[104] Interview with traditional healer (2011-10-22-Hm2), Mecubúri, Nampula, October 22, 2011; Interview with local government officials and religious leaders (2011-10-15-Gr-G/Pm), Mecubúri, Nampula, October 15, 2011.

[105] It is unclear whether this happened in 1987 or 1988. Interview with former Frelimo combatant (2011-10-17-Fm2a), Mecubúri, Nampula, October 17, 2011; Interview with former Naparama combatant (2011-10-22-Nm27), Mecubúri, Nampula, October 22, 2011.

[106] República Popular de Moçambique, Província de Nampula, Distrito de Mecubúri, *Relatório annual – 1988*, December 30, 1988 (AGN, Nampula).

9,000 in 12 accommodation centers by the end of 1989.[107] Two more attacks on the district town occurred in 1989 and 1990.[108]

In its response to the violence, the local administration faced similar challenges to those in Lugela and Namarrói. When the war began, most of the population was settled in communal wards and villages, which allowed Frelimo to surveil the population. However, these wards and villages were also among the major targets of Renamo attacks to pillage relief goods.[109] Moreover, the district had an insufficient number of armed forces to counter the Renamo menace. Youths refused recruitment into compulsory military service by moving to Nampula city, mostly due to the military's problems with food and supplies for the armed forces.[110] After the military battalion stationed in the district had moved to Pemba in Cabo Delgado province, villages remained without any army contingent. Due to limited supplies, the few military forces present preferred working their plots to carrying arms, or even stealing food aid meant for the population.[111]

6.4.2 The Emergence of Naparama in Mecubúri

In the context of this difficult military situation, Naparama emerged in mid-1990, spreading from Murrupula district on the initiative of local residents.[112]

---

[107] República Popular de Moçambique, Província de Nampula, Distrito de Mecubúri, *Relatório annual – 1988*, December 30, 1988 (AGN, Nampula). A provincial government report from 1989 indicates that the number of inhabitants in Mecubúri was 118,887, of which about 80,000 people lived in communal villages; the population density was 16 inhabitants per square kilometer. See República Popular de Moçambique, Governo da Província de Nampula, Direcção Provincial de Apoio e Controlo, Departamento de Assistentes, *Levantamento do Distrito de Mecubúri*, referente a 1989, June 30, 1989 (AGN, Nampula).

[108] On February 17, 1989, well-armed Renamo combatants attacked Mecubúri town and killed 2 people, kidnapped 30, and burned over 110 houses. On March 25, 1990, about 600 Renamo combatants, divided into 5 groups, simultaneously attacked various neighborhoods of the town. They killed 8 people, kidnapped 115, and burnt almost 700 houses. Shortly thereafter, on May 17 and 19, 1990, Renamo attacked the administrative posts of Muite and Milhana. See República Popular de Moçambique, Governo da Província de Nampula, Direcção Provincial de Apoio e Controlo, Departamento de Assistentes, *Levantamento do Distrito de Mecubúri*, referente a 1989, June 30, 1989 (AGN, Nampula); República Popular de Moçambique, Província de Nampula, Distrito de Mecubúri, *Relatório*, March 28, 1990 (AGN, Nampula).

[109] República de Moçambique, Província de Nampula, Distrito de Mecubúri, *Relatório dos meses de Setembro, Outubro e Novembro/91*, December 5, 1991 (AGN, Nampula).

[110] República de Moçambique, Província de Nampula, Administração do Distrito de Mecubúri, *Relatório das actividades do mês Fevereiro/91*, February 28, 1991; República de Moçambique, Província de Nampula, Distrito de Mecubúri, *Relatório de Dezembro/90*, December 1990 (AGN, Nampula).

[111] República de Moçambique, Província de Nampula, Administração do Distrito de Mecubúri, *Relatório das actividades do mês Fevereiro/91*, February 28, 1991 (AGN, Nampula).

[112] Interview with local government official (2011-10-17-Gf1), Mecubúri, Nampula, October 17, 2011; Interview with local government officials and religious leaders (2011-10-15-Gr-G/Pm), Mecubúri, Nampula, October 15, 2011.

The militia was strong in Mecubúri, counting about 200 men in the district town alone.[113] Before Mecubúri residents traveled to Murrupula to meet the Naparama leader Nampila, António, who later became Zambézia's Naparama leader, had visited the district and initiated a few people. According to Mecubúri's residents, however, António's group did not curb the violence, and so António left the district shortly after his arrival.[114]

Naparama units formed in Mecubúri when residents of Nahipa, a village close to the district town, heard of Naparama's successes in Murrupula district. They decided to go and meet Nampila and bring him to Nahipa to form a militia unit. The young men who met the Naparama leader in Murrupula belonged to a community-initiated militia that was formed before Naparama's emergence. Youths in Nahipa sought to counter the activities of "criminals" who stole people's belongings. The group was called the grupo decidido (the committed group), and was presumably linked to the local office of the Mozambican intelligence service (Serviço Nacional de Segurança Popular, SNASP).[115] When the group heard about Naparama, they sent a small group to Murrupula to meet the traditional healer Nampila. Their main motivation was to benefit from the additional protection Naparama promised, as one of the first members narrated:

We heard that there was a traditional healer in Murrupula who vaccinates people and [these people] don't die from weapons. So we said we are the grupo decidido, but we die from weapons, so twelve of us left .... We went to Murrupula, looked for the traditional healer, met him and got vaccinated, returned to Nahipa, introduced ourselves [to the administration] and began to work. From then onward, we took five people from every village and vaccinated them. [Naparama's] center was Nahipa, and when the traditional healer came here from Murrupula, he stayed in Nahipa.

Thus, migration was the mechanism that led to the initial diffusion of Naparama between communities with strong cultural and ethnic bonds. People across Nampula province belong to the Makua-Lomwe linguistic group, and Naparama made use of many of the traditional rituals known to community residents.[116] Naparama's rituals resonated with Mecubúri residents, and the members of the grupo decidido initiated the spread of Naparama to their

---

[113] Interview with former Naparama combatant (2011-10-16-Nm26), Mecubúri, Nampula, October 16, 2011.

[114] Interviews with former Naparama combatants (2011-10-22-Nm27), Mecubúri, Nampula, October 22, 2012; (2011-10-26-Fm6/N), Nahipa, Mecubúri, Nampula, October 26, 2011. One respondent claimed that António later joined Renamo. See interview (2011-10-26-Nm29), Nahipa, Mecubúri, Nampula, October 26, 2011.

[115] República Popular de Moçambique, Província de Nampula, Distrito de Mecubúri, *Relatório mensal – Novembro de 1989*, November 30, 1989 (AGN, Nampula).

[116] For example, before going to battle, Naparama combatants had to perform a ceremony during which they sprinkled flour on the ground. This is a traditional ceremony by which the ancestors are worshipped (*makeya*).

district. In contrast to Lugela and Namarrói, however, the diffusion agents in Mecubúri were local residents in search of new ways to curb the violence, and not the provincial Naparama leaders in search of new members.

As in Lugela, Naparama spread to Mecubúri and across the district because the population learned of Naparama's success in other areas, became convinced that the situation in Mecubúri was sufficiently similar to that of other areas, and that Naparama could be the one to respond to it most effectively. At the time of the community residents' decision to become Naparama followers, Nahipa was a destroyed village and most of the population lived in the bush. When the initial twelve Naparama members returned from their trip to Murrupula, they successfully mobilized displaced people to return to the village, join the new militia, and defend the village.[117] Moreover, after Naparama forces from Nahipa had helped to retake the district town from Renamo occupation, the town's population sought to form its own Naparama force, as a former Naparama combatant from Mecubúri town explained:

At that time, Renamo had come and attacked the district town and the first Naparama combatants here expelled them. We [from Mecubúri] came to the conclusion that they did a good job. We asked these Naparama where they came from, they said they were from Nahipa. Then we decided to go there.[118]

It was only after the Naparama forces from Nahipa had demonstrated their strength that people from Mecubúri realized the value of the new force, as this former Naparama combatant's remarks show:

There was war here and we fled to Nahipa. When we arrived there, we met members of the Naparama militia. They [wanted to] mobilize us, but we didn't agree [to join] and returned here [to Mecubúri town]. Here we met a group of Naparama who had come and rescued the town, and its leaders mobilized us. Then we decided to return to Nahipa to get vaccinated. We came and stayed in the district town to defend [it] in case of any eventualities.[119]

Thus, after learning about the success of Naparama in Mecubúri town, youths joined Naparama on their own initiative.[120] A former Naparama combatant from Nahipa confirms this story:

One of the times [when Renamo attacked], Renamo stayed for one week in Mecubúri. The military force had fled. Reinforcements from Nampula came twice, but without success. So we, twelve men, left [Nahipa for Mecubúri], succeeded in recuperating [the

[117] Interview with former Naparama combatant (2011-10-16-Nm30), Nahipa, Mecubúri, Nampula, October 16, 2011.

[118] Interview with former Naparama combatant (2011-10-15-Nm23), Mecubúri, Nampula, October 15, 2011.

[119] Interview with former Naparama combatant (2011-10-16-Nm26), Mecubúri, Nampula, October 16, 2011.

[120] Interview with former Naparama combatant (2011-10-26-Nm30), Nahipa, Mecubúri, Nampula, October 26, 2011.

town]. So the population accepted and confided in us and followed us here [to Nahipa], they came to receive the vaccine.[121]

The mechanisms of migration and learning led to Naparama's initial diffusion because local residents reacted positively to the cultural tropes used by Naparama and became convinced that the community-initiated militia enhanced the security situation in their area.

6.4.3 Sustained Diffusion of Naparama to Mecubúri

Diffusion was sustained in Mecubúri when elite conflicts could be averted so that the Naparama militia was integrated into the local security apparatus. The militia cooperated closely with the local administration. The local administration not only tolerated, but even promoted the diffusion of Naparama forces across the district, as this former Naparama combatant explains:

What did the local government think of Naparama?

The government felt relieved, that is why it accepted the emergence of other groups. The secretary of [the administrative post] Muite came and requested that we go there and vaccinate the population. From then on, the group emerged in Muite. After here, Nahipa, people were vaccinated in the district town and in Muite.[122]

It was on the initiative of Muite's party secretary that Naparama spread to the village to the north of the district town. In Mecubúri town, a local government official confirmed that there had been a close relationship between the population and the local government in deciding to form a Naparama force:

Because of the fatigue with the burning of houses and random killing of people, when the traditional healer arrived, he contacted the local authorities and since these were tired ... – just imagine an administrator who never slept in his residence! [Naparama emerged] in agreement with the local government to resolve the problem – and we [the people] agreed that this was real because the enemy did not reach areas where Naparama units were [present]. As soon as they founded Naparama, the enemy no longer came here. When the youths went into battle, the enemy died and it was in battle that [Naparama] convinced the people and the local government [to support Naparama].[123]

Traditional leaders and local party secretaries actively mobilized youths to join Naparama, even forcing some to be initiated into the group, as this former Naparama combatant testified:

---

[121] Interview with former Naparama combatant (2011-10-26-Nm30), Nahipa, Mecubúri, Nampula, October 26, 2011.

[122] Interview with former Naparama combatant (2011-10-26-Nm29), Nahipa, Mecubúri, Nampula, October 26, 2011.

[123] Interview with local government official (2011-10-17-Gf1), Mecubúri, Nampula, October 17, 2011.

You mentioned that some youths were forced to receive the vaccine – by whom?

By the leaders, because Naparama worked together with them and the secretaries. There was a meeting, where some volunteered [to receive the vaccine], and since their number was small, they had to force some other youths.[124]

Although there was initial mistrust, elite conflicts did not arise. The reasons for this seem slightly different in Mecubúri than in Lugela. Instead of evolving as equal to the Frelimo armed forces, the Naparama militia simply overpowered the army contingent stationed in Mecubúri and came to replace them with the army's approval. As a former Frelimo combatant stated, Naparama dismissed collaboration with the army contingent, but the army did not challenge Naparama:

Did Naparama coordinate with the armed forces stationed in the district?

No, they did not because Naparama said to the armed forces that they did not do anything. ... They went to battle jointly, but in some cases, Naparama did not accept [joint operations]. Even I told them that I was a soldier and could do anything [to support them], but they refused, saying "You won't succeed." ... [The armed forces] wanted to give [Naparama] [advice on] tactics in case the enemy came, but they didn't want it.[125]

The Naparama militia did not want to collaborate with the armed forces, claiming that the soldiers would die in battle.[126] A former Naparama combatant explained that from Naparama's perspective, militia tactics were incompatible with those of the armed forces. He accused the military of being afraid of Naparama, which is why they did not cooperate:

[The armed forces] were afraid to go with us [into battle]. The manner in which we fought was different. The armed forces fought from a distance and Naparama always wanted to catch the men, this is what made the armed forces afraid [of us].[127]

---

[124] Interview with former Naparama combatant (2011-10-16-Nm-24), Mecubúri, Nampula, October 16, 2011. See also Interview with former Naparama combatant (2011-10-15-Nm22), Mecubúri, Nampula, October 15, 2011. Although some people were forced to join Naparama, most joined voluntarily. A local government report from March 1992 stated that "the majority of schools in the district did not comply with the goals of the 4th and 5th class, due to the fact that many students submit to the organization of Naparama, in particular in the administrative posts of Muite and Milhana." See República de Moçambique, Província de Nampula, Distrito de Mecubúri, *Relatório referente ao mês de Fevereiro de 1992*, March 3, 1992 (AGN, Nampula).

[125] Interview with former Frelimo combatant (2011-10-24-Fm4), Mecubúri, Nampula, October 24, 2011.

[126] Interviews with former Naparama combatants (2011-10-26-Nm29), Nahipa, Mecubúri, Nampula, October 26, 2011, and (2011-10-16-Nm30), Nahipa, Mecubúri, Nampula, October 16, 2011.

[127] Interview with former Naparama combatant (2011-10-16-Nm24), Mecubúri, Nampula, October 16, 2011.

There was some mistrust between Naparama's and Frelimo's armed forces, but mutual mistrust did not undermine the basis of cooperation or provoke lasting conflict. Several respondents confirmed that Naparama militiamen received weapons from the armed forces – in particular those who had been members of the state-initiated popular militias before receiving the Parama vaccine and were trained in using a rifle. Those Naparama combatants with weapons went on missions while the armed forces stayed behind.[128] Rather than rivaling the army, the Naparama militia came to replace the military forces with the latter's approval, as this former Naparama combatant explained:

One time, [Renamo combatants] came from Lalaua and passed by Metuba, and we went to meet them. We confronted each other and we recuperated a mortar. When we went to present it to the army headquarters, [the army] decided to provide all of us with weapons and the troops suspended going to battle. Until the war ended.[129]

In sum, in the case of Mecubúri district, the mechanisms of migration and learning operated in a similar way as they did in Lugela and (in a limited manner) in Namarrói districts. However, the initiative for Naparama's formation in Mecubúri came from the local population instead of the provincial Naparama leaders. This created a basis for strong popular support for the new Naparama force, which in turn translated into a slightly different model of sustained diffusion of Naparama in Mecubúri. Instead of being integrated into the local security apparatus and acting in parallel with local armed forces, Naparama replaced the existing local security apparatus. The few armed forces stationed in the district ceased all their operations when it became clear that Naparama was stronger than the armed forces could ever be.

6.5 CONCLUSION

What explains the differences in the diffusion of Naparama to two adjacent districts, Lugela and Namarrói, in Zambézia province? The two districts faced a similar set of challenges in terms of rebel presence, occupation, and violence, but they followed different trajectories regarding the mobilization of community-initiated militias. Incorporating mechanisms of diffusion and the conditions under which they operate into existing theoretical frameworks helps us to understand this variation.

As discussed in Chapter 5, Naparama spread across communities because of its innovative character, providing a competitive supplement and even an alternative to prevailing local security arrangements at the time. Naparama spread to Lugela and Namarrói because diffusion agents arrived in the district

---

[128] Interviews with former Naparama combatants (2011-10-15-Nm23) and (2011-10-15-Nm22), Mecubúri, Nampula, October 15, 2011.

[129] Interview with former Naparama combatant (2011-10-22-Nm27), Mecubúri, Nampula, October 22, 2011.

and the population learned about Naparama's success in neighboring communities. Naparama was able to become a lasting force in Lugela because its integration into the local security apparatus was not hampered by elite conflicts. A highly regarded community leader took on the role of Naparama leader and was able to mobilize loyal members. Moreover, Naparama enjoyed the trust of the local administration and acted in close coordination with the armed forces. In the adjacent district of Namarrói, people did not perceive their situation as sufficiently similar to that of neighboring communities, so they did not consider Naparama an important force to improve their security situation. The militia also suffered from weak leadership that was unable to overcome the army's suspicions and, in fact, sundered relations with the military and administrative elite altogether.

The case of Mecubúri in Nampula province helps to develop these arguments further. The main difference between sustained diffusion in Mecubúri and Lugela was that in Mecubúri, elite conflicts did not arise because Naparama replaced the weak armed forces with their approval. In Namarrói, the armed forces were strong, and thus they did not allow for a forceful and potentially rival Naparama militia to evolve. The only – limited – chance of survival for Naparama in Namarrói was to evolve into a private army that represented a third party to the conflict and threatened Frelimo hegemony in government-controlled areas.

In sum, even when a "trigger" moment occurs and newly invented collective action repertoires spread from one community to the other, the community's elite constellation influences whether the new militia is maintained. Whether a community-initiated militia is institutionalized does not say much, however, about how the militia can attract more members. The armed organization's growth once it is diffused from one region to another is the subject of Chapter 7.

7

The Power of a Vaccine

The Process of Community-Initiated Militia Formation

In March 1992, the local Mecubúri district government in Nampula province stated in their monthly report that education targets could not be met because students preferred joining Naparama to going to school: "The majority of schools in the district did not comply with the goals for the fourth and fifth grade due to the fact that many students enlisted in the organization of Naparama."[1] As in other districts, the newly formed community-initiated militia units attracted a large number of followers, even a couple of years after their initial formation in the Mecubúri district in 1990.

By contrast, state-initiated militias had difficulty mobilizing militia members and suffered from a high desertion rate, as the local administration of Namarrói stated in a report from 1989:

The key problem has always been the disorganization [of the popular militia] due to the lack of a capable and efficient command, linked to the problem of the lack of weapons; [militia members] often desert and abandon [the militia], for various reasons.[2]

How can the differences between these militias' appeal be explained? How does the mobilization process of community-initiated militias differ from that of the mobilization for state-initiated militias?

While Chapter 6 analyzed the group-level process of how armed organizations and repertoires of violent collective action spread, this chapter focuses on the links between group characteristics and the individual-level process of

---

[1] The fourth and fifth grades correspond to the age group of youths between ten and fourteen years of age. República de Moçambique, Província de Nampula, Distrito de Mecubúri, *Relatório referente ao mês de Fevereiro de 1992*, March 3, 1992 (AGN, Nampula).
[2] República Popular de Moçambique, Província da Zambézia, Administração do Distrito de Namarrói, *Informação do Governo Distrital sobre as actividades realizados referentes aos meses de Janeiro a Setembro 1989*, October 2, 1989 (AGZ, Quelimane).

joining a militia. Once a community adopts a new form of violent collective action and a new institution is established, how does the institution grow and attract new followers?

The conditions and mechanisms of *initial* diffusion identified in Chapter 6 point to the importance of mobilization's social context. Communities learned that forming militias would help protect them from insurgent violence because they considered their situation sufficiently similar to that of a neighboring community. This implies that the security context and the social context of the two communities were similar; forming militias resonated with the receiving community. I further draw on the significance of the social context in this chapter to explore the process of militia mobilization.

I suggest one causal path of militia mobilization: the militia's innovative use of social conventions that invoke collective meaning with community residents, which increases participants' sense of agency and shapes their willingness to join the militia.[3] Naparama's reinterpretation of preexisting rites and rituals – the initiation with a bullet-proof vaccine – gave ordinary men (and women) the power to engage Renamo combatants and prevail over them.[4] The alleged power of the vaccine convinced many to join the newly formed militia, as a former Naparama combatant from Nicoadala declared: "[I joined] because of the suffering, [because] I wanted the war to be over. I heard that [when people were vaccinated], they were not hit by bullets, that's why I joined."[5]

I compare Naparama's mobilization success to the less effective mobilization of state-initiated popular militias (milícias populares), using interview and archival evidence from the Nicoadala district in Zambézia province (see map in Figure 7.1), one of the main districts of Naparama activity. To explore these mechanisms further in a different context, I use interview and archival evidence from Murrupula district in Nampula province, one of the main districts of Naparama activity in the province north to Zambézia (see map in Figure 6.3). In both cases, I focus on the mobilization of combatants, not on the mobilization of collaborators, from among the local population.[6]

This chapter proceeds as follows. I first lay out the empirical puzzle of militia mobilization during Mozambique's civil war and provide some historical

---

[3] As I explain Chapter 6, learning did not lead to sustained diffusion in the Namarrói district because the institutional context – elite conflicts – prevented the militia from being integrated into the local security apparatus. This chapter focuses on the mobilization processes once this institutionalization of the militia is complete.

[4] Interview with local government representative (2011-09-23-Gm4), Nicoadala, Zambézia, September 23, 2011.

[5] Interview with former Naparama combatant (2011-09-14-Nm10), Nicoadala, Zambézia, September 14, 2011.

[6] I exclude the mobilization of collaborators from this analysis, as the processes of mobilizing combatants and collaborators are different. Many civilians provided Naparama with food, but only those with "courage" joined the Naparama militias as combatants. Thus, there are different thresholds for joining as a collaborator or as a combatant.

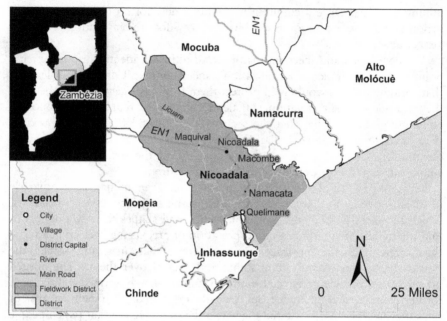

FIGURE 7.1. Map of Nicoadala in Zambézia province
Note: Cartography by Sofia Jorges

background to the war's dynamics in Zambézia and Nampula provinces. I then review the theory of militia mobilization that I introduced in Chapter 2, which frames my analysis of the militia mobilization process. In the second section, I evaluate the different mechanisms by tracing the mobilization process of the community-initiated militia and comparing it to the less successful mobilization process of the state-initiated militia in the Nicoadala district. The final section inquires whether these mechanisms operated in the Murrupula district of Nampula province to explore whether the argument holds in a different context.

7.1 THE PUZZLE OF STATE-INITIATED VERSUS COMMUNITY-INITIATED MILITIA MOBILIZATION

Pro-government militias were not an uncommon sight in wartime Mozambique. Beginning in the early 1980s, Frelimo relied on state-initiated militias as a counterinsurgency instrument for maintaining territorial control and pursuing state-building during the unfolding war with Renamo.[7] Popular militias (milícias populares) – initially created as political forces in communal villages

---

[7] "Mozambique: Frelimo Draws the Battleline," *Africa (London)* (116), 1981, 38. For more detailed historical context of how state-initiated militias were formed, see Chapter 4.

and state companies – were no longer linked to the local party hierarchy but to the military headquarters and received military training. In addition, Frelimo formed territorial defense forces (forças de defesa territorial) in 1985, which received rudimentary military training to defend the rural areas in the districts.[8] Provincial military headquarters trained militias as first defenders of villages, state farms, companies, and towns.[9] Over 400 Tanzanian soldiers assisted with the training of the militias, and Portugal provided weapons and uniforms.[10] An estimated 50 percent of the population of Zambézia had received military training by 1986.[11]

The delegation of military tasks to state-initiated militias backfired in many areas. Uncontrolled distribution of weapons contributed to insecurity on roads and in rural areas.[12] People often complained about the state-initiated militias for being "dangerous, drunken, undisciplined thieves" (Finnegan 1992, 211). In the northern provinces, the local administration sent militias to force people into communal villages (Alexander 1997, 7).[13] In Zambézia province, militiamen were involved in assaults on buses and stole from the local population.[14] Moreover, militia members proved disloyal, as the rebels were able to recruit them as combatants and spies (Alexander 1997, 4).[15] Local administrations, therefore, faced major challenges in mobilizing and retaining militia members.

As a response to the worsening security situation in the late 1980s, the Naparama militia formed as a result of a community initiative. The militia gained in a short amount of time a large number of followers and successfully drove Renamo out of its strongholds in Zambézia and Nampula provinces (see Chapter 5). What explains the large-scale grassroots mobilization for community-initiated militias in the late 1980s, as compared to earlier failed state attempts? This puzzle is especially striking given the apparent lack of firearms and other resources for the grassroots movement.

---

[8] It is unclear what the exact difference is between the popular militias and the territorial defense forces; in many districts, the popular militia appeared to be part of the territorial defense forces.

[9] On state-initiated militias in government-controlled areas in Gorongosa, see Igreja (2007, 132).

[10] "A 'Worst-Case' Security Scenario for Mozambique," *Africa Now* (32), 1983, 86–88.

[11] Gil Lauriciano, "Resistência popular cresce na Zambézia. Dez mil pessoas armadas com zagaias," *Notícias*, November 22, 1986. In areas that were affected by the war in the late 1970s, such as Manica province, Frelimo had already created militias and provided district administrators with weapons (Alexander 1997, 4).

[12] "Distribuição de armas não foi bem controlada reconhece Ministro do Interior," *Notícias*, May 28, 1991.

[13] República Popular de Moçambique, Província da Zambézia, Gabinete do Administrador do Distrito de Morrumbala, *Relatório Informativo*, December 11, 1981 (AGZ, Quelimane).

[14] Interview with local government representative (2011-09-28-Gm5), Nicoadala, Zambézia, September 28, 2011; Interview with civilian (2011-09-14-f1), Nicoadala, Zambézia, September 14, 2011.

[15] Interview with community leader (2011-09-23-Lm1), Nicoadala, Zambézia, September 23, 2011.

State-led militia mobilization is not necessarily doomed to fail, as the sustained mobilization of the civil patrols during Guatemala's civil war and of the self-defense committees (rondas campesinas) in southern Peru show (Stoll 1993; Remijnse 2002; Starn 1995; Degregori 1999). Such state-initiated militias can bring about a "self-reinforcing logic," restoring agency among villagers that previously suffered from insurgent and state violence (Starn 1995, 568). Why was the community-initiated Naparama militia able to instill agency and attract new members where the Mozambican state-initiated militias were unable to do so?

7.1.1 The Experience of Wartime Uncertainty

As outlined in Chapter 2, I start from the premise that the benefits and risks of participating in militia organizations are difficult to calculate and project. In such unstable and uncertain environments as civil wars, individuals oftentimes base their decisions on whether to join armed organizations on other means than rational calculation. They draw on familiar knowledge and institutions from their community that may, if not overcome, then at least stabilize such uncertainty.

To establish the context of uncertainty in Mozambique, it helps to look at how civilians experienced and made sense of the war, as described to me in interviews. All of the armed groups involved in the war targeted civilians due to the "identification problem" in irregular civil wars, which made it difficult to distinguish supporters from collaborators (Kalyvas 2006). In northern Mozambique, the "pattern of violence" (Gutiérrez-Sanín and Wood 2017) of armed organizations was therefore characterized by repertoires of kidnappings, killings, and rape, and selective, collective, and indiscriminate targeting of civilians.

A central theme in my interviews was the notion of "luck": being spared from violence and emphasizing violence's arbitrary nature. Indiscriminate violence mostly occurred in contested zones where few people remained, but through which people traveled (see Kalyvas 2006). When civilians encountered combatants in these zones, they were likely to experience violence whether the combatants were from Frelimo or Renamo, as a pastor in Nicoadala explained: "I'm not going to say that those who killed are those who did not kill. All killed. They killed side by side. Men suffered."[16] According to the pastor, civilians had difficulty convincing combatants that they were loyal: when traveling somewhere, "it was a matter of luck whether you arrived – arrive and you were safe. But on the way – [there was] killing just killing ...".[17]

---

[16] Interview with religious leader (2011-09-06-Pm1), Nicoadala, Zambézia, September 6, 2011.
[17] Interview with religious leader (2011-09-06-Pm1), Nicoadala, Zambézia, September 6, 2011.

In less contested, enemy-controlled zones, civilians were usually targeted either selectively, based on their position within the enemy's organization, or collectively, based on the fact that they lived in enemy-controlled areas.[18] When combatants entered an enemy-controlled zone, they targeted leaders and enemy collaborators based on their association with the rebels:

When Frelimo entered an area controlled by Renamo, they kidnapped half [of the population] and there were also some [people whom] they killed – those conniving, those who had some relationship [with Renamo]. They even asked the people who the leader was in that area.[19]

However, due to the fact that combatants often did not wear uniforms, it was difficult to identify those who were fighting or collaborating with the enemy, and so often all people living under the enemy's control were *collectively* targeted:

Did Frelimo also kill regular people who weren't Renamo combatants?

If you lived in a Renamo-controlled area, [Frelimo] said that you as well belonged to Renamo; as much as Renamo did the same in Frelimo-controlled areas. This was war. When you are in war, you are there to kill.[20]

Most often, little selective targeting occurred, and civilians were targeted just by their location, in particular when they had moved between places and were suspected of being spies:

There was a problem during the war. When Renamo arrived in the [Frelimo-controlled] town and met someone who had fled from the area under their control and they recognized him, they killed him. When Frelimo arrived here [in the Renamo-controlled area], they killed as well, saying that we fed [Renamo].[21]

In line with this perception that violence was omnipresent and arbitrary, community residents felt that among those targeted were often innocent civilians.[22] In addition, it was uncertain whether alleged enemy collaborators would be killed as combatants could decide to kidnap them instead:

Even here [in Frelimo-controlled areas] there were some that had the attitude to kill, others did not; the same was true for over there [with Renamo], [when] they came and

---

[18] On the concept of collective targeting, see Steele (2017). Gutiérrez-Sanín and Wood (2017) refer to the same concept as "identity-based targeting."

[19] Interview with former Frelimo combatant (2011-09-13-Fm1), Nicoadala, Zambézia, September 13, 2011.

[20] Interview with former Frelimo combatant (2011-09-13-Fm1), Nicoadala, Zambézia, September 13, 2011.

[21] Interview with civilian (2011-11-24-m18), Namilasse, Murrupula, Nampula, November 24, 2011.

[22] Interview with community leader (2011-09-23-Lm3), Nicoadala, Zambézia, September 23, 2011.

took us [with them], some killed, while others said we can't kill, we will take them with us.[23]

Many respondents stated that whether they would be spared from being killed was thus arbitrary:

Renamo did not behave badly toward all the people they met, it was a matter of luck for each of us! [When] Frelimo came for rescue, they also mistreated people, it was a matter of luck for each of us![24]

[Renamo] killed us, it was a matter of luck.[25]

It was just war. You needed to be lucky to stay alive.[26]

Pointing to war as a state of exception – "war is war" – and staying alive as a "matter of luck," respondents found it difficult to predict whether they would be alive tomorrow.[27] There was little that they could do to make sure they survived. Even joining Renamo, the military, or the state-initiated militia did not seem to provide assurance that one would be spared, as this former Renamo combatant pointed out: "Where we met each other, we fought; some were wounded, [some] killed and others were saved. It was war."[28] The combatant did not indicate anything that could have explained who was wounded, killed, or saved.

Interviewees recognized that the type of war they had experienced – a guerrilla war "between brothers" whose root causes were difficult to understand – did not leave much room for predictability. In contrast to the anticolonial war between the Portuguese and the Frelimo liberation movement, the reasons for the war were impossible to understand, and the enemy difficult to recognize:

So we thought the following: We already received our country [from the Portuguese] and [among] those that are fighting among Blacks, we can't recognize the enemy as the uniforms are the same, and the weapons are the same. If they had been white, we would have understood that they were the enemy.[29]

Respondents perceived the particular type of war – the guerrilla war – as one in which anyone could be potentially affected by violence. Violence therefore seemed somewhat limitless, as this former local government official explained:

---

[23] Interview with community leader (2011-09-23-Lm3), Nicoadala, Zambézia, September 23, 2011.

[24] Interview with local government representative (2011-10-03-Gm6), Nicoadala, Zambézia, October 3, 2011.

[25] Interview with civilian (2011-11-28-f12), Chinga, Murrupula, Nampula, November 28, 2011.

[26] Interview with civilian (2011-11-28-m22), Chinga, Murrupula, Nampula, November 28, 2011.

[27] Interview with civilian (2011-11-28-m22), Chinga, Murrupula, Nampula, November 28, 2011.

[28] Interview with former Renamo combatant (2011-11-25-Rm9), Murrupula, Nampula, November 25, 2011.

[29] Interview with civilian (2011-09-14-f1), Nicoadala, Zambézia, September 14, 2011.

"In whatever guerrilla war, there is not much control. Only in wars between regular armies, there is control."[30]

My conversations with civilians, community representatives, and combatants thus affirm the importance of uncertainty during the civil war in Mozambique. Especially after the initial years of the war when Renamo switched from selective to collective and indiscriminate violence, the war's context provided few hints about who would be spared from violence. Joining an armed group – whether a rebel or government force, or a state-initiated or a community-initiated militia – was not an obvious choice with measurably less risk of experiencing violence.

7.1.2 Explaining Militia Mobilization

The Naparama militia helped manage the uncertainty of war by relying on preexisting social conventions. I suggest two main mechanisms through which social conventions facilitate militia mobilization: First, *commonality*, whereby the militia represented an innovative institutionalization of common, preexisting social conventions, and second, a *context for self-empowerment*, which instilled a belief in agency and enabled the large-scale mobilization of members. Table 7.1 provides a schematic of the argument's key components and the indicators relevant for analyzing the empirical material.[31]

In addition to these proposed mechanisms from my theory on militia mobilization, I also explore alternatives in this chapter. While classic approaches to mobilization do not directly respond to decision-making under

TABLE 7.1. *Overview of factors, mechanisms, and indicators explaining militia mobilization*

Factor	Mechanisms	Indicators

Social conventions	Commonality	Militia resonates with communities:
		    Credible expertise of leaders
		    Salient purpose
		Militia provides innovation:
		    Reinterprets and adapts social conventions

	Context for self-empowerment	Belief in agency/claim of ownership: Identification with militia Hope and sense of purpose: Expression of pride; expectation of success

[30] Interview with local government representative (2011-11-10-Gm13), Nampula, November 10, 2011.
[31] Chapter 2 outlines this theory in more detail.

uncertainty, they can still serve as a template for alternative explanations. The main alternative explanation is to receive (reliable) information that allows people to make projections about future trajectories of being a civilian versus being a militia member.

First of all, people may directly or indirectly experience members of the militia being spared from violence, thereby updating their expectations by *learning*. If learning was sufficient to explain mobilization success, we should see interviewees linking their decision to join militias exclusively to having experienced that militia members are spared from violence and being sure that this information is correct.

Second, the state might provide resources and institutional support to militias to enlist them in their counterinsurgency efforts, which could make a militia more attractive to joiners. These mechanisms would be *resource allocation* and *political opportunity* (McAdam 1982). If such support was sufficient to explain mobilization success, we should see evidence of the local government and military providing resources such as weapons, food, and transport to militias and a willingness to cooperate with militias in the form of information exchange. Individual recruits would report that they joined to receive a salary or other material benefits.

A third option would be that there is little risk calculation because people are desperate to change something in their lives. The security situation may deteriorate in such a way that *discontent* becomes salient, which motivates participation in new armed groups (Gurr 1970; Paige 1975; Scott 1976). If discontent was sufficient to explain mobilization success, we should see people referring exclusively to their hardship when speaking about their motivation to join the militias.

When tracing the mobilization process of the Naparama militia and comparing it to that of the popular militias, I evaluate each of the mobilization mechanisms – those I propose and the alternatives – and the validity of the causal chain to explain why the Naparama militia was more successful than the state-initiated popular militia in mobilizing.

7.2 EXPLAINING NAPARAMA MOBILIZATION IN NICOADALA, ZAMBÉZIA PROVINCE

7.2.1 The War in Nicoadala

Using evidence from Nicoadala district in Zambézia province – which was one of the main districts of Naparama activity and also its headquarters for most of the time that Naparama was active – I develop and evaluate the different mechanisms to explain how Naparama mobilized (see map in Figure 7.1).

The war came to Nicoadala in central Mozambique for the first time in early August 1984 during Renamo's second offensive in Zambézia province.

Renamo attacked the outer boroughs of the district town close to the railway line that connects Quelimane to Zambézia's second-largest city, Mocuba. Renamo combatants looted people's belongings and abducted people, mostly to carry goods back to their base in Mabadane, in the border area between Mocuba and Namacurra districts to the northwest of Nicoadala (Lemia 2001, 36).[32] Nicoadala's district capital lies at the crossroads of the main Highway Number 1, and the road to the coastal provincial capital Quelimane. Nicoadala served as a buffer zone for the advancing rebels that sought to occupy the provincial capital, and convoys on roads around the town were targets of constant ambushes.[33]

A second wave of attacks reached Nicoadala in 1986. Renamo pillaged and destroyed stores, the main administrative building, and the hospital. In late 1988 and early 1989, Nicoadala experienced a few confrontations between Renamo and Frelimo, and Renamo advanced up to ten kilometers from Quelimane. However, Renamo never occupied the district town.[34] Direct confrontations remained limited. Small groups of Renamo combatants often attacked the town in the early mornings when most of the population and military were hiding in surrounding areas.[35] By the late 1980s, many displaced people had settled in the district capital in government-organized displacement camps (centros de acomodação).[36] These villages were frequent targets for Renamo attacks; in particular, right after people had received relief goods.[37]

---

[32] Before July 25, 1986, Nicoadala was part of the Namacurra district.

[33] Interview with local government representative (2011-10-03-Gm6), Duguduia, Nicoadala, Zambézia, October 3, 2011.

[34] Interview with former Naparama combatant (2011-09-09-Nm1), Nicoadala, Zambézia, September 9, 2011.

[35] Interview with local government representative (2012-02-25-Gm16), Quelimane, Zambézia, February 25, 2012.

[36] The population called these settlements *aldeias* (villages), since in their structure and organization they resembled communal villages, which Frelimo had attempted to construct right after independence to introduce socialist forms of production in the countryside. Frelimo's villagization policy met lots of resistance in Zambézia. By 1982, only 2 percent of the population in Zambézia lived in communal villages (Legrand 1993, 90). During the war, the local administration registered all newly arrived displaced people and then allocated land to them to build a hut in a displacement camp in which other people with the same origin had settled. The displacement camp then received the name of the village from where most of its residents originated.

[37] Interviews with local government representatives (2011-09-15-Gm1), Nicoadala, Zambézia, September 15, 2011; and (2011-09-28-Gm5), Nicoadala, Zambézia, September 28, 2011. The displaced population put a heavy burden on the local residents and conflicts arose. After several neighborhoods had experienced the first assaults, Nicoadala's residents accused those coming from war-affected areas to have brought the war to the district capital. The residents also complained that they did not receive any relief goods like the displaced population did. See interview with former Naparama combatant (2011-09-22-Nm15), Nicoadala, Zambézia, September 22, 2011.

Although Frelimo military units were stationed in Nicoadala's district capital, their response to Renamo attacks was ineffective, as this former Naparama combatant reported:

The suffering that people experienced – Frelimo could not cope [with it]. Renamo came at night, hammering against front doors [so that] people came out and they [could] arrest them, take them with them and collect all their belongings. This meant that the population did not live at ease. Every morning [we] talked about the number of people kidnapped during the night.[38]

Community members told stories of soldiers failing to pursue Renamo combatants to their base and fleeing rather than defending the town as they were too few to succeed.[39] The army units stationed in Nicoadala usually retreated to wait for reinforcement from Quelimane.[40] In 1988, the Russian-trained Red Berets (Boina Vermelha) Special Forces and Tanzanian soldiers were stationed in the district to prevent Renamo from attacking Quelimane. One of Renamo's targets was the water facility in the Licuar locality, which Frelimo protected by enlisting *antigos combatentes*, former combatants from the liberation struggle, who had settled in the area.[41] However, these forces only improved the situation in or close to the district capital; rural areas continued to be targets for frequent attacks.[42]

The state-initiated popular militias were not an effective counterinsurgency force either. They were organized as early as 1980 by a subunit of the provincial unit of the national army's chief of staff, with the relevant unit reporting that it had trained 3,000 militias across Zambézia province by February 1980.[43] The popular militias were recruited locally and their task was primarily defensive. They were organized similarly to the army in sections, platoons, companies, and battalions, patrolled their communities at night, and informed the population of any imminent threat.[44] Popular militias had limited access to weapons, which meant shooting them primarily to warn the population in case

[38] Interview with former Naparama combatant (2011-09-19-Nm12), Nicoadala, Zambézia, September 19, 2011.
[39] Interviews with former Frelimo combatant and civilian (2011-09-13-Fm1), Nicoadala, Zambézia, September 13, 2011; (2011-09-14-fi), Nicoadala, Zambézia, September 14, 2011.
[40] Interview with community leader (2011-09-29-Lf2), Nicoadala, Zambézia, September 29, 2011.
[41] Interview with religious leader (2011-09-06-Pm1), Nicoadala, Zambézia, September 6, 2011.
[42] Interview with community leader (2011-09-23-Lm3a), Nicoadala, Zambézia, September 23, 2011.
[43] República Popular de Moçambique, Ministério da Defesa Nacional, Comando do 1º Batalhão de Infantaria Zambézia, Comissariado Político das Forças Populares de Libertação de Moçambique, Secção de Milícias Populares, *Relatório*, February 18, 1980 (AGZ, Quelimane).
[44] República Popular de Moçambique, Ministério da Defesa Nacional, Comando do 1º Batalhão da 7º Brigada Infantaria da Zambézia/Mocuba, Estado Maior do 1º Batalhão da Zambézia/Mocuba, Secção de Milícias Populares. *Nota N.º 083/MM/80, Assunto: Pedido de Viatura*, May 14, 1980 (AGZ, Quelimane); Interview with local government representative (2011-09-15-Gm1), Nicoadala, Zambézia, September 15, 2011.

of an assault.[45] Militias only received a salary if they were employed by a company to protect factory sites; none of the others received any pay and the population was expected to support them with food.[46] In 1987, there were attempts to professionalize the militias through increased military training and political education.[47]

The state-initiated militias had a bad reputation among some respondents, and they could not mobilize enough community residents. Several respondents claimed that militias did not have a specific task during the war as they were either absent or fled.[48] It was unclear how joining the militia would or could help manage residents' uncertainty: joining could just as easily increase the chances that they would suffer violence as if they were to remain civilians. The popular militias were part of Frelimo's restructuring of society after independence that served to politically educate and control the population through its involvement in mass organizations and the eradication of anything "traditional" (Frelimo 1978). However, communities in Zambézia, historically a region of resistance (Isaacman and Isaacman 1976), successfully refused to move into communal villages and were suspicious of efforts to strengthen the state's reach into rural areas (Chichava 2007). Across Mozambique, militia desertion rates were high, the government had to resort to forced recruitment, and the population often complained about militias mistreating the people they were supposed to protect (Finnegan 1992; Alexander 1997). Many militiamen joined Naparama when they had the chance to do so.[49]

The state-initiated militia could not mobilize and retain enough community residents, as the militia did not resonate with local communities and did not provide an opportunity for self-empowerment. Community residents did not identify with the militiamen and their limited ability to confront Renamo did not provide the agency that community residents required to address the difficult situation they found themselves in. As I will show in the following section, these two mechanisms, commonality and the context for self-empowerment, operated in the social mobilization of Naparama.

[45] Interview with former Frelimo combatant (2011-09-13-Fm1), Nicoadala, Zambézia, September 13, 2011.
[46] Interview with community leader (2011-09-23-Lm1), Nicoadala, Zambézia, September 23, 2011.
[47] República Popular de Moçambique, Província de Zambézia, Direcção Provincial de Apoio e Controlo, *Relatório*, September 12, 1987 (AGZ, Quelimane).
[48] Interviews with civilian (2011-09-14-f1), Nicoadala, Zambézia, September 14, 2011; community leader (2011-09-23-Lm3), Nicoadala, Zambézia, September 23, 2011; and government representative (2011-09-28, Gm5), Nicoadala, Zambézia, September 28, 2011.
[49] Interview with former Naparama combatant (2011-11-05-Nm43), Nicoadala, Zambézia, November 5, 2011; Interview with community leader (2011-09-21-Lm2), Nicoadala, Zambézia, September 21, 2011.

7.2.2 Mobilizing Naparama in Nicoadala

The difficult conditions in Nicoadala in 1988–89 led residents to welcome the relief Naparama promised. The displaced community invited Naparama leader António to Nicoadala after hearing stories about his activities in other regions. The local government had no knowledge of this initiative and tried to prevent Naparama from mobilizing in Nicoadala. However, when the administration saw the groups' benefit – the "recuperation" of weapons and population from Renamo-held territories – they tolerated Naparama's activities.[50]

Commonality. In its mobilization process, the Naparama leadership made references to (traditional) religion, which resonated with local communities and attracted followers. As discussed earlier, António claimed that he had received a mission from God to liberate the Mozambican people from war by use of a bulletproof medicine (Nordstrom 1997, 58).[51] Traditional medicine for personal defense has historical roots in Mozambique, in particular in the region where Naparama formed, the area of the Makua-Lomwe linguistic group (Do Rosário 2009, 327; Dos Santos Peixe 1960; Isaacman and Isaacman 1983).[52] Protective measures featured during the liberation struggle and the civil war (Wilson 1992; Wiegink 2020). But the reference to Christian symbols also resonated in a society in which Catholicism was strong.[53] The reference to well-known conventions thus was salient within communities.

In addition, the leader's expertise provided the necessary credibility for resonance to occur. Whenever António introduced himself to the people and the local administration, he did so by first demonstrating his powers. When he first arrived in Nicoadala, he asked local leaders to call all the town residents together for a meeting:[54]

[António] dug a ditch, it seemed as if he wanted to bury a person. Dug, and put a mat on the ground. He entered, closed [the ditch], ... and then spoke from underneath the

---

[50] Interview with former Naparama combatant (2011-09-19-Nm13), Nicoadala, Zambézia, September 19, 2011.

[51] Rachel Waterhouse, "Antonio's Triumph of the Spirits," *Africa South (Harare)* (May), 1991, 14.

[52] See Do Rosário (2009, 327) on a medicine against the danger of lions; see also interview with a civilian, (2012-05-03-m25), Namarrói, Zambézia, May 3, 2012, who told me about a medicine against cobra bites; see Dos Santos Peixe (1960) on a potion historically used during war. Scholars also point to the use of such a medicine during the Barue rebellion against the Portuguese in 1917 (Isaacman and Isaacman 1976).

[53] António often mixed Christian and Muslim with African traditions. See Rachel Waterhouse, "Antonio's Triumph of the Spirits," *Africa South (Harare)* (May), 1991, 14–15. Aside from the story of his resurrection, the reenactment of the resurrection, and claiming to have received the mission to liberate the Mozambican people from Jesus Christ, António often prayed from a bible during his ceremonies (Interview [2012-03-12-Jm3], Quelimane, Zambézia, March 12, 2012).

[54] António repeated this ceremony in places where he was unknown and whenever journalists or researchers visited him. See interview with journalist (2012-03-12-Jm3), Quelimane, Zambézia, March 12, 2012.

ground and we heard [him]. . . . Then he woke up, went to the fire with clothes [that melt when they burn], and started to take firewood and [touched] his arms until the fire was extinguished. And he didn't burn himself.[55]

This demonstration of invincibility was crucial for people to believe that António could mobilize the necessary resources to save them from violence, and served as a major motivation to join.[56] António's power over life and death created confidence in the new movement: "We were left with admiration. There existed a person in the world who treated people so that they wouldn't die? But this [must be] God [himself]!"[57]

Individual protective medicine was common during the war, but Naparama's *innovation* was to provide an organizational framework for the use of such medicine, thereby turning it into a collective practice.[58] Every new member had to go through an initiation ritual that took place as follows:

Thirty youths were taken to be treated. [António] vaccinated us with razor blades. [He] cut our bodies with razor blades and put the medicine [into the wound]. Others he rubbed the whole body [with the medicine]. After all this, we were put to a test, [he] took sharpened machetes and attempted to cut [us], but because of the medicine, the machetes did not hurt us. He took a rifle and shot in our direction and nothing happened with us. And then we were told the rules that we had to respect. We paid five meticais for a small ceremony.[59]

Protective measures during war usually focused on personal protection. Spirit mediums, traditional healers, or traditional chiefs could be accessed on an individual basis and they often limited access to those in power such as chiefs or commanders of higher rank (see Wilson 1992, 544). Access to spiritual power was an expression of social differentiation, emphasizing the elite individual more than the group. For the state army, the popular militias, and the rebels, the use of protective measures was therefore not a means to mobilize people to join their forces; Renamo, as well as the state army in the late 1980s, mostly relied on forced recruitment (Vines 1991; Weinstein 2007; Schafer 2007, 78–79).

---

[55] Interview with former Naparama combatant (2011-09-12-Nm6), Nicoadala, Zambézia, September 12, 2011.

[56] Interview with former Naparama combatant (2011-09-14-Nm8), Nicoadala, Zambézia, September 14, 2011.

[57] Interview with former Naparama combatant (2011-09-09-Nm4), Nicoadala, Zambézia, September 9, 2011.

[58] Naparama was organized similarly to military forces into sections, platoons, companies, and battalions; group interview with former Naparama commanders (2011-08-23-Gr-Nm1), Nicoadala, Zambézia, August 23, 2011. The initiation rituals also had a socialization effect to teach members about norms of behavior within the group, but I focus here on the *mobilizational* effect of the initiation (Cohen 2016, 21).

[59] Interview with former Naparama combatant (2011-09-09-Nm2), Nicoadala, Zambézia, September 9, 2011.

To ensure the effect of Naparama's medicine, each member had to follow a strict code of conduct that concerned his or her behavior in the household, within the family, and on the battlefield. On the battlefield, Naparama combatants were

not allowed to look back, only look ahead; no one was allowed to be in front of the other; no fighting in the shade, always in the sun; if the enemy was in the shade, we were not allowed to be in the shade as well; . . . we could not retreat when we heard shots, we had to go there where they [Renamo] were.[60]

These rules demonstrate how the militia adapted social conventions to the new social context. By continuously advancing, often while singing, and not turning back, Naparama created such fear among Renamo combatants that direct confrontations between the two forces were often averted. Renamo combatants left their bases as soon as they heard Naparama approaching. If a Naparama combatant violated any of these rules, he or she forfeited the protection of the medicine: "when someone shot, the bullet chased you until it hit you."[61] All deaths among Naparama combatants were explained by reference to violations of these rules.

At first glance, inoculation against violence might be interpreted simply as reducing individuals' risk of injury or death in battle when joining the militia. But it was more than that: it tapped into shared beliefs and built institutions to make the militia effective in battle, effectiveness which in turn reinforced those beliefs and generated a context for self-empowerment.

Context for Self-Empowerment. The promise of relief from the suffering turned Naparama into a movement that reclaimed civilians' agency over a war that had reduced them to spectators. Respondents frequently claimed ownership over the movement:

It was a movement that emerged from within the population, it just emerged like this, they fought with spears and supported Frelimo in their fight against Renamo. It was the population that fought against Renamo in order to capture Renamo bandits.[62]

The people idealized Naparama as their prime solution to constant flight and damage to family and property, and the passivity that these experiences created. Interviewees frequently repeated that they had been "tired of war" and had needed to do something about it:

It was the people revolting, the people were tired of war, so they preferred to volunteer, encounter those that made war and neutralize [Renamo].[63]

---

[60] Interview with former Naparama combatant (2011-09-09-Nm2), Nicoadala, Zambézia, September 9, 2011.

[61] Interview with former Naparama combatant (2011-09-09-Nm2), Nicoadala, Zambézia, September 9, 2011.

[62] Interview with civilian (2011-09-09-m2), Nicoadala, Zambézia, September 9, 2011.

[63] Interview with former local government representative (2011-09-15-Gm1), Nicoadala, Zambézia, September 15, 2011.

What did Manuel [António] say to the people to encourage them to receive the vaccine?
Nothing, they just volunteered because they were tired of war. Each one's courage is
what incentivized them to go. An example: If you didn't get to eat for one or two days,
wouldn't you search for something to eat?[64]

When the war began, we always had to flee to the bush. My alternative was to join
Naparama to defend myself and my family.[65]

We were tired of all the suffering, and since we saw that the Naparama combatants did
not flee, I decided to be vaccinated to protect myself and my family.[66]

Naparama thus provided the tools to strive toward greater autonomy and
empower the people to confront those that made war. The vaccine offered the
necessary courage for self-defense instead of flight. Most members thus joined
voluntarily.[67]
Naparama nurtured people's belief in agency by responding to two important hardships. The militia provided the opportunity for people to reclaim their
farmland and the ability to provide for themselves,[68] and to bring back family
members abducted by Renamo. People no longer had to rely on the absent and
inefficient state armed forces:

I was in my house, one time [Renamo] came during the night and abducted my sister and
my brother and took all of my documents. It was during the night, it was raining, no one
noticed anything, and so they were kidnapped and [Renamo] left. We did not have any
way to defend ourselves, we were simple people. Everyone was just suffering. The
moment when this man [António] appeared, I volunteered in order to search for my
family. ... That's what led me to be a Naparama.[69]

Those most exposed to Renamo violence sought to overcome their passivity
the most. In Nicoadala, many of the Naparama members came from displacement camps that had formed in several neighborhoods of the district capital.[70]
It was in these camps – that people referred to as "villages" – where many
Naparama combatants in the Nicoadala district were mobilized:

---

[64] Interview with former Naparama combatant (2011-09-30-Nm20), Nicoadala, Zambézia,
September 30, 2011.
[65] Interview with former Naparama combatant (2011-09-28-Nm17), Nicoadala, Zambézia,
September 28, 2011.
[66] Interview with former government representative (2011-09-23-Gm4), Nicoadala, Zambézia,
September 23, 2011.
[67] Interview with former Naparama combatant (2011-09-28-Nm17), Nicoadala, Zambézia,
September 28, 2011.
[68] Interview with community leader (2011-09-23, Lm3a), Nicoadala, September 23, 2011.
[69] Interview with former Naparama combatant (2011-09-12-Nm6), Nicoadala, Zambézia,
September 12, 2011.
[70] Rachel Waterhouse, "Antonio's Triumph of the Spirits," *Africa South (Harare)* (May), 1991,
14–15; Interviews with former Naparama combatants (2011-09-09-Nm1), Nicoadala,
Zambézia, September 9, 2011; and (2011-09-22-Nm15), Nicoadala, Zambézia, September
22, 2011.

Where did Manuel António mobilize people for the Naparama?

That was in the village. Because many displaced people lived in the village – people tired of the war. So when [António] Naparama came and said "I am bringing [the Parama medicine]," all these people that were there in the village and suffered accepted [António's offer], and the [Naparama] commando was set up in the village.[71]

Thus, the most vulnerable population, which lived in simple huts, had limited access to food, and was often in conflict with the local population over scarce resources, was the most attracted to the Naparama militia.[72]

Community residents therefore became the main agents and beneficiaries of the new movement, which led them to identify with the Naparama. The movement was independent of any existing political, religious, or traditional organizations (Wilson 1992, 563).[73] This openness along with António's attention to the plea for agency by the people made community residents believe that there was no difference between Naparama and the people. When asked for their views on Naparama, respondents repeatedly emphasized that Naparama and the people were the same – "Naparama *was* the population. Because they were the sons of the people."[74]

In addition to the claim of ownership and belief in agency, the hope that Naparama generated was crucial for the context of self-empowerment. Naparama's arrival nourished people's hope to be reunited with abducted family members:

There were seventeen people in my house, all of them were abducted. . . . I recuperated my mother and three children, I lost the remaining [family members]. [The wish to be reunited with my family] is what gave me determination and courage to join [Naparama] to recuperate the people.[75]

When I thought about everything that had happened with my mother [who was shot by Renamo combatants], I gained the courage to agree to join Naparama.[76]

---

[71] Interview with former Naparama combatant (2011-09-09-Nm1), Nicoadala, Zambézia, September 9, 2011.

[72] Interview with former government representative (2011-10-03-Gm6), Nicoadala, Zambézia, October 3, 2011; Interview with former Naparama combatant (2011-09-22-Nm15), Nicoadala, Zambézia, September 22, 2011.

[73] It is important to note that António did not refer to any historical roots of the medicine or his powers himself. This fact increased the impression that people had of him of being "one of them." It also demonstrates that Naparama was not simply reproducing certain traditional spiritual practices, but innovating in the sense of using various social conventions to create something new, which served to mobilize the population in a much more effective way.

[74] Interview with religious leader (2011-09-06-Pm1), Nicoadala, Zambézia, September 6, 2011.

[75] Interview with former Naparama combatant (2011-09-09-Nm4), Nicoadala, Zambézia, September 9, 2011. See also Interview with former Naparama combatant (2011-09-09-Nm2), Nicoadala, Zambézia, September 9, 2011.

[76] Interview with former Naparama combatant (2011-09-09-Nm2), Nicoadala, Zambézia, September 9, 2011.

Naparama combatants expressed pride in fulfilling this dream by bringing back their families from areas under Renamo control:

My family had been abducted by Renamo, so I thought about becoming a Naparama to try and recuperate my family. ... After receiving the vaccine, I proceeded to go to the bush and recuperate my brothers and my mother.[77]

This courage created "a sense of purpose despite the surrounding violence and chaos" (Beal 2006, 235). Community residents were proud that they were able to capture Renamo combatants without any military training and equipment:

It was normal for a peasant to engage the enemy because he was vaccinated. There were even peasants who captured [Renamo combatants] in their fields and took their weapons because they prevailed over the enemy.[78]

In sum, the resonantly familiar and innovative militia institution provided people with the necessary courage to manage uncertainty, defend themselves and confront Renamo, hoping to end a war that had reduced them to passive victims.

Alternative explanations. The fact that Naparama combatants frequently pointed to the protective force of the vaccine as a motivation for joining could be understood as learning. Potential members could update their information and make a rational calculation that joining would protect them from violence. While such information influenced people's sense of purpose and expectation of success of the militia, there is little evidence that learning alone led recruits to manage the uncertain environment and to decide to join for guaranteed personal protection. The explanation of why people joined was always linked to the fact that members had to have the courage to go through the initiation ritual and confront the enemy in the bush; their fear of being killed did not completely subside with joining:

They came with a vaccinated person. They had their magic and invited those who showed courage to come and he treated the courageous person, and then they went and did their work and returned.[79]

In fact, those who decided not to join emphasized their fear. As a response to my question whether he joined the Naparama, a community resident replied: "No, because I was afraid to kill."[80]

---

[77] Interview with former Naparama combatant (2011-09-28-Nf1), Nicoadala, Zambézia, September 28, 2011.

[78] Interview with local government representative (2011-09-23-Gm4), Nicoadala, Zambézia, September 23, 2011.

[79] Interview with local government representative (2011-09-15-Gm1), Nicoadala, Zambézia, September 15, 2011.

[80] Interview with civilian (2011-10-02-m5), Nicoadala, Zambézia, October 2, 2011. I collected similar evidence from other areas of Naparama activity in Nampula, where interviewees pointed out that those who did not join did not have the necessary courage.

As to the mechanism of discontent, there had been plenty of previous opportunities for community residents to get involved in local self-defense through the state-initiated militias, opportunities that many did not avail themselves of. In addition, many members of the popular militia subsequently joined Naparama to improve their chances of survival in battle. So, it is clear that discontent alone did not motivate people to join.

The allocation of resources and new political opportunities and state support for Naparama also do not sufficiently explain the success of mobilization. The local government was skeptical of Naparama, as the self-proclaimed Marxist-Leninist ideology of the Frelimo party had led to abandoning traditional authorities and all forms of religion. Local governments allowed António to hold a meeting to present his case to the people, but they did not provide the militia with any resources, institutional capacity, or information sharing. Confronted with the hesitant attitude of the local government, António did not ask for any support other than people for his troops.[81] In fact, the district administrator in Nicoadala at the time refused to allow Naparama to operate; as the administrator spent his nights in Quelimane, however, his substitute signed the necessary papers to allow Naparama to recruit members.[82] Much later, António received material support such as transport, but this did not seem to have influenced members to join.[83] None of the respondents mentioned that they received a salary or individual material benefit as Naparama members. In fact, they complained that they had never been paid for their services even after the war had ended and mobilized to receive demobilization benefits.

In sum, evidence from Nicoadala supports the argument that social conventions, through the commonality and the context for self-empowerment that they provided, were integral to mobilization, and weakens the case for alternative explanations. While learning, opportunities, and discontent may have played a role in mobilization processes, they were not sufficient to bring about large-scale mobilization. By providing a template based on social conventions and turning it into an innovative institution, Naparama provided community residents with the agency they thought they had lost.

7.3 EXPLORING NAPARAMA MOBILIZATION IN MURRUPULA, NAMPULA PROVINCE

To establish whether the argument applies more broadly, I explore whether the same causal path can explain Naparama mobilization in Murrupula district in Nampula province. Murrupula had similar relevance for Naparama, as the

---

[81] Interview with former Naparama combatant (2011-09-09-Nm4), Nicoadala, Zambézia, September 9, 2011.
[82] Interview with former Naparama combatant (2011-09-19-Nm13), Nicoadala, Zambézia, September 19, 2011.
[83] Interview with local government representative (2011-09-15, Gm1), Nicoadala, Zambézia, September 15, 2011.

militia's provincial headquarters were located close to Murrupula's district town. Nampula's Naparama evolved independently of the militia in Zambézia (see Chapter 5). The district's strategic situation was similar to the one in Nicoadala. The national highway crosses the district (see map in Figure 6.3) and, as in Nicoadala, Renamo frequently targeted Frelimo military convoys for ambushes. The district is, therefore, a suitable comparative case to analyze whether the mechanisms present in the Nicoadala case also explain community-initiated militia mobilization in Murrupula.

7.3.1 The War in Murrupula

Shortly after Renamo had reached Nampula province in April 1983 (see Chapter 4), Murrupula experienced its first attacks on the outer wards of the district town, communal villages, and traffic on the main Highway number 1. While attacks remained scattered during the first years of the war in Murrupula, the district experienced an increased level of insecurity starting in 1986. Travel from Murrupula to Nampula city was only possible in military columns, and the trip of about fifty miles could take up to three days.[84]

Murrupula was home to an important Renamo base at Namilasse, in the Chinga administrative post, to the west of the main highway (see map in Figure 6.3). Combatants frequently transported goods from Namilasse to a base in Mogovolas to the east of Murrupula, attacking cars and trucks between the district town Murrupula and the Kazuzo village when crossing the main highway. Although Frelimo armed forces captured the Namilasse base in 1989, and Renamo moved the military commando to Muecate district further north, the district remained a target of frequent attacks.

Similar to the situation in Nicoadala, community residents of Murrupula were frustrated with how the military responded to the frequent attacks by Renamo. When the district administration called for military support from Nampula city, it came late and the soldiers left promptly after responding to an attack. On their way out of the district, soldiers pillaged the local population's belongings, which, from this former Naparama combatant's perspective, resembled Renamo's behavior:

> [Naparama] were not part of the government, but we emerged due to the suffering. When the war came here, [Renamo] took all our property, because we had fled. The military arrived late, after the enemy had already left. So we decided to defend ourselves. The military came here and didn't do anything; while leaving, they took our livestock instead of protecting us.[85]

Thus, the people were open to alternative means of self-defense.

---

[84] Interview with former Frelimo combatant (2011-11-25-Fm12), Nampaua, Murrupula, Nampula, November 25, 2011.

[85] Interview with former Naparama commander (2011-11-03-Nm32), Mothi, Murrupula, Zambézia, November 3, 2011.

7.3.2 Mobilizing Naparama in Murrupula

As outlined in Chapter 5, similarly to what happened in Zambézia, Naparama spread across Nampula province because diffusion agents traveled and made Naparama known to people, and communities proved receptive to new means to end the suffering imposed on them by the war. In Nampula province, it was António's acquaintance from Ribáuè, Ambrósio Albino, who formed the first Naparama unit in Murrupula. He was living in Nampula city working as a traditional healer when Gregório Nampila, the son of the local leader and traditional healer Nampila of Mothi, a village five miles of the district town of Murrupula, met him in the city in 1989.[86] In his narrative, Gregório Nampila depicts how Naparama formed in Murrupula as an unanticipated by-product of searching for a cure for his father's illness:

I went to Nampula [city], and when I arrived, I met a traditional healer who was practicing divination. My father here [in Mothi] was sick, and so I decided to [ask for] divination as well. After the divination, I said to the traditional healer, "I could not bring you my father, it's complicated, let's go together [to Mothi]," and the healer accepted and we came here.

When we arrived here, I told my father that I had brought a traditional healer because I saw him falling ill. He accepted and said he would call his brother. That's when they started to practice divination. The traditional healer said that he had another medicine that would prevent the war from coming here. My father said okay, my brother, son and I are here, so you can prepare the medicine. Ambrósio taught me and my father [how to prepare the medicine], and from then on we started to work.

People from other areas began to hear that the bandits did not reach the area of Nampila, and they started asking us [for the medicine]. We said that if they wanted the medicine, they had to talk to the party in their areas – secretaries and régulos – and bring a document, and we would take the document to the administration so that they would know about it.[87]

Proving their power against the rebels, the Naparama militia quickly attracted recruits. Local Naparama leaders claimed that on the day that they mobilized the first youths to join the militia, Renamo attacked, and Naparama combatants pursued them and recuperated a weapon, thereby demonstrating their effectiveness.[88] After this first day of Naparama activity, the Naparama

---

[86] I took the date of the meeting between Gregório Nampila and Ambrósio Albino from the report about the formation of Naparama in Murrupula written by the provincial Frelimo party committee. Partido Frelimo, Comité Provincial, Departamento de Trabalho Ideológico, Nampula, *Relatório do levantamento e estudo efectuado sobre o fenómeno "Napharama" no distrito de Murrupula*, November 15, 1990 (personal archive of Ambrósio Albino).

[87] Interview with Naparama commander (2011-11-03-Nm32), Mothi, Murrupula, Nampula, November 3, 2011.

[88] Some respondents claimed that Ambrósio had called the Renamo soldiers to be able to show the effectiveness of the vaccine. Interview with Naparama commander (2011-11-03-Nm32), Mothi, Murrupula, Nampula, November 3, 2011.

leaders did not only recruit residents from Murrupula, but also from neighboring districts.

Commonality. The militia quickly formed in Murrupula, as the social conventions on which it built resonated with the community. Before Naparama formed, Mothi's residents had used other means to defend themselves against attacks by Renamo's local police, the mujeeba. For example, traditional healers sprinkled a certain powder in a circle around the village for protection.[89] Several residents, including Nampila's wife, claimed that Nampila already had a medicine, to which he added Ambrósio's to make it more powerful.[90] Thus, the use of a medicine and rituals to protect the village from Renamo attacks were a well-established practice. The idea of introducing another medicine that would be able to ward off Renamo was salient – congruent with people's real-life experiences – and resonated with the community.

Without the credibility of the Naparama leaders, however, members would not have been sufficiently convinced to join the militia. The traditional healer from Nampula, Ambrósio Albino, had to prove that his medicine would have the desired effect. People believed in the power of his vaccine when Albino was able to heal Nampila's illness. After demonstrating newly initiated Naparama combatants were able to defeat Renamo combatants, more community residents volunteered to become Naparama combatants.[91] As Albino and Nampila worked closely together – Nampila being a well-respected community leader – Naparama's power to mobilize new members built on both leaders' credibility.

While Naparama's use of social conventions resonated with the community, it also mobilized members by innovating and adapting preexisting rites and rituals to new contexts. The previously used types of medicine were different from Parama in the sense that they protected individuals or the entire village. The Parama medicine, in contrast, created a collective armed force that could patrol, pursue, and even confront Renamo combatants in the event of an attack.

In sum, in the Murrupula case, the same mechanism of commonality as in the Nicoadala case was at work to convince community residents to join the new militia.

[89] According to residents, a traditional healer from Ligonha close to Zambézia province, Razak, had come to Mothi to lay a medicine around the limits of the village, so that mujeeba would not be able to enter the village. See interview with local government representative (2011-11-04-Gm10), Mothi, Murrupula, Nampula, November 4, 2011. Other respondents attribute this method to the traditional healer Nampila.

[90] See, for instance, interview with former Naparama combatant (2011-11-05-Nm38), Mothi, Murrupula, Nampula, November 5, 2011. See also interview with community leader (2012-06-27-Lm21), Murrupula, Nampula, June 27, 2012, who claimed that Ambrósio's and Nampila's medicine complemented each other.

[91] Interview with former Naparama combatant (2011-11-05-Nm39), Mothi, Murrupula, Nampula, November 5, 2011; Interview with civilian (2011-11-06-m11), Mothi, Murrupula, Nampula, November 6, 2011.

Empowerment. Given the powerlessness of the local administration when faced with Renamo's rising threat, community residents were increasingly convinced that they had to organize themselves without the help of the government to protect themselves. This belief was strengthened when the provincial government actively called on the people to rely on community strategies of self-defense. Several respondents remembered an instance in which the armed forces' political commissar and Frelimo political bureau member Major General António da Silva Nihia came to Murrupula and encouraged the people to defend themselves, as told by this religious leader in Murrupula:

General Nihia came when the war was intense to talk to the population and ask them to help the government. From then on Naparama started. [The general] did not know about the existence of this group, but he knew that there was a medicine that would prevent people from being hit by bullets.[92]

A commander from Nampula came and asked us why there was so much war here. The people responded, "You deploy men, but when they come back from a mission, they return to Nampula [city]." The people said they wanted to move to the city together with the commander, because they were tired. [The commander] asked them to prepare themselves with traditional weapons to confront [the enemy] rather than fleeing to Nampula. When the general left, the population came together and searched for a medicine. The medicine's creator was Nampila .... He started vaccinating people and the war started to decrease.[93]

As the religious leader's testimony demonstrates, community residents understood the general's call to use "any means at their disposal"[94] to refer to traditional practices of defense.

As in the Nicoadala case, Naparama formed as a people's movement on the initiative of community residents, without the knowledge of the local administration. Community residents said they "were tired" of fleeing; thus, they no longer wanted to be passive victims of war. The following quotes from former Naparama combatants show how people wanted to turn their passivity into active resistance:

[Naparama] were volunteers; the population was tired [of the war].[95]

Why did you become a Naparama? I was tired of fleeing, suffering, [and] sleeping outside [my house].[96]

---

[92] Interview with religious leader (2011-11-02-Pm3), Murrupula, Nampula, November 2, 2011.
[93] Interview with religious leader (2011-11-02-Pm4), Murrupula, Nampula, November 2, 2011.
[94] This is how the report about the investigation into Naparama in Murrupula describes the administration's appeal to self-defense: Partido Frelimo, Comité Provincial, Departamento de Trabalho Ideológico, Nampula, *Relatório do levantamento e estudo efectuado sobre o fenómeno "Napharama" no distrito de Murrupula*, November 15, 1990 (personal archive of Ambrósio Albino).
[95] Interview with religious leader (2011-11-02-Pm4), Murrupula, Nampula, November 2, 2011.
[96] Interview with former Naparama combatant (2011-11-03-Nm33), Murrupula, Nampula, November 3, 2011.

Why did you become a Naparama? It was because of the suffering and the necessity to defend oneself, and we family members were called to receive the vaccine.[97]

I became a Naparama in order to help the elderly who were suffering, didn't sleep in their houses, [and] lost their belongings.[98]

Bandits came at night. This led me to join Naparama. Bandits came and captured families, some of them had to go with them, others they killed. And then [I said to myself] why flee? I will join [Naparama]. This war is the worst. My brother in law had already been captured. I and my group went to receive the vaccine and started to work.[99]

How did Ambrósio mobilize people to receive the vaccine? It was the will of the people because they were tired. During that time, it was normal [that when Renamo] fired [shots], we fled without eating dinner to the bush. It was the strength of the people, they offered themselves to fight. [They were] tired.[100]

As a form of violent resistance, Naparama in Murrupula thus emphasized their independence from the government and claimed ownership of the new movement. They were not interested in collaborating with the armed forces, as these had a negative image among the population. In fact, criticizing the behavior of the military and the state-initiated militia, the community welcomed the different attitude of Naparama:

The people liked [Naparama] because the military sometimes retreated; it didn't succeed. When there were only militiamen, they just fired shots from afar, but Naparama, when they heard [something] in Namiope, they came to help and when [Renamo] attacked the district town, all of them went [there].[101]

Word traveled fast that Naparama offered a sense of purpose and an expectation of success, and thus an opportunity for self-empowerment. Those Naparama combatants who came from other villages to receive the vaccine in Mothi expected that forming a Naparama militia in their village would bring long-sought peace:

We heard from other people that the war did not reach [the area of] Nampila, [as] there was a medicine that people received as a vaccine, [and so] people on their own went to receive the vaccine.[102]

---

[97] Interview with former Naparama combatant (2011-11-04-Nm36), Murrupula, Nampula, November 4, 2011.

[98] Interview with former Naparama combatant (2011-11-04-Nm37), Murrupula, Nampula, November 4, 2011.

[99] Interview with former Naparama combatant (2011-11-05-Nm38), Murrupula, Nampula, November 5, 2011.

[100] Interview with community leader (2012-06-27-Lm21), Murrupula, Nampula, June 27, 2012.

[101] Interview with community leader (2012-06-27, Lm21), Murrupula, Nampula, June 27, 2012.

[102] Interview with former Naparama combatant (2011-11-05-Nm39), Mothi, Murrupula, Nampula, November 5, 2011.

Alternative Explanations. Similarly to the situation in Nicoadala, the district administration provided little if any support to Naparama. In fact, the district administration was very skeptical of Naparama when it first heard about the new movement and started an investigation:[103]

When the district [administration] took notice [of Naparama], the administrator Massina who replaced Avila Wahua sent the information to Nampula to the provincial party committee of Frelimo. [The committee members] were afraid when they heard that there was a group that could not be hit by bullets, so they sent the information to Maputo. [Maputo] responded and asked [the provincial party committee of] Nampula to come here to understand what was happening.

[The delegation] wanted to know whether we wanted to take over the country or what kind of treatment [we were hoping for] when the war ended. They met us and we told them that we were the people, we were tired and we were not trained, but we were losing many of our belongings and that is why we prepared ourselves so that we could go and search for these belongings in the bush. We wrote this down, but the commission that came didn't believe us and asked that one of us would accompany them to meet the provincial governor, Amórico Mfumo. Ambrósio and my secretary went.

When they arrived in Nampula, they told the governor that we were defending our area, our belongings, and family members who had been killed. They asked us if we wanted to be paid, but we said that we were not sent [by the government], we had our medicines just to defend ourselves.

The government report about the visit of the delegation confirms the hesitance of the local administration and military to engage with Naparama. In fact, one of the fact-finding mission's delegates told me that the military was ashamed that Naparama were more successful than them.[104] Other than some limited information exchange and the return of population and weapons to the local government and military, there was no other form of support or collaboration between Naparama and the local government. Similarly to the case of Nicoadala, learning and discontent also did not play a significant role in the mobilization of Naparama in Murrupula.

In sum, Naparama offered community residents in Murrupula who were targeted by Renamo combatants or the mujeeba a familiar, but innovative form of organized violent resistance, which promised to provide the people with an opportunity for self-empowerment. One of the major differences between the mobilization of Naparama in Murrupula and Nicoadala was that community residents in Mothi, in the first village where Naparama formed, were mainly

---

[103] This is interesting in light of the appeals to self-defense by the provincial military commander cited earlier. Even if respondents remembered that the general appealed to traditional forms of defense, it is unlikely that the Frelimo government and military had a traditional force that was independent of the local party structure in mind.

[104] Interview with provincial government representative (2011-10-10-Gm7), Nampula, October 10, 2011.

concerned about looting and future, more violent attacks. Their aim was to shield the village from any future attacks. In Nicoadala, community residents also sought to protect their houses and their belongings, but in addition, the large number of displaced people also saw Naparama as a tool to bring back their abducted family members from Renamo-held areas.

7.4 CONCLUSION

To understand the militia mobilization process in Mozambique, the context of an uncertain environment makes more sense than the context of traditional approaches to collective action that emphasize calculable risk. Comparing the mobilization processes of the Naparama militia with that of the state-initiated militias during the war in Mozambique in the Nicoadala district in Zambézia province, I argue that the former mobilized more successfully because Naparama created commonality by both appealing to and innovating upon social conventions and providing the context for collective empowerment. A similar causal path applies to militia mobilization in Murrupula. The reference to social conventions in Mozambique – a bullet-proof vaccine and Christian symbols – resonated with community residents and gave ordinary men and women the power to engage rebel combatants. The belief in the power of the vaccine provided people with the necessary hope and sense of purpose. Community residents did not identify with the state-initiated militia influenced by Frelimo's socialist ideology, and its limited ability to confront Renamo did not provide the agency that community residents required to address the difficult situation they found themselves in. Naparama helped to manage the uncertainty that people were confronted with in their daily lives.

8

Conclusion

Violence and Civilian Agency in Civil Wars

"It was *Naparama* who ended the war," an elder told me in a village in northern Mozambique.[1] For the peasants who experienced the war in the rural areas of Zambézia and Nampula provinces, the community-initiated militia provided much-needed relief. Residents I spoke with perceived Naparama as being crucial to pacify and return their villages to some level of order and stability. As a community resident in Nicoadala stated, "[w]hen [Manuel António] Naparama came, he said that no one will ever [have to] flee again from their home. And indeed, we were able to sleep in our homes."[2] Not all claimed that the end of the war was due to Naparama, but many granted the militia an important role in reducing violence.

The case of Mozambique shows how important militias are for civilian self-protection and the dynamics of war. But the Naparama militia is not unique. Stories of spontaneous and more organized community initiatives to arm residents and protect communities come up in many civil wars. Scholars and policy makers alike have acknowledged that militias can upend the military balance and impact the dynamics of war and their aftermath and they have studied the causes and consequences of militia formation. Due to the use of different concepts and approaches, however, the field of militia studies has become fragmented and a unified body of research is yet to form.

In this book, I begin to define a research agenda on militias. The book brings conceptual clarity to the phenomenon of militias and explains when, where, and how communities form militias to defend themselves against violence. The book makes two important distinctions: first, between grassroots initiatives (*community-initiated militias*) and militias that are formed by state agents

---

[1] Interview with male civilian (2011-10-26-m10), Nahipa, Mecubúri, Nampula, October 26, 2011.
[2] Interview with civilian (2011-09-14-f1), Nicoadala, Zambézia, September 14, 2011.

(*state-initiated militias*); and second, between militias that exercise their tasks part-time, and those that are committed full-time to their work as militias. The militia's access to resources such as weapons and training and its level of professionalism has consequences for the type of operations that militias perform and the violence they perpetrate. The focus of this book lies on militias that are formed by communities and initially only complete their tasks during the day or night but otherwise go about their regular activities (community-initiated part-time forces). These are militias with few resources and little professional training. Parts of the book compare these militias to part-time state-initiated militias, which have the advantage of state resources.

The book analyzes how militias form from three perspectives and develops arguments for when, where, and how communities include such forms of self-protection in their repertoire of collective action. Community-initiated militias form when community residents' lives are in danger and local military stalemates provide windows of opportunity for militia formation. This strategic situation shapes community incentives to form militias rather than flee or rely on the state military to protect them from insurgent violence. In the absence of sufficient support from the national armed forces, the local administrative elite tolerate or even support additional armed groups to fight insurgents.

While this strategic context may explain the timing, it does not fully explain the location of militia emergence. When militias form in neighboring communities and demonstrate their success against insurgents, residents may seek to form community-initiated militias in their own communities. This may lead to forms of collective action diffusing across community boundaries due to ethnic, cultural, or historical bonds between those communities. Such initial diffusion of militias is only transformed into sustained diffusion, however, if relative unity among elites allows the militia's integration into the local security apparatus, which facilitates broad-based support from the local population, the administration, and the army.

Once a community includes militias in its repertoire of violent collective action, several factors may explain the rapid growth of the organization. When communities appeal to preexisting social conventions and base their creation of innovative institutions on them, they help residents to manage the uncertainty of war. Community-initiated militias attract a large number of recruits when they provide a new and innovative opportunity for self-empowerment, creating a sense of agency and hope among residents to address their hardship during war.

The book develops and illustrates these arguments with a diverse set of evidence from interviews and archival data on the Naparama militia and the Mozambican civil war from thirteen months of fieldwork in central and northern Mozambique. Naparama formed at a time in which local military stalemates between Frelimo and Renamo, characterized by much indiscriminate and collective violence, prevented a solution to the conflict. Community residents in Zambézia and Nampula provinces considered forming Naparama units as their best option in a war about control over people. The local Frelimo administration considered the indirect support for Naparama as their only chance to retain some level of military and political control over district towns in Zambézia and Nampula provinces.

Once Naparama leaders had demonstrated their power over Renamo in the first districts in which they operated, the militia spread from one district to another. Community residents longed for the same stability that neighboring communities were experiencing. However, elite conflicts prevented the militia from forming durable organizations in some districts, as individual elites abused Naparama units to pursue political ambitions.

Community residents were convinced that the Naparama militia provided a solution to their hardship because Naparama's social and cultural references resonated with them and the militia provided an innovative institution that seemed more promising than preexisting ones. Residents felt empowered to not only protect themselves from violence, but also to regain agency over their life course and provide for themselves and their families.

Analyzing the origins of militias in Mozambique helps us understand wartime civilian agency and violent resistance, as well as how the rise of third actors affects the dynamics of civil war. As a result, this study sheds light on similar movements beyond Mozambique.

8.1 CIVILIAN AGENCY AND VIOLENT RESISTANCE

When Naparama emerged in Mozambique in the late 1980s, it was treated as a story of surprising civilian resilience. An international journalist who reported on the militia's formation at the time spoke of a "rag-tag army" confronting the rebels and a surprising "triumph of spears over guns."[3] Armed with spears and machetes, the grassroots movement fought back Renamo's military organization of about 20,000 men and pacified many areas in northern and central Mozambique, an achievement the army had been unable to accomplish alone. This was a surprising story as civilians are often depicted as passive victims of war, and even if they try to organize, they often have the challenge of limited resources to defend themselves. Paying attention to the various ways in which civilians can claim agency helps us to understand how and why they would want to protect themselves and to recognize the challenges that come with such violent displays of agency.

The stories from Zambézia and Nampula show the ways in which the Naparama militia offered civilians agency. The militia empowered civilians to respond to their hardships and protect themselves. For militia members,

---

[3] Karl Maier, "Renamo Flee at Sight of Rag-Tag Army," *Independent*, July 27, 1990, 12; Karl Maier, "Triumph of Spears Over Guns Brings Refugees Home," *Independent*, February 23, 1990.

becoming a Naparama was an opportunity to overcome the passivity that they felt was forced upon them, and to regain the ability to secure their own livelihoods:

My experience was the following: During the time when the country was at war, I didn't succeed in doing anything far [from my home] to provide for my family. But when I became a Naparama [combatant], I went to the bush to fish and could at least get some fish and bring it here to sell and use [the money] for expenses at home. This was important. For example, from [Nicoadala] to Namacurra, the road was full of bandits. If you didn't drink [the Naparama medicine], you didn't arrive there [because you were killed], but since I had taken the Naparama medicine, I went there, ran my errands and returned [alive]. This was good! Yes, this was good.[4]

But for those who did not formally join the militia, Naparama's activities also had an empowering effect. As a community leader explained to me, when Naparama arrived, "the people began to experience the war [first-hand] and face the enemy, [and the war] became a popular war. Before, when it was just Frelimo, it was the army that engaged in war and the people fled."[5] As with the Naparama combatant above, regained agency meant not only to survive but also to provide for one's livelihoods. In the same conversation, the community leader explained that before Naparama arrived, "people were put into pro- tected zones (villages). They received food and clothes in these villages. When Naparama arrived and vaccinated people, the community was able to return to the fields."[6] Thus, the agency that community residents were longing for was to secure their survival *and* to ensure that they could provide for themselves.

The type of community empowerment we see in Mozambique fits with a new research agenda on civilian agency and civilian self-protection in civil war (Jose and Medie 2015, 2016; Kaplan 2017; Krause 2018), and elucidates what civilian self-protection can encompass and how it emerges. Concepts and typologies of civilian self-protection often include violent means, but in-depth analyses mainly refer to nonviolent individual or collective means to protect noncombatants. The book shows that the analysis of agency and self-protection can and should also encompass violent means of self-protection. I consider the type of militia under study in this book, community-initiated part-time militias, to be a form of civilian self-protection.

While civilians may seek protection from government or rebel forces by joining or supporting them, this book contributes to our understanding of why community residents opt for a "third" or neutral strategy in response to war – in other words, when they engage in "noncooperation" with armed

---

[4] Interview with former Naparama combatant (2011-09-09-Nm1), Nicoadala, Zambézia, September 9, 2011.

[5] Interview with community leader (2011-09-23-Lm3a), Nicoadala, Zambézia, September 23, 2011.

[6] Interview with community leader (2011-09-23-Lm3a), Nicoadala, Zambézia, September 23, 2011.

groups (Masullo 2021). The military situation civilians find themselves in – indiscriminate or collective forms of violence – requires civilians to come up with a new, innovative response that allows for self-protection. My analysis of the Mozambican civil war, therefore, confirms Masullo's (2015, 47) argument that conditions of indiscriminate violence are unlikely to lead individuals to join and rely on insurgents or state forces as "indiscriminate targeting makes cooperation in exchange for protection ineffective." In such violent and uncertain environments, community residents look for innovative ways to respond to the violence, and adopting violent or nonviolent means of resistance is such a response. What remains to be refined, however, is our understanding of the conditions under which communities and individuals opt for violent as opposed to nonviolent forms of resistance. Attention to civilian tactical choices will allow researchers, policy makers, and practitioners take into account the challenges that come along with the rise of third actors in civil war.

8.2 THE RISE OF THIRD ACTORS AND ORDER IN CIVIL WAR

Ignoring realities on the ground, the national and provincial Frelimo government adamantly tried to suppress civilian mobilization into community-initiated militias. Already weakened from the civil war against the rebels, the government feared that if it had to fight an additional armed group, an end to the war would be out of sight. What the Mozambican government realized – and conflict research has confirmed – is that multiple armed actors complicate the solution to civil wars. Though militias often support the government, they can turn on their sponsors and target the population they are supposed to protect. More systematic attention to third actors in civil war is needed to specify the ways in which such actors influence levels and types of violence, and the length and outcomes of civil wars.

This book shows that if local military stalemates are conducive to forming community-initiated militias, we should see more militias in prolonged irregular wars, or civil wars in which the adversaries are from the outset relatively equal in their military capabilities, such as symmetric nonconventional wars (Kalyvas and Balcells 2010). In this sense, although the book's theoretical arguments apply primarily to wars in which an asymmetry exists between state and rebel forces, it can also apply to wars with a range of armed groups of equal military capability that exercise high levels of indiscriminate violence. Violent military stalemates do not only prevent incumbents and insurgents from winning the war, they also make settlements between them more difficult, thereby contributing to the length of civil wars. In such situations, militias proliferate. The state may attempt to gain a military advantage over the insurgent by multiplying its forces and delegating tasks to militias. The incumbent may also increase pressure on the insurgent by outsourcing violence against civilians under the insurgent's control to militias. Communities may form militias in prolonged civil wars, as they do not see any other option to protect themselves. War-weary communities may want to bring an end to the war themselves and so form militias. What is difficult to ascertain here, however, and what needs more research, is the precise causal direction; though I argue that prolonged civil war leads communities to adopt militias, there is some cross-national evidence that militias themselves make wars last longer (Aliyev 2020a).

What is important to recognize is that militias are not just any additional armed group. They do have distinct characteristics that distinguish them from other armed groups, at least in irregular wars.[7] For example, a key distinction between community-initiated militias and insurgent groups appears to be the locally rooted character of militias. Militia recruitment is generally more localized than rebel recruitment, which enables reliance – and innovation – upon previously existing forms of organization. Such use of social conventions may help manage wartime uncertainty and explain the rapid growth of some community-initiated militias. It is therefore likely that in some contexts, counterinsurgent recruitment is less ideologically determined and more security-related, as community residents may participate in militias to signal their loyalty to the government to receive protection (Schubiger 2021). This focus on security represents militia members' short-term motivations. For example, in contrast to the supporters of the insurgents in El Salvador, on which Wood's (2003) concept of pleasure of agency is based, Naparama members did not have a vision of social justice and did not think they were making history. The objective to bring back family members and reclaim land resulted from the concern for the family's short-term survival, and did not include any long-term political goals. However, as this book shows, even short-term goals may only be met with participation in an armed group that allows for sufficient empowerment, which raises the sense of purpose and expectation of success. Such short-term vision also points to a source of armed group cohesion that is different from ideology or socialization, and therefore worthy of further study.

The importance of social conventions for attracting militia members also has implications for state-initiated militias. When states or occupying forces rely on preexisting forms of organization or social conventions, they are more likely to create sustainable militia organizations. Policy makers have recognized how important familiarity of new organizational structures is for mobilizing new militia members. For example, the US military in Afghanistan built on previously existing forms of community policing to create militias that were later united into the new Afghan Local Police (Goodhand and Hakimi 2014). As with community-initiated militias, the institutional context of communities influences whether militia organizations form for the long term. In the Khan Abad district in Afghanistan's Kunduz province, for example, militias quickly fell apart due to elite conflicts that turned newly formed militias into private

---

[7] For symmetric nonconventional wars, militias could be grouped into a category of community-based armed groups.

armies.[8] Scholars have begun to analyze the consequences of the "familiar" character of militias, showing that recruitment based on ethnicity is associated with less lethal wars (Aliyev and Souleimanov 2019). These examples show, however, that we need to go beyond ethnicity as a proxy for familiarity. To fully understand how and why familiar structures create sustainable militia organizations, we need to trace their precise origins and analyze how social conventions structure their relation to the population.

More generally, militias represent informal institutions of security governance that emerge during civil wars to create alternative forms of political and social order. Debates both on how rebels "rule," build proto-states, and provide public goods and social order to civilian communities, as well as how warlords contribute to "multiple layers of authority" in war-torn countries have dominated the discussion of governance in civil wars (Mampilly 2011; Arjona 2016; Malejacq 2019). Scholars usually assume that governments are "unitary" actors. Together with the emerging research agenda on (pro-government) militias in civil wars, this book challenges this assumption as it shows that states are fragmented and rely on multiple armed groups to respond effectively and efficiently to rebel threats. Theories on the dynamics of war should therefore take into account the potentially fragmented nature of the state.

8.3 BEYOND MOZAMBIQUE

Grassroots initiatives, which seek to protect the local population from insurgent violence, have influenced and continue to influence the dynamics of war in many other cases. A prominent case is the rise of militias in Sierra Leone's civil war from 1991 to 2002, which provides a fitting example of the militia mobilization process as theorized in this book, albeit in a different kind of civil war. A variety of community-initiated militias influenced the dynamics of war in Sierra Leone: Kamajors, Tamaboros, Donsos, Kapra, Gbethis, and the Organized Body of Hunting Societies (OBHS), whose membership was largely defined by ethnicity and geographic origin (Wlodarczyk 2009, 62). Similar to Naparama, Sierra Leone's militias relied on the belief in a bullet-proof medicine that every new member would receive during an initiation ceremony.

The case of Sierra Leone helps to explore the scope of my arguments. In contrast to the militias in Mozambique that formed toward the end of the war, many of the groups in Sierra Leone formed in the early years of war in order to protect communities against insurgent violence and support or even substitute the army (Ferme and Hoffman 2004; Muana 1997). This could be explained by reference to the type of war; the war in Sierra Leone is considered a symmetric nonconventional war as the rebels challenged a relatively weak state (Kalyvas

---

[8] Jan Köhler, personal communication, July 2014.

and Balcells 2010). In wars that are characterized by relative symmetry among the armed groups, community-empowering stalemates can emerge much earlier than in irregular wars, which would explain the rise of militias in the early stages of war. A second important difference to the case of Naparama is that militias in Sierra Leone evolved into more autonomous forces over time, eventually replacing the state army. Recognizing the militias' power and its own military weakness, the newly elected government of the Sierra Leone People's Party (SLPP) officially recognized the militias in 1996/97 and united them into the Civilian Defense Forces (CDF). This aligns with the expectation that militias in wars characterized by more symmetry between armed groups gain more autonomy (Kalyvas 2006, 107n44). The focus of this book on militia formation provides a limited perspective, however, on how and why militias in Sierra Leone evolved, professionalized, became co-opted, and perpetrated violence against those they were supposed to protect. Sierra Leone's President Kabbah formed the CDF in order to unify the different hunter militias in the country. Yet the government's intervention to unite all militias diluted leadership, slackening the once-strict selection and initiation procedure that every young man had to undergo and contributing to indiscipline and increased levels of violence against civilians (SL TRC 2005; Forney 2012). That the militias lost some of their original structures and processes through the government's interference can explain parts of these developments, but this is an important question to take up in further research (Hoffman 2011).

As for the mobilization process, we see interesting similarities among the two cases that point to the importance of innovation when civilians face a security crisis. As in Mozambique, militias in Sierra Leone mobilized members by creating innovative institutions that relied on preexisting social conventions, which resonated with the relevant communities. The Tamaboro in the north among the Kuranko ethnic group were among the first militias to form. In 1992–93, they worked as guides to the Gola Forrest to support the National Provisional Ruling Council (NPRC), a military junta that ousted President Momoh in a coup in April 1992 (Fithen and Richards 2005, 127). The NPRC valued the hunters' knowledge of the local terrain and their reliability, which exceeded that of the regular army. The NPRC decided to mobilize militia members through Poro societies, the traditional initiation societies for adolescents. The Kamajor militia in the south of the country was modeled on the Tamaboro in the north. A hunter in the Jong chiefdom (Bonthe district) among the Mende ethnic group began training a local militia based on hunting rituals (Fithen and Richards 2005, 127). The example of the Tamaboro provided a crucial innovation for the southern communities: the hunter (kamajô) in the south had much more individualist connotations and was less connected to war traditions than in the north (Ferme 2001, 121). The first initiators brought together craft hunting and organizational modalities from youth initiations to transform the "mysterious individual hunter" tradition into a mass movement: "The hunter civil defence might thus best be understood not as a preexisting institution but a syncretic institutional response to the security threat posed by the RUF" (Fithen and Richards 2005, 128). This innovation successfully mobilized a large number of militia combatants. By 1996, almost all chiefdoms in the south and east had Kamajor societies and mobilization mechanisms (Wlodarczyk 2009, 64). The community-initiated militias empowered the people in Sierra Leone to respond to the increasing threat posed by the RUF – the Revolutionary United Front. Militia mobilization "took place in the context of the national army's failure to protect villagers in the east and south of the country against the initial excesses of RUF 'special forces'" (Fithen and Richards 2005, 127).

Both cases, Mozambique and Sierra Leone, demonstrate the power of storytelling for mobilization processes. In Mozambique, stories of Naparama's "magic" – their invulnerability to bullets and António's alleged powers – resonated with community experiences of spirit mediums and traditional medicine. In Benford and Snow's (2000) terms, Naparama's framing had "narrative fidelity" and resonated culturally. The heroic and magical stories about the capabilities and success of both Naparama and Kamajor were crucial in creating hope and motivated many to join. The importance of such framing can be found across civil wars in Africa. As Ellis (1999) has shown in the context of the civil war in Liberia, existing spiritual practices may serve as a source of invention to mobilize and prepare fighters for war. For Sierra Leone, Hoffman (2011, 76) argues that storytelling that referenced social conventions was more important in the Kamajor civil defense movement's growth than preexisting kinship groups and social networks. It shows that social embeddedness of armed groups needs to be understood in much broader terms – beyond social and ethnic ties to also include social conventions and organizational repertoires that may account for how armed groups form and mobilize their members.

While this study has focused on a particular case of community-initiated militia formation during Mozambique's civil war, the theoretical and empirical implications illuminate similar processes in other types of wars and contribute to our understanding of political violence, civilian agency, and collective action more generally. This book deals with the important questions of when, where, and how community-initiated militias form. Yet, other relevant themes need to be explored. For example, the social embeddedness of community-initiated militias gives rise to various questions: Are community-initiated militias better at protecting civilians than state-initiated ones? What about the trajectory of community-initiated militias? Under what conditions can they retain their relative autonomy from the state? Under what conditions do they turn on the people they are supposed to protect? And (when) should we expect such militias to provide more than just security to communities and establish more complex forms of governance parallel to the state?

The limitations of my theory point to important future avenues of research. Understanding why community-initiated militias emerge is just a first step. To evaluate their impact, we need to study how they evolve over time, when they ally with other (armed) actors, and why they sometimes violently target civilians they are supposed to protect.

8.4 DEMOBILIZED AT LAST?

The 1992 Rome agreement ended the Mozambican civil war and ushered in a long peace process that was challenged by renewed violence. Tensions between the rebel-turned-political party Renamo and the government escalated twenty-one years after the war's end, in 2013, and led to violent confrontations between Renamo-affiliated armed forces and government forces. It took several rounds of peace talks and two new peace agreements to bring that renewed conflict to an end in August 2019 (Darch 2015; Pearce 2020). The long-time Renamo leader Afonso Dhlakama died in May 2018, which helped to bring about a new phase in Renamo's transformation into a political party. In addition to tensions with their long-time political rival, the Mozambican government has faced a new insurgency in the far north of the country since October 2017 (Habibe, Forquilha, and Pereira 2019; Morier-Genoud 2020). The Islamist movement, which pledged allegiance to the Islamic State of Iraq and the Levant (ISIL, known as ISIS) in July 2019, grew over two years to a serious armed challenge and was able to capture and occupy territory in early 2020.

Contrary to what we might expect, the political violence of recent years has not reactivated Naparama. But this is mostly due to Mozambique's political geography. The resurgence of Renamo violence took place in the center of the country, in the Sofala province, where the rebels maintained their main headquarters during the civil war and loyal supporters remained living there throughout the postwar period. The Islamist insurgency is mostly confined to the northernmost province of Cabo Delgado, thousands of miles away from where Naparama had operated.

After the war had ended, the Naparama militia disintegrated in all the districts I worked in, except Nicoadala in Zambézia province, where the militia's headquarters were located during the war. Nicoadala was also among the districts where former Naparama combatants (and soldiers) revolted after the war. Although no official relationship between the Frelimo government and Naparama forces existed, Naparama combatants in Namapa (Nampula) and Nicoadala districts demanded inclusion into the demobilization scheme to receive pensions and other benefits (see Dinerman 2006).[9] Naparama units in these districts sought recognition from the government, as the demobilization process conducted by ONUMOZ did not include combatants for the state-initiated and community-initiated militias.

---

[9] "Mutinying Troops in Quelimane Threaten to Shell City, Seize Airport," *Radio Mozambique (Maputo)*, August 3, 1994; "Zambezia Troop Mutiny Continues; Nearly 9,000 Naparamas Irregulars Mutiny," *Radio Mozambique (Maputo)*, August 3, 1994.

In 2011, these conflicts resurfaced when Hermínio dos Santos, leader of one of the associations for demobilized soldiers (the Forum for the Demobilized of the War [Fórum dos Desmobilizados da Guerra]), staged demonstrations to demand that the government raise demobilized soldiers' pensions and include state- and community-initiated militias into such pension schemes. The protests were a reaction to a new law that redefined the status of demobilized soldiers, which previously only applied to combatants from the independence war. The new statute for former combatants sought to include combatants from the civil war under the umbrella category of "former combatants." While other (Frelimo-loyal) associations for demobilized soldiers supported the new law, dos Santos criticized the statute for not including former members of the state security agency, the police forces, and (state- and community-initiated) militias.[10]

The Naparama leadership in Nicoadala welcomed dos Santos's support, as efforts to collect signatures from former Naparama members and other documents had not brought them any closer to official recognition by the provincial government. In my interviews with them, former Naparama combatants repeatedly complained that Frelimo had never officially recognized that Naparama had contributed to the war effort. "We worked, too" was a common expression with which former militia members demanded access to benefits similar to those that officially demobilized soldiers currently receive. But the renewed mobilization did not gain any traction. Dos Santos died in 2017, so the former militia members lost an important spokesperson and, therefore, political relevance.

The theme of incomplete demobilization is one that has dominated the continued tensions between the Frelimo and Renamo parties after the 1992 peace accord, as Renamo kept a small armed force throughout the years, which facilitated the return to violence in 2013. Incomplete demobilization represents a broader theme of unequal access to economic and political opportunities. The Frelimo party has long marginalized certain social groups and regions and more recently turned to repression of the opposition. While the precise origins of the recent insurgent violence in Cabo Delgado are difficult to ascertain, it appears that the violence was fueled by a government that did not sufficiently respond to citizen concerns, and early repression led to an escalation that escaped the army's control. Mozambique's transition to democracy and peace will remain a struggle for citizens' political, social, and economic equality. *A luta continua.*

---

[10] Hélio Norberto, "Estatuto do Combatente: enquanto uns discutem, outros desconhecem-no," *Verdade*, August 4, 2011; Cláudio Saúte, "Manifestações vão acontecer a qualquer momento," *CanalMoz*, March 16, 2011.

Appendix

Data Collection and Analysis

To collect the necessary data for my analysis, I conducted twelve months of fieldwork in Mozambique between July 2010 and July 2012 in five districts and two provincial capitals, and went on a shorter repeat visit in 2016. In Zambézia province, I conducted research in the Nicoadala, Namarrói, and Lugela districts, and in the provincial capital of Quelimane. In Nampula province, I worked in Murrupula and Mecubúri districts and in the provincial capital Nampula (see map in Figure 5.1 for an overview of fieldwork sites). For most of my fieldwork, I was based in Nampula city and traveled to the districts for repeated stays ranging from one to four weeks. In addition, I stayed in the Nicoadala district for one month and in Quelimane for five weeks, both in Zambézia province.

I began my fieldwork in Nicoadala in Zambézia province, as Naparama's headquarters were in the district town by the end of the war and its main leaders still live in Nicoadala today. Similarly, Murrupula was the center of Naparama activity during the war in Nampula province. In both districts I was introduced to respondents by a trusted person who knew the Naparama combatants living there. The main objective of my work in these districts was to collect background material and data on temporal and spatial variation of militia activity in the two provinces. In addition, evidence from both districts served to explore and test the mechanisms that explain why individuals joined Naparama, allowing me to compare mobilization processes for state- and community-initiated militias.

I selected the remaining field sites depending on the presence or absence of Naparama forces and the severity of the war in that district (see Table 2.2 for an overview of the research design and case selection). I chose Lugela and Namarrói districts in the northwest of Zambézia province because both districts are similar in their geographic, cultural, and wartime characteristics, but the Naparama militia spread to Lugela district in a sustained manner, while it did not to Namarrói. I used evidence from Mecubúri district in the northwest of Nampula province to explore the argument developed in Lugela and Namarrói, since – like Namarrói and Lugela – it was one of the most war-affected districts in the region and one to which Naparama spread.

To reconstruct local histories of war and militia formation, I carried out more than 250 oral histories and semi-structured interviews with community residents, former Naparama combatants, Frelimo soldiers, and Renamo combatants, current and former government representatives, and community leaders, with an average of 46 respondents in each of the 5 districts (see Table A.1). Usually, interviews took place in a semi-private place in the respondents' compounds, but in cases in which local authorities helped me to organize interviews, we met at the residence of the chief, headman, local administrator, or at the local adminis-trative building. In addition to these interviews in the districts, I spoke to journalists, politicians, and researchers in Maputo, Quelimane, and Nampula about the history of the war and its legacy.

The interviews took between thirty minutes and five hours, sometimes in repeated sessions. If the respondent agreed (which happened in almost all cases), I recorded the interview with a digital audio recorder. I conducted the interviews in Portuguese or with the aid of an interpreter who translated the local language – Chuabo in Nicoadala, Makua in Mecubúri and Murrupula, Lomwe in Namarrói, and Manyawa in Lugela district – into Portuguese. The respondents spoke in the language they were most comfortable with, and sometimes mixed or changed the language during the interview. I did not remunerate respondents for their time, but in cases when I met respondents repeatedly, or when respondents had to wait to be interviewed, I brought small necessities such as food or soap or provided refreshments.

For most of my interviews, I worked with an assistant who translated during the interview and prepared translated transcriptions of the recorded interviews afterward. The assistants I worked with in the field were both Mozambican. My assistant in Nicoadala grew up in a locality in the district, but had lived in the provincial capital Quelimane for several years. He was not known to the respondents but, having grown up in the district, was not a stranger, which proved useful for establishing rapport with the respondents. The assistant I worked with in Mecubúri, Murrupula, Namarrói, and Lugela was originally from Zambézia province but had lived in Nampula province for a long time, thus being able to speak the local languages of both provinces fluently. As someone living in the city, he was perceived more as a stranger than my assistant in Nicoadala (see Chapter 3). In both cases, my assistants did not come from the communities we worked in but possessed the necessary know-ledge of cultural codes and social rules that were valuable for setting up interviews and ensuring that respondents felt comfortable. They were also able to explain responses I would not have understood myself due to the social and cultural barriers or lack of context. Both assistants possessed lots of field research experience since they had worked for other researchers before, either translating interviews or conducting surveys. However, the focus on open-ended questions and narratives in interviews was new to both of them, and

TABLE A.I. *Overview of interviews conducted in Mozambique*

	Frelimo	Renamo	Naparama	Local Leaders	Government Reps	Civilians	Total Men	Total Women	Total
Zambézia									
Nicoadala	2	5	22	11	5	6	46	5	51
Lugela	7	3	4	11	1	11	34	3	37
Namarrói	7	4	7	15	2	15	42	8	50
Quelimane	2	1	0	1	7	1	12	0	12
Nampula									
Mecubúri	7	6	12	8	4	14	47	4	51
Murrupula	6	3	13	6	3	9	38	2	40
Nampula City	1	0	3	1	9	2	16	0	16
Maputo	1	1	0	0	1	0	3	0	3
Total	33	23	61	53	32	58	238	22	260

thus it took several interviews to practice the type of questions to ask and the right moments for translation. All translations from Portuguese to English of quotes used in the book are mine unless noted otherwise.

Before my research assistant and I began each interview, we explained our project and asked for (oral) informed consent to be interviewed. At the beginning and end of each interview, we also encouraged the respondents to let us know if they had any concerns or questions about the objectives of the interview and the project. Asking for questions after the interview was crucial, as some respondents felt more comfortable coming forward with their questions after we built up rapport during the interview. I never asked directly about the experience of or participation in violence and waited for the respondent to divulge such information to protect the respondents from retelling painful experiences. The project was approved by the Human Subjects Committee of Yale University, under the IRB protocol number 110308177.

Since data sources can have distinct biases (Davenport and Ball 2002), I aimed to collect data from a variety of sources. To supplement and cross-check the information from the interviews, I collected documents from the provincial government archives in Quelimane (Zambézia province) and Nampula city (Nampula province). I collected, digitally preserved, and organized more than 10,000 of government documents produced during the period 1975–94 by state and party agencies on the provincial and district level. The collection of documents includes monthly reports about political, economic, and social developments in the districts; reports about special visits by administrative personnel to the districts; and radio messages from the districts to the provincial government about special occurrences. Most of these documents have never been used by other researchers.[1]

I selected documents for digital preservation depending on their relevance to my research; that is, I made sure to collect all the reports I found that provided information about violent events, security, military affairs, and relevant social affairs such as communal villages and the effects of war on daily life. To illustrate the coverage of the collected documents, Figures A.1 and A.2 provide an overview of the number of documents by location and by year, collected in the archive in Quelimane, Zambézia province. The figure for "Zambézia" in Figure A.1 is high as the provincial office often summarized the monthly reports from the district. The figure for 1992 and 1993 reflects reports collected on the violation of the ceasefire and peace accord that was signed on October 4, 1992.

A research assistant and I created a dataset of violent events using the archival reports from Zambézia province. The codebook builds on other efforts to collect violent event data, such as the Uppsala Conflict Data Program's (UCDP) Georeferenced Event Dataset (Sundberg and Melander 2013), the Armed Conflict Location and Event Dataset (ACLED) (Raleigh et al. 2010),

---

[1] The researchers Sérgio Chichava, who worked in the archive of Quelimane, and Domingos do Rosário, who worked in the archive of Nampula, made use of a few of the same documents in their studies (Chichava 2007; Do Rosário 2009).

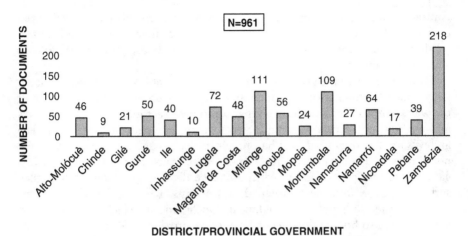

FIGURE A.1. Number of documents collected from the Zambézia archive by district

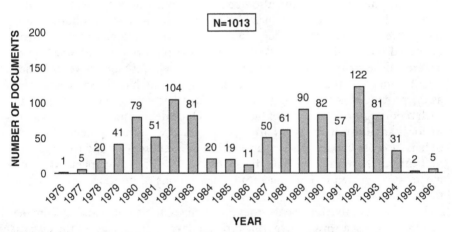

FIGURE A.2. Number of documents collected from the Zambézia archive by year

and the Sierra Leone Local-Location Event Dataset (Bruijne 2014). This ensures that the dataset is compatible with other quantitative data collection efforts and can be combined with existing datasets to extend the analysis. The dataset for Zambézia province includes over 1,300 events from the time period between 1974 and 1994. Each event is categorized into different types of violence so that the analysis can differentiate between violence against civilian and military targets and demonstrate patterns of violence across space and time. The dataset focuses on the following actors: government armed forces, rebel forces, state-initiated militias, and community-initiated militias. The typology of events the dataset includes builds on ACLED, which focuses on changes in territorial control (Raleigh et al. 2010). Battles can result in changes in territorial control or allow a conflict party to remain in control. The dataset also codes violence against civilians as a separate category.

Gaining access to the archives to collect government documents was difficult. Government documents in Nampula and Zambézia provinces from the time of the war are not stored in official archives, and the exact location of the archives and the rules for access were unknown to many government employees. The archives are not organized, so I had to sift through many documents that were not of relevance to my project. In Nampula, documents were stored in boxes in a garage that was part of the provincial finance division guesthouse where they suffered damage from heat, water, dust, and rats. I found similar conditions in Quelimane. Although the building in Quelimane in which the documents were stored also housed documents from other provincial departments, the air-conditioning unit that should have preserved the documents was broken.[2]

Although my collection of documents spans many districts and time periods, it may contain some bias due to the difficult conditions in which the documents are stored and also due to time constraints, but it is difficult to ascertain how systematic the bias is. The office of the district administrator, the police, the security agency, and the military stationed in the district produced reports, but the level of detail in the reports varied. Some reports covered all security-related events, while others left out violent events I knew about from other sources. In general, though, they all had the same structure, as the provincial government provided the districts with guidelines to prepare such reports. Another source of bias may include deliberate selective reporting by local administrative staff. I attempted to deal with these potential sources of bias by cross-checking information from different reports and triangulating that information with evidence from interviews and newspapers. All documents were written in Portuguese; the translations of quotes from the documents are all mine.

In addition to the documents from the archives in Nampula and Quelimane, I collected newspaper and magazine articles; development plans of the districts I worked in that provide basic geographic, administrative, social, cultural, and economic information; and presidential speeches and TV reports. I obtained this material in the archive of the Mozambican News Agency (Agência de

---

[2] Since the early 2000s, there are legal regulations in Mozambique for the preservation and archiving of local and provincial government documents; however, there are limited to no resources for adequate buildings and staff to organize the documents. When Domingos do Rosário conducted archival work in Nampula city, he talked to the permanent secretary at the time to draw attention to the state of the archive. When do Rosário visited the archives the next time, the rooms in which the documents were stored had been cleaned up (Do Rosário 2009). However, when I visited the archives in Nampula, they had been moved to a garage and another site outside the main government building, so conditions for preservation had deteriorated again.

Informação de Moçambique), in the National Historical Archives (Arquívo Nacional Histórico), and from the national TV channel Televisão Moçambique (TVM), all in Maputo, and from Yale University Library.

From the interviews and documents, I obtained detailed information on community histories; levels of violence and territorial control by insurgents and the government; motivations for joining the militia; the relationship between the militia, government, and the population; and current activities of former militia members who demand pensions from the government for their wartime contribution.

References

Abelvik-Lawson, Helle. 2014. "Sustainable Development for Whose Benefit? Brazil's Economic Power and Human Rights Violations in the Amazon and Mozambique." *The International Journal of Human Rights* 18 (7–8): 795–821.

Abrahams, Ray G. 1998. *Vigilant Citizens: Vigilantism and the State.* Malden, MA: Polity Press.

Acemoglu, Daron, James A. Robinson, and Rafael Santos. 2009. "The Monopoly of Violence: Evidence from Colombia." NBER Working Paper 15578. Cambridge, MA: National Bureau of Economic Research.

Acharya, Amitav. 2004. "How Ideas Spread: Whose Norms Matter? Norm Localization and Institutional Change in Asian Regionalism." *International Organization* 58 (2): 239–75.

Adams, Laura L. 1999. "The Mascot Researcher: Identity, Power, and Knowledge in Fieldwork." *Journal of Contemporary Ethnography* 28 (4): 331–63.

Ahram, Ariel I. 2011. *Proxy Warriors: The Rise and Fall of State-Sponsored Militias.* Stanford, CA: Stanford University Press.

2014. "The Role of State-Sponsored Militias in Genocide." *Terrorism and Political Violence* 26 (2): 1–16.

2016. "Pro-Government Militias and the Repertoires of Illicit State Violence." *Studies in Conflict & Terrorism* 39 (3): 207–26.

Alexander, Jocelyn. 1997. "The Local State in Post-War Mozambique: Political Practice and Ideas about Authority." *Africa: Journal of the International African Institute* 67 (1): 1–26.

Aliyev, Huseyn. 2020a. "Pro-Regime Militias and Civil War Duration." *Terrorism and Political Violence* 32 (3): 630–50.

2020b. "Why Are Some Civil Wars More Lethal Than Others? The Effect of Pro-Regime Proxies on Conflict Lethality." *Political Studies* 68 (3): 749–67.

Aliyev, Huseyn, and Emil A. Souleimanov. 2019. "Ethnicity and Conflict Severity: Accounting for the Effect of Co-Ethnic and Non-Ethnic Militias on Battlefield Lethality." *Third World Quarterly* 40 (3): 471–87.

Allen, Tim, and Koen Vlassenroot, eds. 2010. *The Lord's Resistance Army: Myth and Reality*. London: Zed Books.

Arjona, Ana. 2016. *Rebelocracy: Social Order in the Colombian Civil War*. New York: Cambridge University Press.

    2019. "Subnational Units, the Locus of Choice, and Concept Formation: Conceptualizing Civilian Behavior in Contexts of Civil War." In *Inside Countries: Subnational Research in Comparative Politics*, edited by Richard Snyder, Eduardo Moncada, and Agustina Giraudy, 214–42. New York: Cambridge University Press.

Arjona, Ana M., and Stathis N. Kalyvas. 2012. "Recruitment into Armed Groups in Colombia: A Survey of Demobilized Fighters." In *Understanding Collective Political Violence*, edited by Yvan Guichaoua, 143–74. New York: Palgrave Macmillan.

Armando, Hassane. 2018. *Tempos de fúria. Memórias do massacre de Homoíne, 18 de Julho de 1987*. Lisbon: Edições Colibri.

Armon, Jeremy, Dylan Hendrickson, and Alex Vines. 1998. *The Mozambican Peace Process in Perspective*. London: Conciliation Resources.

Bakke, Kristin M., Kathleen Gallagher Cunningham, and Lee J. M. Seymour. 2012. "A Plague of Initials: Fragmentation, Cohesion, and Infighting in Civil Wars." *Perspectives on Politics* 10 (2): 265–83.

Balcells, Laia. 2017. *Rivalry and Revenge: The Politics of Violence during Civil War*. New York: Cambridge University Press.

Bamidele, Seun. 2017. "The Civilian Joint Task Force and the Struggle against Insurgency in Borno State, Nigeria." *African Conflict and Peacebuilding Review* 7 (2): 85–98.

Barnes, Sam. 1997. "The Socio-Economic Reintegration of Demobilised Soldiers in Mozambique: The Soldiers' View." Maputo: United Nations Development Program (UNDP).

Barter, Shane J. 2013. "State Proxy or Security Dilemma? Understanding Anti-Rebel Militias in Civil War." *Asian Security* 9 (2): 75–92.

    2014. *Civilian Strategy in Civil War: Insights from Indonesia, Thailand, and the Philippines*. New York: Palgrave Macmillan.

Bateson, Regina. 2017. "The Socialization of Civilians and Militia Members: Evidence from Guatemala." *Journal of Peace Research* 54 (5): 634–47.

    2020. "The Politics of Vigilantism." *Comparative Political Studies* 54 (6): 923–55.

Beal, Sophia. 2006. "Terra Sonâmbula: Mythmaking and the Naparama in the Work of Mia Couto." In *Studies in Witchcraft, Magic, War, and Peace in Africa*, edited by Beatrice Nicolini, 227–37. Lewiston, NY: Edwin Mellen Press.

Behrend, Heike. 1999. *Alice Lakwena and the Holy Spirits: War in Northern Uganda, 1985–97*. Oxford: James Currey.

Beissinger, Mark R. 2002. *Nationalist Mobilization and the Collapse of the Soviet State*. Cambridge and New York: Cambridge University Press.

Benford, Robert D., and David A. Snow. 2000. "Framing Processes and Social Movements: An Overview and Assessment." *Annual Review of Sociology* 26: 611–39.

Bennett, Andrew. 2008. "Process Tracing: A Bayesian Perspective." In *Oxford Handbook of Political Methodology*, edited by Janet Box-Steffensmeier, Henry Brady, and David Collier, 703–21. Oxford: Oxford University Press.

Bennett, Andrew, and Jeffrey T. Checkel. 2014. "Process Tracing: From Philosophical Roots to Best Practices." In *Process Tracing in the Social Sciences: From Metaphor to Analytic Tool*, edited by Andrew Bennett and Jeffrey T. Checkel, 3–38. New York: Cambridge University Press.

Bennett, Andrew, and Colin Elman. 2006. "Qualitative Research: Recent Developments in Case Study Methods." *Annual Review of Political Science* 9: 455–76.

Bennett, Huw C. 2013. *Fighting the Mau Mau: The British Army and Counter-Insurgency in the Kenya Emergency*. New York: Cambridge University Press.

Bertelsen, Bjørn Enge. 2009. "Sorcery and Death Squads: Transformation of State, Sovereignty, and Violence in Postcolonial Mozambique." In *Crisis of the State: War and Social Upheaval*, edited by Bruce Kapferer and Bjørn Enge Bertelsen, 210–40. New York: Berghahn.

2016. *Violent Becomings: State Formation, Sociality, and Power in Mozambique*. New York: Berghahn.

Biberman, Yelena. 2018. "Self-Defense Militias, Death Squads, and State Outsourcing of Violence in India and Turkey." *Journal of Strategic Studies* 41 (5): 751–81.

2019. *Gambling with Violence: State Outsourcing of War in Pakistan and India*. New York: Oxford University Press.

Blocq, Daniel S. 2014. "The Grassroots Nature of Counterinsurgent Tribal Militia Formation: The Case of the Fertit in Southern Sudan, 1985–1989." *Journal of Eastern African Studies* 8 (4): 710–24.

Boudon, R., and F. Bourricaud. 1989. *A Critical Dictionary of Sociology*. Chicago: University of Chicago Press.

Boutros-Ghali, Boutros. 1995. *The United Nations and Mozambique, 1992–1995*. New York: United Nations Department of Public Information.

Bowen, Merle L. 2000. *The State against the Peasantry: Rural Struggles in Colonial and Postcolonial Mozambique*. Charlottesville: University Press of Virginia.

Branch, Daniel. 2007. "The Enemy Within: Loyalists and the War against Mau Mau in Kenya." *The Journal of African History* 48 (02): 291–315.

2009. *Defeating Mau Mau, Creating Kenya: Counterinsurgency, Civil War, and Decolonization*. New York: Cambridge University Press.

Brown, Richard Maxwell. 1975. *Strain of Violence: Historical Studies of American Violence and Vigilantism*. New York: Oxford University Press.

Browne, Brendan Ciarán, and Ruari-Santiago McBride. 2015. "Politically Sensitive Encounters: Ethnography, Access, and the Benefits of 'Hanging Out'." *Qualitative Sociology Review* 11 (1): 34–48.

Bruijne, Kars de. 2014. "Introducing the Sierra Leone Local-Location Event Dataset." www.acleddata.com/wp-content/uploads/2015/01/Introducing-SLL-LED_de-Bruijne-2014.pdf (accessed August 16, 2021).

Buhaug, Halvard, and Kristian Skrede Gleditsch. 2008. "Contagion or Confusion? Why Conflicts Cluster in Space." *International Studies Quarterly* 52 (2): 215–33.

Cabá, Sérgio Nathú. 1998. "A guerra na província da Zambézia e o papel do Malawi, 1975–1988." Licenciatura diss., Universidade Eduardo Mondlane.

Cabrita, João M. 2000. *Mozambique: The Tortuous Road to Democracy*. New York: Palgrave.

Cahen, Michel. 1985. "État et pouvoir populaire dans le Mozambique indépendant." *Politique Africaine* (19): 36–60.

1987. *Mozambique, la révolution implosée. Études sur 12 ans d'indépendance, 1975–1987.* Paris: L'Harmattan.

1989. "Is RENAMO a Popular Movement in Mozambique?" *Southern African Review of Books* (December/January): 20–21.

1993. "Check on Socialism in Mozambique – What Check? What Socialism?" *Review of African Political Economy* 20 (57): 46–59.

1999. "The Mueda Case and Maconde Political Ethnicity: Some Notes on a Work in Progress." *Africana Studia* (2): 29–46.

2000. "Nationalism and Ethnicities: Lessons from Mozambique." In *Ethnicity Kills? The Politics of War, Peace and Ethnicity in Sub-Saharan Africa,* edited by Einar Braathen, Morten Bøås, and Gjermund Sæther, 163–87. New York: St. Martin's Press.

2006. "Lutte d'émancipation anticoloniale ou mouvement de libération nationale? Processus historique et discours idéologique." *Revue historique* (1): 113–38.

2008a. "La 'fin de l'histoire'... unique: trajectoires des anticolonialismes au Mozambique." *Portuguese Studies Review* 16 (1): 171–207.

2008b. "À la recherche de la défaite." *Politique Africaine* (4): 161–81.

2018. "The War as Seen by RENAMO: Guerilla Politics and the 'Move to the North' at the Time of the Nkomati Accord, 1983–1985." In *The War Within: New Perspectives on the Civil War in Mozambique, 1976–1992,* edited by Michel Cahen, Eric Morier-Genoud, and Domingos Do Rosário, 100–46. Woodbridge, UK: James Currey.

2019. *"Não somos bandidos". A vida diária de uma guerrilha de direita. A Renamo na época do Acordo de Nkomati (1983–1985).* Lisbon: ICS. Imprensa de Ciências Sociais.

Cahen, Michel, Eric Morier-Genoud, and Domingos Do Rosário, eds. 2018a. *The War Within: New Perspectives on the Civil War in Mozambique, 1976–1992.* Woodbridge, UK: James Currey.

2018b. "Introduction: The Civil War in Mozambique. A History Still to Be Written." In *The War Within: New Perspectives on the Civil War in Mozambique, 1976–1992,* edited by Michel Cahen, Eric Morier-Genoud, and Domingos Do Rosário, 1–14. Woodbridge, UK: James Currey.

Campbell, Bruce B., and Arthur D. Brenner, eds. 2000. *Death Squads in Global Perspective. Murder with Deniability.* New York: St. Martin's Press.

Campbell, John L. 2002. "Where Do We Stand? Common Mechanisms in Organizations and Social Movements Research." Paper presented at the Conference on Social Movements and Organizations Theory, University of Michigan, Ann Arbor, May.

Campbell, Lisa M., Noella J. Gray, Zoë A. Meletis, James G. Abbott, and Jennifer J. Silver. 2006. "Gatekeepers and Keymasters: Dynamic Relationships of Access in Geographical Fieldwork." *Geographical Review* 96 (1): 97–121.

Caporaso, James A. 2009. "Is There a Quantitative-Qualitative Divide in Comparative Politics? The Case of Process Tracing." In *The Sage Handbook of Comparative Politics,* edited by Todd Landman and Neil Robinson, 67–83. London: Sage Publications.

Carey, Sabine C., Michael P. Colaresi, and Neil J. Mitchell. 2015. "Governments, Informal Links to Militias, and Accountability." *Journal of Conflict Resolution* 59 (5): 850–76.

2016. "Risk Mitigation, Regime Security, and Militias: Beyond Coup-Proofing." *International Studies Quarterly* 60 (1): 59–72.

Carey, Sabine C., and Neil J. Mitchell. 2017. "Pro-Government Militias." *Annual Review of Political Science* 20: 127–47.

Carey, Sabine C., Neil J. Mitchell, and Will Lowe. 2013. "States, the Security Sector and the Monopoly of Violence: A New Database on Pro-Government Militias." *Journal of Peace Research* 50 (2): 249–58.

Cederman, Lars-Erik, Kristian Skrede Gleditsch, and Halvard Buhaug. 2013. *Inequality, Grievances, and Civil War*. New York: Cambridge University Press.

Chan, Stephen. 1990. *Exporting Apartheid: Foreign Policies in Southern Africa, 1978–1988*. London: Macmillan.

Checkel, Jeffrey T. 2008. "Process Tracing." In *Qualitative Methods in International Relations. A Pluralist Guide*, edited by Audie Klotz and Deepa Prakash, 114–27. Basingstoke, UK, and New York: Palgrave Macmillan.

ed. 2013. *Transnational Dynamics of Civil War*. New York: Cambridge University Press.

Chichava, Sérgio Inácio. 2007. "Le 'vieux Mozambique'. Étude sur l'identité politique de la Zambézie." PhD diss., Université Montesquieu/Bordeaux IV.

Chichava, Sérgio Inácio, and Jimena Durán. 2016. "Civil Society Organisations' Political Control over Brazil and Japan's Development Cooperation in Mozambique: More Than a Mere Whim?" LSE Global South Unit Working Paper Series 2, LSE Global South Unit, London.

Christia, Fotini. 2012. *Alliance Formation in Civil Wars*. New York: Cambridge University Press.

Clarence-Smith, Gervase. 1989. "The Roots of the Mozambican Counter-Revolution." *Southern African Review of Books* (April/May): 7–10.

Clayton, Anthony. 1999. *Frontiersmen. Warfare in Africa since 1950*. London: University College London Press.

Clayton, Govinda, and Andrew Thomson. 2014. "The Enemy of My Enemy Is My Friend … the Dynamics of Self-Defense Forces in Irregular War: The Case of the Sons of Iraq." *Studies in Conflict & Terrorism* 37 (11): 920–35.

2016. "Civilianizing Civil Conflict: Civilian Defense Militias and the Logic of Violence in Intra-State Conflict." *International Studies Quarterly* 60 (3): 499–510.

Clifford, James, and George E. Marcus. 1986. *Writing Culture: The Poetics and Politics of Ethnography*. Berkeley: University of California Press.

Coelho, João Paulo Borges. 2002. "African Troops in the Portuguese Colonial Army, 1961–1974: Angola, Guinea-Bissau and Mozambique." *Portuguese Studies Review* 10 (1): 129–50.

Coelho, João Paulo Borges, and Alex Vines. 1992. Pilot Study on Demobilization and Re-Integration of Ex-Combatants in Mozambique, Usaid's Mozambique Demobilization and Reintegration Support Project (656-0235). Oxford: University of Oxford, Refugee Studies Programme, Queen Elizabeth House.

Cohen, Dara Kay. 2016. *Rape during Civil War*. Ithaca, NY: Cornell University Press.

Cohen, Nissim, and Tamar Arieli. 2011. "Field Research in Conflict Environments: Methodological Challenges and Snowball Sampling." *Journal of Peace Research* 48 (4): 423–35.

Collier, Paul, and Anke Hoeffler. 2004. "Greed and Grievance in Civil War." *Oxford Economic Papers* 56 (4): 563–95.

Cordesman, Anthony H., and Emma R. Davies. 2008. *Iraq's Insurgency and the Road to Civil Conflict*. Westport, CT: Praeger Security International.

Couto, Mia. 1996. *Terra Sonâmbula*. Maputo: Ndjira.

Cronin-Furman, Kate, and Milli Lake. 2018. "Ethics Abroad: Fieldwork in Fragile and Violent Contexts." *PS: Political Science & Politics* 51 (3): 607–14.

Cuahela, Ambrósio. 1998. "Análise da estratégia da Frelimo para o desenvolvimento rural integrado: Experiências em Namarrói (1975–1983)." Licenciatura diss., Universidade Eduardo Mondlane.

Cunningham, Kathleen Gallagher, Kristin M. Bakke, and Lee J.M. Seymour. 2012. "Shirts Today, Skins Tomorrow Dual Contests and the Effects of Fragmentation in Self-Determination Disputes." *Journal of Conflict Resolution* 56 (1): 67–93.

Daly, Sarah Zukerman. 2016. *Organized Violence after Civil War. The Geography of Recruitment in Latin America*. New York: Cambridge University Press.

Darch, Colin. 2015. "Separatist Tensions and Violence in the 'Model Post-Conflict State': Mozambique since the 1990s." *Review of African Political Economy* 43 (148): 320–27.

Davenport, Christian, and Patrick Ball. 2002. "Views to a Kill: Exploring the Implications of Source Selection in the Case of Guatemalan State Terror, 1977–1995." *Journal of Conflict Resolution* 46 (3): 427–50.

Davies, Robert H. 1985. *South African Strategy towards Mozambique in the Post-Nkomati Period: A Critical Analysis of Effects and Implications*. Uppsala: Scandinavian Institute of African Studies.

De Bragança, Aquino, and Jacques Depelchin. 1986. "From the Idealization of FRELIMO to the Understanding of the Recent History of Mozambique." *African Journal of Political Economy* 1 (1): 162–80.

De Bragança, Aquino, and Immanuel Maurice Wallerstein, eds. 1982. *The African Liberation Reader. Documents of the National Liberation Movements*, Vol. 2. London: Zed Press.

De Bruin, Erica. 2020. *How to Prevent Coups d'État: Counterbalancing and Regime Survival*. Ithaca, NY: Cornell University Press.

Degregori, Carlos Iván. 1999. "Reaping the Whirlwind. The Rondas Campesinas and the Defeat of Sendero Luminoso in Ayacucho." In *Societies of Fear: The Legacy of Civil War, Violence and Terror in Latin America*, edited by Kees Koonings and Dirk Kruijt, 63–87. London and New York: Zed Books.

Dhada, Mustafah. 2016. *The Portuguese Massacre of Wiriyamu in Colonial Mozambique, 1964–2013*. New York: Bloomsbury Academic.

Dinerman, Alice. 2001. "From 'Abaixo' to 'Chiefs of Production': Agrarian Change in Nampula Province, Mozambique, 1975–87." *The Journal of Peasant Studies* 28 (2): 1–82.

  2006. *Revolution, Counter-Revolution and Revisionism in Post-Colonial Africa: The Case of Mozambique, 1975–1994*. London and New York: Routledge.

2009. "Regarding Totalities and Escape Hatches in Mozambican Politics and Mozambican Studies." *Politique Africaine* (1): 187–210.

Do Rosário, Domingos. 2009. "Les Mairies des 'autres': une analyse politique, socio-historique et culturelle des trajectoires locales. Le cas d'Angoche, de l'Île de Moçambique et de Nacala Porto." PhD diss., Université Montesquieu/Bordeaux IV.

Dobbin, Frank, Beth Simmons, and Geoffrey Garrett. 2007. "The Global Diffusion of Public Policies: Social Construction, Coercion, Competition, or Learning?" *Annual Review of Sociology* 33 (1): 449–72.

Dos Santos Peixe, Júlio. 1960. "Emparrámê." *Separata do Boletim do Museu de Nampula* 1 (1): 145–47.

Eck, Kristine. 2010. "Raising Rebels: Participation and Recruitment in Civil War." PhD diss., Uppsala Universitet.

Ekeh, Peter P. 1975. "Colonialism and the Two Publics in Africa: A Theoretical Statement." *Comparative Studies in Society and History* 17 (1): 91.

Elbadawi, Ibrahim, and Nicholas Sambanis. 2002. "How Much War Will We See? Explaining the Prevalence of Civil War." *Journal of Conflict Resolution* 46 (3): 307–34.

Elkins, Zachary, and Beth Simmons. 2005. "On Waves, Clusters, and Diffusion: A Conceptual Framework." *Annals of the American Academy of Political and Social Science* 598 (1): 33–51.

Ellis, Stephen. 1999. *The Mask of Anarchy: The Destruction of Liberia and the Religious Dimension of African Civil War*. London: Hurst.

Emerson, Stephen A. 2014. *The Battle for Mozambique. The FRELIMO-RENAMO Struggle, 1977–1992*. Pinetown, South Africa: 30° South Publishers.

England, Kim V. L. 1994. "Getting Personal: Reflexivity, Positionality, and Feminist Research." *The Professional Geographer* 46 (1): 80–89.

Esteban, Joan, and Gerald Schneider. 2008. "Polarization and Conflict: Theoretical and Empirical Issues." *Journal of Peace Research* 45 (2): 131–41.

Fauvet, Paul. 1989. "Clarence-Smith on Mozambique." *Southern African Review of Books* (August/September): 26–27.

1990. "Clarence-Smith on Mozambique." *Southern African Review of Books* (June/July): 21.

Fauvet, Paul, and Marcelo Mosse. 2003. *Carlos Cardoso: Telling the Truth in Mozambique*. Cape Town: Double Storey.

Fearon, James D. 2004. "Why Do Some Civil Wars Last So Much Longer Than Others?" *Journal of Peace Research* 41 (3): 275–301.

Fearon, James D., and David D. Laitin. 2003. "Ethnicity, Insurgency, and Civil War." *American Political Science Review* 97 (1): 75–90.

Ferme, Mariane C. 2001. "La figure du chasseur et les Chasseurs-miliciens dans le conflit sierra-Léonais." *Politique Africaine* (82): 119–32.

Ferme, Mariane C., and Danny Hoffman. 2004. "Hunter Militias and the International Human Rights Discourse in Sierra Leone and Beyond." *Africa Today* 50: 73–95.

Finnegan, William. 1992. *A Complicated War: The Harrowing of Mozambique*. Berkeley: University of California Press.

Fithen, Caspar, and Paul Richards. 2005. "Making War, Crafting Peace: Militia Solidarities and Demobilisation in Sierra Leone." In *No Peace, No War: An*

Anthropology of Contemporary Armed Conflicts, edited by Paul Richards, 117–36. Oxford: James Currey.

Flint, Julie. 2009. *Beyond "Janjaweed": Understanding the Militias of Darfur*. Geneva: Small Arms Survey, Graduate Institute of International and Development Studies.

Flint, Julie, and Alexander De Waal. 2005. *Darfur: A Short History of a Long War*. London: Zed Books.

Flower, Ken. 1987. *Serving Secretly: Rhodesia's CIO Chief on Record*. Alberton, Republic of South Africa: Galago.

Forney, Jonathan. 2012. "Who Can We Trust with a Gun? Social Networks and Private Information in Militia Recruitment." Paper presented at the Conference on Paramilitaries, Militias, and Civil Defense Forces in Civil Wars, October 19–20, Yale University, New Haven, CT.

Francis, David J., ed. 2005. *Civil Militia: Africa's Intractable Security Menace?* Aldershot: Ashgate.

Franzese, Robert J., and Jude C. Hays. 2008. "Interdependence in Comparative Politics: Substance, Theory, Empirics, Substance." *Comparative Political Studies* 41 (4–5): 742–80.

Frelimo. 1978. *Central Committee Report to the Third Congress of FRELIMO*. London: Mozambique, Angola and Guiné Information Centre.

Fujii, Lee Ann. 2010. "Shades of Truth and Lies. Interpreting Testimonies of War and Violence." *Journal of Peace Research* 47 (2): 231–41.

———. 2012. "Research Ethics 101: Dilemmas and Responsibilities." *PS: Political Science & Politics* 45 (4): 717–23.

Fumerton, Mario. 2001. "Rondas Campesinas in the Peruvian Civil War: Peasant Self-Defence Organisations in Ayacucho." *Bulletin of Latin American Research* 20 (4): 470–97.

Geffray, Christian. 1990. *La cause des armes au Mozambique. Anthropologie d'une guerre civile*. Paris: Karthala.

George, Alexander L., and Andrew Bennett. 2005. *Case Studies and Theory Development in the Social Sciences*. Cambridge, MA: MIT Press.

Gerharz, Eva. 2009. "Ambivalent Positioning: Reflections on Ethnographic Research in Sri Lanka during the Ceasefire of 2002." Working Papers in Development Sociology and Social Anthropology 361. Bielefeld: Universität Bielefeld.

Gerring, John. 2010. "Causal Mechanisms: Yes, But." *Comparative Political Studies* 43 (11): 1499–526.

Gersony, Robert. 1988. Summary of Mozambican Refugee Accounts of Principally Conflict-Related Experience in Mozambique. Report Submitted to Ambassador Jonathon Moore: Director, Bureau for Refugees Program and Dr. Chester Crocker: Assistant Secretary of African Affairs. Washington, DC: State Department, US Government.

Gilardi, Fabrizio. 2010. "Who Learns from What in Policy Diffusion Processes?" *American Journal of Political Science* 54 (3): 650–66.

Givan, Rebecca Kolins, Kenneth M. Roberts, and Sarah Anne Soule. 2010. *The Diffusion of Social Movements: Actors, Mechanisms, and Political Effects*. New York: Cambridge University Press.

Gleditsch, Kristian Skrede, and Michael D. Ward. 2006. "Diffusion and the International Context of Democratization." *International Organization* 60 (4): 911–33.

Gleditsch, Nils Petter, Peter Wallensteen, Mikael Eriksson, Margareta Sollenberg, and Håvard Strand. 2002. "Armed Conflict 1946–2001: A New Dataset." *Journal of Peace Research* 39 (5): 615–37.

Goodhand, Jonathan. 2000. "Research in Conflict Zones: Ethics and Accountability." *Forced Migration Review* 8 (4): 12–16.

Goodhand, Jonathan, and Aziz Hakimi. 2014. *Counterinsurgency, Local Militias, and Statebuilding in Afghanistan*. Washington, DC: United States Institute of Peace.

Gramsci, Antonio. 2000. "Socialism and Culture." In *The Antonio Gramsci Reader. Selected Writings, 1916–1935*, edited by David Forgacs, 56–59. New York: New York University Press.

Greenhill, Kelly M., and Ben Oppenheim. 2017. "Rumor Has it: The Adoption of Unverified Information in Conflict Zones." *International Studies Quarterly* 61 (3): 660–76.

Groger, Lisa, Pamela S. Mayberry, and Jane K. Straker. 1999. "What We Didn't Learn Because of Who Would Not Talk to Us." *Qualitative Health Research* 9 (6): 829–35.

Gurr, Ted Robert. 1970. *Why Men Rebel*. Princeton, NJ: Princeton University Press.

Gutiérrez-Sanín, Francisco. 2008. "Telling the Difference: Guerrillas and Paramilitaries in the Colombian War." *Politics & Society* 36 (1): 3–34.

Gutiérrez-Sanín, Francisco, and Elisabeth J. Wood. 2014. "Ideology in Civil War: Instrumental Adoption and Beyond." *Journal of Peace Research* 51 (2): 213–26.

2017. "What Should We Mean by 'Pattern of Political Violence'? Repertoire, Targeting, Frequency, and Technique." *Perspectives on Politics* 15 (1): 20–41.

Habibe, Saide, Salvador Forquilha, and João Pereira. 2019. "Islamic Radicalization in Northern Mozambique: The Case of Mocímboa Da Praia." *Cadernos IESE* 17, Maputo.

Hale, Charles R. 1996. *Resistance and Contradiction. Miskitu Indians and the Nicaraguan State, 1894–1987*. Palo Alto, CA: Stanford University Press.

Hall, Margaret. 1990. "The Mozambican National Resistance Movement (RENAMO): A Study in the Destruction of an African Country." *Africa* 60 (1): 39–68.

Hall, Margaret, and Tom Young. 1997. *Confronting Leviathan: Mozambique since Independence*. Athens: Ohio University Press.

Hall, Peter. 2003. "Aligning Ontology and Methodology in Comparative Research." In *Comparative Historical Analysis in the Social Sciences*, edited by James Mahoney and Dietrich Rueschemeyer, 373–404. New York: Cambridge University Press.

Hanlon, Joseph. 1984. *Mozambique. The Revolution under Fire*. London: Zed Books.

1996. *Peace without Profit: How the IMF Blocks Rebuilding in Mozambique*. Oxford: James Currey.

Hedges, David. 1989. "Notes on Malawi–Mozambique Relations, 1961–1987." *Journal of Southern African Studies* 15 (4): 617–44.

Hermele, Kenneth. 1986. *Contemporary Land Struggles on the Limpopo: A Case Study of Chokwe, Mozambique, 1950–1985*. Uppsala: AKUT.

Hills, Alice. 1997. "Warlords, Militias, and Conflict in Contemporary Africa. A Reexamination of Terms." *Small Wars and Insurgencies* 8 (1): 35–51.

Hobsbawm, Eric J. 1969. *Bandits*. London: Weidenfeld & Nicolson.

Hobsbawm, Eric J., and Terence O. Ranger. 1983. *The Invention of Tradition*. Cambridge: Cambridge University Press.

Hoffman, Danny. 2003. "Like Beasts in the Bush: Synonyms of Childhood and Youth in Sierra Leone." *Postcolonial Studies* 6 (3): 295–308.

2011. *The War Machines: Young Men and Violence in Sierra Leone and Liberia.* Durham, NC: Duke University Press.

Honwana, Alcinda Manuel. 2002. *Espíritos vivos, tradições modernas: possessão de espíritos e reintegração social pós-guerra no sul de Moçambique.* Maputo: Promédia.

Hultman, Lisa. 2009. "The Power to Hurt in Civil War: The Strategic Aim of RENAMO Violence." *Journal of Southern African Studies* 35 (4): 821–34.

Humphreys, Macartan, and Jeremy M. Weinstein. 2008. "Who Fights? The Determinants of Participation in Civil War." *American Political Science Review* 52 (2): 436–55.

Igreja, Victor. 2007. "The Monkeys' Sworn Oath. Cultures of Engagement for Reconciliation and Healing in the Aftermath of the Civil War in Mozambique." PhD diss., University of Leiden.

Igreja, Victor, Béatrice Dias-Lambranca, and Annemiek Richters. 2008. "Gamba Spirits, Gender Relations, and Healing in Post-Civil War Gorongosa, Mozambique." *Journal of the Royal Anthropological Institute* 14 (2): 353–71.

International Monetary Fund. 2016. "Republic of Mozambique: Selected Issues." IMF Country Report 16/10. International Monetary Fund, Washington, DC.

Isaacman, Allen F., and Barbara Isaacman. 1976. *The Tradition of Resistance in Mozambique. The Zambesi Valley, 1850–1921.* Berkeley: University of California Press.

1983. *Mozambique: From Colonialism to Revolution, 1900–1982.* Boulder, CO: Westview Press Gower.

Jentzsch, Corinna. 2017. "Auxiliary Armed Forces and Innovations in Security Governance in Mozambique's Civil War." *Civil Wars* 19 (3): 325–47.

2018a. "Intervention, Autonomy and Power in Polarised Societies." In *Experiences in Researching Conflict & Violence: Fieldwork Interrupted*, edited by Althea-Maria Rivas and Brendan C. Browne, 75–94. Bristol: Policy Press.

2018b. "Spiritual Power and the Dynamics of War in the Provinces of Nampula and Zambézia in Mozambique." In *The War Within: New Perspectives on the Civil War in Mozambique, 1976–1992*, edited by Michel Cahen, Eric Morier-Genoud, and Domingos Do Rosário, Woodbridge, UK: James Currey.

Jentzsch, Corinna, Stathis N. Kalyvas, and Livia I. Schubiger. 2015. "Militias in Civil Wars." *Journal of Conflict Resolution* 59 (5): 755–69.

Jentzsch, Corinna, and Juan Masullo. 2019. "Resisting Armed Groups in Colombia and Mozambique. Tactical Choice in Civilian Resistance." Paper presented at the American Political Science Association Annual Meeting, August 29–September 1, Washington, DC.

Johnson, Phyllis, David Martin, and Julius K. Nyerere, eds. 1986. *Destructive Engagement: Southern Africa at War.* Harare: Zimbabwe Publishing House.

Jose, Betcy, and Peace A. Medie. 2015. "Understanding Why and How Civilians Resort to Self-Protection in Armed Conflict." *International Studies Review* 17 (4): 515–35.

2016. "Civilian Self-Protection and Civilian Targeting in Armed Conflicts: Who Protects Civilians." In *Oxford Research Encyclopedia of Politics*, Oxford: Oxford University Press. https://oxfordre.com/politics/view/10.1093/acrefore/9780190228637 .001.0001/acrefore-9780190228637-e-216 (accessed August 16, 2021).

Justino, Patricia. 2009. "Poverty and Violent Conflict: A Micro-Level Perspective on the Causes and Duration of Warfare." *Journal of Peace Research* 46 (3): 315–33.

Kalyvas, Stathis N. 2003. "The Ontology of 'Political Violence': Action and Identity in Civil Wars." *Perspectives on Politics* 1 (3): 475–94.

2006. *The Logic of Violence in Civil War.* New York: Cambridge University Press.

2008a. "Ethnic Defection in Civil War." *Comparative Political Studies* 41 (8): 1043–68.

2008b. "Promises and Pitfalls of an Emerging Research Program: The Microdynamics of Civil War." In *Order, Conflict and Violence,* edited by Stathis N. Kalyvas, Ian Shapiro, and Tarek Masoud, 397–421. New York: Cambridge University Press.

Kalyvas, Stathis N., and Ana M. Arjona. 2005. "Paramilitarismo: una perspectiva Teórica." In *El poder paramilitar,* edited by Alfredo Rangel, 25–45. Bogotá: Planeta.

Kalyvas, Stathis N., and Laia Balcells. 2010. "International System and Technologies of Rebellion: How the End of the Cold War Shaped Internal Conflict." *American Political Science Review* 104 (03): 415–29.

Kalyvas, Stathis N., and Matthew A. Kocher. 2007. "How "Free" Is Free Riding in Civil Wars? Violence, Insurgency, and the Collective Action Problem." *World Politics* 59 (2): 177–216.

Kaplan, Oliver R. 2017. *Resisting War: How Communities Protect Themselves.* New York: Cambridge University Press.

Kastfelt, Niels. 2005. *Religion and African Civil Wars.* New York: Palgrave Macmillan.

Keynes, John Maynard. 1921. *A Treatise on Probability.* London: MacMillan.

Knight, Frank H. 1921. *Risk, Uncertainty and Profit.* New York: Houghton Mifflin.

Knox, Colin. 2001. "Establishing Research Legitimacy in the Contested Political Ground of Contemporary Northern Ireland." *Qualitative Research* 1 (2): 205–22.

Kovats-Bernat, J. Christopher. 2002. "Negotiating Dangerous Fields: Pragmatic Strategies for Fieldwork amid Violence and Terror." *American Anthropologist* 104 (1): 208–22.

Krause, Jana. 2018. *Resilient Communities. Non-Violence and Civilian Agency in Communal War.* New York: Cambridge University Press.

Lake, David A., and Donald S. Rothchild. 1998. *The International Spread of Ethnic Conflict: Fear, Diffusion, and Escalation.* Princeton, NJ: Princeton University Press.

Lan, David. 1985. *Guns & Rain: Guerrillas & Spirit Mediums in Zimbabwe.* London and Berkeley: James Currey and University of California Press.

Larson, Jennifer M., and Janet I. Lewis. 2017. "Ethnic Networks." *American Journal of Political Science* 61 (2): 350–64.

Le Billon, Philippe. 2001. "The Political Ecology of War: Natural Resources and Armed Conflicts." *Political Geography* 20 (5): 561–84.

Leenders, Reinoud, and Antonio Giustozzi. 2019. "Outsourcing State Violence: The National Defence Force, 'Stateness' and Regime Resilience in the Syrian War." *Mediterranean Politics* 24 (2): 157–80.

Legrand, Jean-Claude. 1993. "Logique de guerre et dynamique de la violence en Zambézie, 1976–1991." *Politique Africaine* 50 (June): 88–104.

Legum, Colin. 1988. *The Battlefronts of Southern Africa.* New York: Africana.

Lemia, Rosário Jaime. 2001. "Pós-Independência, Guerra E Reassentamento Da População No Distrito de Namacurra (1975–1998/9)." Licenciatura diss., Universidade de Eduardo Mondlane.

Lerma Martínez, Francisco. 2008. *O povo macua e a sua cultura. Análise dos valores culturais do povo macua no ciclo vital, Maúa, Moçambique 1971–1985*. Maputo: Paulinas Editorial.

Lichbach, Mark Irving. 1995. *The Rebel's Dilemma*. Ann Arbor: University of Michigan Press.

Licklider, Roy E. 1993. *Stopping the Killing: How Civil Wars End*. New York: New York University Press.

Lillywhite, Serena, Deanna Kemp, and Kathryn Sturman. 2015. *Mining, Resettlement and Lost Livelihoods: Listening to the Voices of Resettled Communities in Mualadzi, Mozambique*. Melbourne: Oxfam.

Lloyd-Jones, Stewart, and António Costa Pinto. 2003. *The Last Empire: Thirty Years of Portuguese Decolonization*. Portland, OR: Intellect Books.

Lubkemann, Stephen C. 2005. "Migratory Coping in Wartime Mozambique: An Anthropology of Violence and Displacement in 'Fragmented Wars'." *Journal of Peace Research* 42 (4): 493–508.

Lyall, Jason. 2015. "Process Tracing, Causal Inference, and Civil War." In *Process Tracing: From Metaphor to Analytic Tool*, edited by Andrew Bennett and Jeffrey T. Checkel, 186–208. New York: Cambridge University Press.

Lynch, Meghan. 2013. "Civilian-on-Civilian Violence: An Ethnography of Choices during Civil War." PhD diss., Yale University.

Macamo, Elísio. 2016. "Violence and Political Culture in Mozambique." *Social Dynamics* 42 (1): 85–105.

Machava, Benedito Luís. 2011. "State Discourse on Internal Security and the Politics of Punishment in Post-Independence Mozambique (1975–1983)." *Journal of Southern African Studies* 37 (3): 593–609.

    2018. "The Morality of Revolution: Urban Cleanup Campaigns, Reeducation Camps, and Citizenship in Socialist Mozambique (1974–1988)." PhD diss., University of Michigan.

Mackey, Robert R. 2017. "Militia." In *Oxford Bibliographies in Military History*, Oxford: Oxford University Press. http://dx.doi.org/10.1093/obo/9780199791279-0116.

Mahon, John K. 1983. *History of the Militia and the National Guard*. New York: Macmillan.

Maier, Karl. 1998. *Into the House of the Ancestors: Inside the New Africa*. New York: Wiley.

Malejacq, Romain. 2016. "Warlords, Intervention, & State Consolidation: A Typology of Political Orders in Failed & Failing States." *Security Studies* 25 (1): 85–110.

    2017. "Pro-Government Militias." In *Oxford Bibliographies in International Relations*. Oxford: Oxford University Press. http://dx.doi.org/10.1093/obo/9780199743292-0213.

    2019. *Warlord Survival. The Delusion of State Building in Afghanistan*. Ithaca, NY: Cornell University Press.

Malejacq, Romain, and Dipali Mukhopadhyay. 2016. "The 'Tribal Politics' of Field Research: A Reflection on Power and Partiality in 21st-Century Warzones." *Perspectives on Politics* 14 (4): 1011–28.

Mampilly, Zachariah Cherian. 2011. *Rebel Rulers: Insurgent Governance and Civilian Life during War*. Ithaca, NY: Cornell University Press.

Marcum, John A., Edmund Burke III, and Michael W. Clough. 2017. *Conceiving Mozambique*. London: Palgrave Macmillan.

Masullo, Juan. 2015. *The Power of Staying Put: Nonviolent Resistance against Armed Groups in Colombia*. Washington, DC: International Center on Nonviolent Conflict.

———. 2021. "Refusing to Cooperate with Armed Groups: Civilian Agency and Civilian Noncooperation in Armed Conflicts." *International Studies Review* 23 (3): 887–913.

Mazula, Brazão, ed. 1995. *Eleições, democracia e desenvolvimento*. Maputo: A Embaixada do Reino dos Paises Baixos.

———. 1997. *Moçambique. Dados estatísticos do processo eleitoral 1994*. Maputo: STAE.

Mazurana, Dyan E., Karen Jacobsen, and Lacey Andrews Gale, eds. 2013. *Research Methods in Conflict Settings: A View from Below*. New York: Cambridge University Press.

Mazzei, Julie. 2009. *Death Squads or Self-Defense Forces? How Paramilitary Groups Emerge and Challenge Democracy in Latin America*. Chapel Hill: The University of North Carolina Press.

McAdam, Doug. 1982. *Political Process and the Development of Black Insurgency, 1930–1970*. Chicago: University of Chicago Press.

Meldrum, Andrew. 1991. "Railway of Refuge." *Africa Report* (May–June): 63–66.

Metelits, Claire. 2010. *Inside Insurgency: Violence, Civilians, and Revolutionary Group Behavior*. New York: New York University Press.

Meyns, Peter. 1988. *Agrargesellschaften im portugiesischsprachigen Afrika*. Saarbrücken: Verlag Breitenbach.

Minter, William. 1989. "Clarence-Smith on Mozambique." *Southern African Review of Books* (June/July): 22–23.

———. 1994. *Apartheid's Contras: An Inquiry into the Roots of War in Angola and Mozambique*. London: Zed Books.

Mitchell, Neil J., Sabine Carey, and Christopher Butler. 2014. "The Impact of Pro-Government Militias on Human Rights Violations." *International Interactions* 40 (5): 812–36.

Mondlane, Eduardo. 1969. *The Struggle for Mozambique*. Harmondsworth: Penguin.

Morier-Genoud, Eric. 2018. "War in Inhambane. Reshaping State, Society, and Economy." In *The War Within: New Perspectives on the Civil War in Mozambique, 1976–1992*, edited by Michel Cahen, Eric Morier-Genoud, and Domingos Do Rosário, 149–80. Woodbridge, UK: James Currey.

———. 2020. "The Jihadi Insurgency in Mozambique: Origins, Nature and Beginning." *Journal of Eastern African Studies* 14 (3): 396–412.

Muana, Patrick K. 1997. "The Kamajoi Militia. Civil War, Internal Displacement and the Politics of Counter-Insurgency." *Africa Development* 22 (3/4): 77–100.

Muiuane, Armando Pedro. 2006. *Datas e documentos da história da FRELIMO: De 1960 a 1974, ano da independência de Moçambique*. Maputo: CIEDIMA.

Munslow, Barry. 1988. "Mozambique and the Death of Machel." *Third World Quarterly* 10 (1): 23–36.

Nash, June. 1976. "Ethnology in a Revolutionary Setting." In *Ethics and Anthropology. Dilemmas in Fieldwork*, edited by Michael A. Rynkiewich and James P. Spradley, 148–66. New York: Wiley & Sons.

Nelson, Stephen C., and Peter J. Katzenstein. 2014. "Uncertainty, Risk, and the Financial Crisis of 2008." *International Organization* 68 (2): 361–92.

Newitt, Malyn. 1995. *A History of Mozambique.* Bloomington: Indiana University Press.

Nicolini, Beatrice. 2006. *Studies in Witchcraft, Magic, War, and Peace in Africa.* Lewiston, NY: Edwin Mellen Press.

Nordstrom, Carolyn. 1997. *A Different Kind of War Story.* Philadelphia: University of Pennsylvania Press.

Nordstrom, Carolyn, and Antonius C. G. M. Robben. 1995. *Fieldwork under Fire: Contemporary Studies of Violence and Culture.* Berkeley: University of California Press.

Norman, Julie M. 2009. "Got Trust? The Challenge of Gaining Access in Conflict Zones." In *Surviving Field Research: Working in Violent and Difficult Situations,* edited by Chandra Lekha Sriram, John C. Kind, Julie A. Mertus, Olga Martin-Ortega, and Johanna Herman, 71–90. London and New York: Routledge.

O'Laughlin, Bridget. 1992. "A base social da guerra em Moçambique." *Estudos Moçambicanos* (10): 107–42.

Okumu, Wafula, and Augustine Ovuoronye Ikelegbe. 2010. "Introduction: Towards Conceptualisation and Understanding of the Threats of Armed Non-State Groups to Human Security and the State in Africa." In *Militias, Rebels and Islamist Militants,* edited by Wafula Okumu and Augustine Ovuoronye Ikelegbe, 1–44. Tshwane (Pretoria), South Africa: Institute for Security Studies.

Olson, Mancur. 1965. *The Logic of Collective Action: Public Goods and the Theory of Groups.* Cambridge, MA: Harvard University Press.

Ortega, Marvin. 1990. "The State, the Peasantry and the Sandinista Revolution." *The Journal of Development Studies* 26 (4): 122–42.

Otto, Sabine. 2018. "The Grass Is Always Greener? Armed Group Side Switching in Civil Wars." *Journal of Conflict Resolution* 62 (7): 1459–88.

Pachter, Elise Forbes. 1982. "Contra-Coup: Civilian Control of the Military in Guinea, Tanzania, and Mozambique." *The Journal of Modern African Studies* 20 (4): 595–612.

Paige, Jeffery M. 1975. *Agrarian Revolution: Social Movements and Export Agriculture in the Underdeveloped World.* New York: Free Press.

Parkinson, Sarah E. 2013. "Organizing Rebellion: Rethinking High-Risk Mobilization and Social Networks in War." *American Political Science Review* 107 (3): 418–32.

Parkinson, Sarah E., and Elisabeth J. Wood. 2015. "Transparency in Intensive Research on Violence: Ethical Dilemmas and Unforeseen Consequences." *Qualitative and Multi-Method Research: Newsletter of the American Political Science Association's QMMR Section* 13 (1): 22–27.

Pearce, Justin. 2020. "History, Legitimacy, and RENAMO's Return to Arms in Central Mozambique." *Africa* 90 (4): 774–95.

Pearlman, Wendy. 2009. "Spoiling Inside and Out: Internal Political Contestation and the Middle East Peace Process." *International Security* 33 (3): 79–109.

Pearlman, Wendy, and Kathleen Gallagher Cunningham. 2012. "Nonstate Actors, Fragmentation, and Conflict Processes." *Journal of Conflict Resolution* 56 (1): 3–15.

Peic, Goran. 2014. "Civilian Defense Forces, State Capacity, and Government Victory in Counterinsurgency Wars." *Studies in Conflict & Terrorism* 37 (2): 162–84.

Pereira, Fabião Manuel. 1999a. "Particularidades da dinâmica do conflito armado no distrito do Alto Molócuè, 1982–1992: Violência armada e guerra mágica." Licenciatura diss., Universidade Eduardo Mondlane.

Pereira, João Candido Graziano. 1999b. "The Politics of Survival. Peasants, Chiefs and RENAMO in Maringue District, Mozambique 1982–1992." MA diss., University of the Witwatersrand.

Petersen, Roger. 2001. *Resistance and Rebellion: Lessons from Eastern Europe*. New York: Cambridge University Press.

Pettersson, Thérése, Stina Högbladh, and Magnus Öberg. 2019. "Organized Violence, 1989–2018 and Peace Agreements." *Journal of Peace Research* 56 (4): 589–603.

Pfister, Roger. 2005. *Apartheid South Africa and African States: From Pariah to Middle Power, 1961–1994*. London: Tauris Academic Studies.

Politique Africaine. 1988. *Mozambique. Guerre et nationalismes*. Paris: Karthala.

Popkin, Samuel L. 1979. *The Rational Peasant: The Political Economy of Rural Society in Vietnam*. Berkeley: University of California Press.

Raleigh, Clionadh. 2016. "Pragmatic and Promiscuous Explaining the Rise of Competitive Political Militias across Africa." *Journal of Conflict Resolution* 60 (2): 283–310.

Raleigh, Clionadh, and Roudabeh Kishi. 2020. "Hired Guns: Using Pro-Government Militias for Political Competition." *Terrorism and Political Violence* 32 (3): 582–603.

Raleigh, Clionadh, Andrew Linke, Håvard Hegre, and Joakim Karlsen. 2010. "Introducing ACLED: An Armed Conflict Location and Event Dataset Special Data Feature." *Journal of Peace Research* 47 (5): 651–60.

Ranger, Terence O. 1985. *Peasant Consciousness and Guerrilla War in Zimbabwe: A Comparative Study*. London: James Currey.

Reid-Daly, Ron. 1999. *Pamwe Chete. The Legend of the Selous Scouts*. South Africa: Covos-Day.

Reis, Bruno C., and Pedro A Oliveira. 2012. "Cutting Heads or Winning Hearts: Late Colonial Portuguese Counterinsurgency and the Wiriyamu Massacre of 1972." *Civil Wars* 14 (1): 80–103.

Remijnse, Simone. 2001. "Remembering Civil Patrols in Joyabaj, Guatemala." *Bulletin of Latin American Research* 20 (4): 454–69.

———. 2002. *Memories of Violence. Civil Patrols and the Legacy of Conflict in Joyabaj, Guatemala*. Amsterdam: Rozenberg Publishers.

Renamo. 1988. "Manifeste-programme de la RENAMO." *Politique Africaine* (30): 106–12.

Robinson, David Alexander. 2006. "Curse on the Land: A History of the Mozambican Civil War." PhD diss., University of Western Australia.

Roesch, Otto. 1989. "Is RENAMO a Popular Movement in Mozambique?" *Southern African Review of Books* (December/January): 20–22.

———. 1992. "RENAMO and the Peasantry in Southern Mozambique: A View from Gaza Province." *Canadian Journal of African Studies* 26 (3): 462–84.

Romano, David. 2006. "Conducting Research in the Middle East's Conflict Zones." *PS: Political Science & Politics* 39 (3): 439–41.

Romero, Mauricio. 2003. *Paramilitares y autodefensas, 1982–2003*. Bogotá: Planeta.

Saideman, Stephen M. 2002. "Discrimination in International Relations: Analyzing External Support for Ethnic Groups." *Journal of Peace Research* 39 (1): 27–50.

Salehyan, Idean. 2007. "Transnational Rebels. Neighboring States as Sanctuary for Rebel Groups." *World Politics* 59 (2): 217–42.

Salehyan, Idean, and Kristian S. Gleditsch. 2006. "Refugees and the Spread of Civil War." *International Organization* 60 (2): 335–66.

Saul, John S. 2005. "Eduardo Mondlane and the Rise and Fall of Mozambican Socialism." *Review of African Political Economy* 32 (104–105): 309–15.

Schafer, Jessica. 2007. *Soldiers at Peace: Veterans and Society after the Civil War in Mozambique.* New York: Palgrave Macmillan.

Schuberth, Moritz. 2015. "The Challenge of Community-Based Armed Groups: Towards a Conceptualization of Militias, Gangs, and Vigilantes." *Contemporary Security Policy* 36 (2): 296–320.

Schubiger, Livia I. 2021. "State Violence and Wartime Civilian Agency: Evidence from Peru." *Journal of Politics* 83 (4): (Online First).

Schulhofer-Wohl, Jonah. 2019. *Quagmire in Civil War.* New York: Cambridge University Press.

Scott, James C. 1976. *The Moral Economy of the Peasant. Rebellion and Subsistence in Southeast Asia.* New Haven, CT: Yale University Press.

1998. *Seeing Like a State: How Certain Schemes to Improve the Human Condition Have Failed.* New Haven, CT: Yale University Press.

Seibert, Gerhard. 2003. "The Vagaries of Violence and Power in Post-Colonial Mozambique." In *Rethinking Resistance: Revolt and Violence in African History,* edited by Jon Abbink, Mirjam de Bruijn, and Klaas van Walraven, 253–76. Leiden: Brill.

Serapião, Luis Benjamin. 1985. "Mozambican Foreign Policy and the West 1975–1984." Munger Africana Library Notes 76. Pasadena, CA: California Institute of Technology.

2004. "The Catholic Church and Conflict Resolution in Mozambique's Post-Colonial Conflict, 1977–1992." *Journal of Church and State* 46: 365–87.

Serra, Carlos. 2003. *Cólera e catarse.* Maputo: Imprensa Universitária.

Shesterinina, Anastasia. 2016. "Collective Threat Framing and Mobilization in Civil War." *American Political Science Review* 110 (3): 411–27.

Simmons, Erica S., and Nicholas Rush Smith. 2017. "Comparison with an Ethnographic Sensibility." *PS: Political Science & Politics* 50 (1): 126–30.

Singer, J. David, and Melvin Small. 1994. *Correlates of War Project: International and Civil War Data, 1816–1992 (ICPSR 9905).* Ann Arbor, MI: Inter-University Consortium for Political and Social Research.

Sirnate, Vasundhara. 2014. "Positionality, Personal Insecurity, and Female Empathy in Security Studies Research." *PS: Political Science & Politics* 47 (2): 398–401.

SL TRC. 2005. *Witness to Truth: Report of the Sierra Leone Truth and Reconciliation Commission.* Freetown: Sierra Leone Truth and Reconciliation Commission.

Slater, Dan, and Daniel Ziblatt. 2013. "The Enduring Indispensability of the Controlled Comparison." *Comparative Political Studies* 20 (10): 1–27.

Sluka, Jeffrey A. 1990. "Participant Observation in Violent Social Contexts." *Human Organization* 49 (2): 114–26.

1995. "Reflections on Managing Danger in Fieldwork: Dangerous Anthropology in Belfast." In *Fieldwork under Fire: Contemporary Studies of Violence and Culture,* edited by Carolyn Nordstrom and Antonius C. G. M. Robben, 276–94. Berkeley: University of California Press.

Smith, Nicholas Rush. 2019. *Contradictions of Democracy: Vigilantism and Rights in Post-Apartheid South Africa*. New York: Oxford University Press.

Snyder, Richard, Eduardo Moncada, and Agustina Giraudy. 2019. *Inside Countries: Subnational Research in Comparative Politics*. New York: Cambridge University Press.

Sriram, Chandra Lekha, John C. King, Julie A. Mertus, Olga Martin-Ortega, and Johanna Herman. 2009. *Surviving Field Research. Working in Violent and Difficult Situations*. London and New York: Routledge.

Staniland, Paul. 2012. "Organizing Insurgency: Networks, Resources, and Rebellion in South Asia." *International Security* 37 (1): 142–77.

2014. *Networks of Rebellion: Explaining Insurgent Cohesion and Collapse*. Ithaca, NY: Cornell University Press.

2015. "Militias, Ideology, and the State." *Journal of Conflict Resolution* 59 (5): 770–93.

Stanton, Jessica A. 2015. "Regulating Militias. Governments, Militias, and Civilian Targeting in Civil War." *Journal of Conflict Resolution* 59 (5): 899–923.

Starn, Orin. 1995. "To Revolt against the Revolution: War and Resistance in Peru's Andes." *Cultural Anthropology* 10 (4): 547–80.

1999. *Nightwatch: The Making of a Movement in the Peruvian Andes*. Durham, NC: Duke University Press.

Stearns, Jason K. 2011. *Dancing in the Glory of Monsters. The Collapse of the Congo and the Great War of Africa*. New York: PublicAffairs.

Stedman, Stephen John. 1997. "Spoiler Problems in Peace Processes." *International Security* 22 (2): 5–53.

Steele, Abbey. 2017. *Democracy and Displacement in Colombia's Civil War*. Ithaca, NY: Cornell University Press.

Stoll, David. 1993. *Between Two Armies in the Ixil Towns of Guatemala*. New York: Columbia University Press.

Strang, David, and Sarah Anne Soule. 1998. "Diffusion in Organizations and Social Movements: From Hybrid Corn to Poison Pills." *Annual Review of Sociology* 24: 265–90.

Sumich, Jason. 2013. "Tenuous Belonging: Citizenship and Democracy in Mozambique." *Social Analysis* 57 (2): 99–116.

Sumich, Jason, and João Honwana. 2007. "Strong Party, Weak State? FRELIMO and State Survival through the Mozambican Civil War: An Analytical Narrative on State-Making." Crisis States Working Papers Series 2, LSE Development Studies Institute, London.

Sundberg, Ralph, and Erik Melander. 2013. "Introducing the UCDP Georeferenced Event Dataset." *Journal of Peace Research* 50 (4): 523–32.

Tapscott, Rebecca. 2019. "Conceptualizing Militias in Africa." In *Oxford Research Encyclopedia of Politics*, Oxford: Oxford University Press. http://dx.doi.org/10.1093/acrefore/9780190228637.013.834.

Tarrow, Sidney G., and Doug McAdam. 2005. "Scale Shift in Transnational Contention." In *Transnational Protest and Global Activism*, edited by Donatella Della Porta and Sidney G. Tarrow, 121–47. Lanham, MD: Rowman & Littlefield.

Taylor, Michael. 1982. *Community, Anarchy, and Liberty*. New York: Cambridge University Press.

Thaler, Kai M. 2012. "Ideology and Violence in Civil Wars: Theory and Evidence from Mozambique and Angola." *Civil Wars* 14 (4): 546–67.

Themnér, Lotta. 2012. *UCDP/PRIO Armed Conflict Dataset Codebook*, Version 4-2012. Uppsala, Oslo: Uppsala Conflict Data Program, Centre for the Study of Civil Wars, International Peace Research Institute, Oslo (PRIO).

Themnér, Lotta, and Peter Wallensteen. 2012. "Armed Conflicts, 1946–2011." *Journal of Peace Research* 49 (4): 565–75.

Tilly, Charles. 1978. *From Mobilization to Revolution*. Reading, MA: Addison-Wesley.

Tullock, Gordon. 1971. "The Paradox of Revolution." *Public Choice* 11 (1): 89–99.

UN Security Council. 1994. *Final Report of the Secretary General on ONUMOZ, S/1994/1449*. New York: United Nations.

Üngör, Ugur Ümit. 2020. *Paramilitarism: Mass Violence in the Shadow of the State*. Oxford: Oxford University Press.

Vines, Alex. 1991. *RENAMO: Terrorism in Mozambique*. London: Centre for Southern African Studies, University of York in association with James Currey.

Vlassenroot, Koen. 2006. "War and Social Research." *Civilisations* 54 (1–2): 191–98.

Walter, Barbara F. 1997. "The Critical Barrier to Civil War Settlement." *International Organization* 51 (3): 335–64.

Wedeen, Lisa. 2010. "Reflections on Ethnographic Work in Political Science." *Annual Review of Political Science* 13: 255–72.

Weinstein, Jeremy M. 2002. "Mozambique: A Fading UN Success Story." *Journal of Democracy* 13 (1): 141–56.

2007. *Inside Rebellion. The Politics of Insurgent Violence*. New York: Cambridge University Press.

Weinstein, Matthew. 2012. "Tams Analyzer for Macintosh OS X: The Native Open Source, Macintosh Qualitative Research Tool." http://tamsys.sf.net. http://tamsys.sf .net (accessed August 16, 2021).

Wiegink, Nikkie. 2020. *Former Guerrillas in Mozambique*. Philadelphia: University of Pennsylvania Press.

Wilson, Kenneth B. 1992. "Cults of Violence and Counter-Violence in Mozambique." *Journal of Southern African Studies* 18 (3): 527–82.

Wlodarczyk, Nathalie. 2009. *Magic and Warfare: Appearance and Reality in Contemporary African Conflict and Beyond*. New York: Palgrave Macmillan.

Woldemariam, Michael. 2018. *Insurgent Fragmentation in the Horn of Africa. Rebellion and Its Discontents*. New York: Cambridge University Press.

Wood, Elisabeth Jean. 2003. *Insurgent Collective Action and Civil War in El Salvador*. New York: Cambridge University Press.

2006. "The Ethical Challenges of Field Research in Conflict Zones." *Qualitative Sociology* 29 (3): 373–86.

2007. "Field Research during War: Ethical Dilemmas." In *New Perspectives in Political Ethnography*, edited by Lauren Joseph, Matthew Mahler, and Javier Auyero, 205–23. New York: Springer.

2013. "Transnational Dynamics of Civil War: Where Do We Go from Here?" In *Transnational Dynamics of Civil War*, edited by Jeffrey T. Checkel, 231–58. New York: Cambridge University Press.

Young, Tom. 1990. "The MNR/RENAMO: External and Internal Dynamics." *African Affairs* 89 (357): 491–509.

Zahar, Marie-Joëlle. 2000. "Protégés, Clients, Cannon Fodder: Civilians in the Calculus of Militias." *International Peacekeeping* 7 (4): 107–28.

Zartman, I. William. 1989. *Ripe for Resolution. Conflict and Intervention in Africa.* New York: Oxford University Press.

Zech, Steven T. 2016. "Between Two Fires: Civilian Resistance during Internal Armed Conflict in Peru." PhD diss., Washington University.

Zhukov, Yuri M. 2015. "Population Resettlement in War. Theory and Evidence from Soviet Archives." *Journal of Conflict Resolution* 59 (7): 1155–85.

Index

Books in the Series (continued from p.ii)